D1083920

The Development
of Scientific
Thinking Skills

DEVELOPMENTAL PSYCHOLOGY SERIES

SERIES EDITOR
HARRY BEILIN

Developmental Psychology Program
City University of New York Graduate School
New York, New York

A complete list of titles in this series is available from the publisher.

The Development of Scientific Thinking Skills

Deanna Kuhn

Department of Psychology
Teachers College
Columbia University
New York, New York

Eric Amsel

Department of Psychology
Yale University
New Haven, Connecticut

Michael O'Loughlin

Department of Educational Foundations and Inquiry
Bowling Green State University
Bowling Green, Ohio

with the assistance of

Leona Schauble
Learning Research
  and Development Center
University of Pittsburgh
Pittsburgh, Pennsylvania

Bonnie Leadbeater
Department of Psychology
Barnard College
New York, New York

William Yotive
Department of Psychology
Teachers College
Columbia University
New York, New York

ACADEMIC PRESS, INC.
Harcourt Brace Jovanovich, Publishers
San Diego   New York   Berkeley   Boston
London   Sydney   Tokyo   Toronto

ACADEMIC PRESS, INC.
1250 Sixth Avenue
San Diego, California 92101

United Kingdom Edition published by
ACADEMIC PRESS INC. (LONDON) LTD.
24-28 Oval Road, London NW1 7DX

Library of Congress Cataloging in Publication Data

Kuhn, Deanna.
   The development of scientific thinking skills.

   (Developmental psychology series)
   Bibliography: p.
   Includes index.
   1. Science—Methodology.   2. Thought and thinking.
3. Evidence.   I. Amsel, Eric.   II. O'Loughlin,
Michael, Date .   III. Title.   IV. Series.
Q175.K927   1988   502'.8   87-19476
ISBN 0-12-428430-2   (alk. paper)

PRINTED IN THE UNITED STATES OF AMERICA
88 89 90 91   9 8 7 6 5 4 3 2 1

CONTENTS

v

4. The Interpretation of Covariation and Noncovariation Evidence   57

5. The Influence of Theory on Evaluation of Evidence   69

6. The Reconstruction of Theory and Evidence   92

III.   The Coordination of Theory and Evidence
Deanna Kuhn and Michael O'Loughlin
with the assistance of William Yotive

7. Replication: The Evaluation of Evidence   105

PREFACE

The impetus for this book was our desire for a satisfactory framework in terms of which changes in scientific reasoning strategies from middle childhood to adulthood might be conceptualized. The pioneering effort in this respect by Inhelder and Piaget has three significant drawbacks, each of which has led to a diminishment of its influence. The first is the central role that propositional logic plays in their model, and the second the dominating role played by the concept of stage. Cheng, Holyoak, Nisbett, and their colleagues have made a convincing case against the utility of formal logic as a model of thinking, as we discuss in Chapter 2. The concept of stage has proven equally problematic. Little evidence exists to support the presence of global stages in the strong sense that Piaget and Inhelder portrayed them, though, unfortunately, this fact has led many developmentalists to swing to the opposite, and equally unlikely, extreme of maintaining that developmental change is entirely localized. Third, there has arisen an increasing awareness that thinking occurs in a context that significantly shapes its form and expression, and these contextual factors are not ones that formal structural theories of development readily accommodate.

Despite the drawbacks of their theoretical model, an evolution in thought along the lines that Inhelder and Piaget attempted to characterize is of crucial theoretical importance. Are the cognitive processes of exploration and induction significantly different in the child, the adolescent, the lay adult, the scientist? If so, we wondered, is there a useful framework in which such development might be conceptualized and examined?

A recent line of research that reflects a recognition of context is the work on conceptual change and the development of scientific understanding, which we consider in Chapter 2. This work has fostered recognition of the fact that an individual's existing knowledge of the world is organized into mental models, or theories, that provide the context for the assimilation of new information and undergo repeated revision. In many ways, this body of work provided a starting point for the research and ideas presented in this volume. The conceptual change literature, however, has thus far focused on identifying and describing these conceptual structures themselves and has not addressed the mechanisms in terms of which conceptual change occurs. If the revision of theories underlies cognitive development, we need to know more about how it occurs.

The question we posed, then, was how existing knowledge is reconciled with new information, or—in the terminology we use—how existing theories are coordinated with new evidence. The central thesis advanced in this volume is that these processes undergo developmental change—that the strategies used by the young child to reconcile naïve theories and new evidence differ significantly from those used by the more sophisticated thinker. This thesis distinguishes the present work from that of the conceptual change researchers, who tend to argue against strategic change. One of the things we shall suggest is that the metaphor of child as scientist, while useful in one sense, may be fundamentally misleading in another: Theory and evidence—the alleged hallmarks of science—are conceived only in a very restricted sense by the young child.

We have framed the present work in the context of scientific thinking and its development, arguing that skills in the coordination of theories and evidence are the most central and fundamental skills that define scientific thinking. Yet, it is in the context of children and adults as intuitive scientists in everyday life that our work probably has the greatest significance. At the same time, the theoretical framework that we propose offers a way to conceptualize the relationship between thinking in formal scientific and everyday contexts.

A final goal we have for the present work is to provide empirical data of value to the burgeoning group of researchers and practitioners concerned with teaching thinking skills. Too often, in our view, identification of the thinking skills that become the object of an instructional program is based on armchair analysis of the kinds of thinking skills the program creator believes it would be good for students to have. Very little program development has been based on empirical data regarding specific thinking skills that students do (or do not) display in their own thinking, and, most important, *the directions in which such skills develop naturally.*

The present work began when the two junior authors and the senior author were in a student–teacher relationship, but the collaboration and the development of ideas have extended beyond that context. All of the people whose names appear on the title page contributed to establishing an intellectual environment in which the working and reworking of ideas flourished. Early on in the work we decided to publish the series of studies as a book rather than submit them to journals for publication as individual articles; we wanted the reader to be able to regard them within the context of the broader theoretical framework we were developing and in relation to one another. All of these studies were carried out without external funding, which means the students involved labored without the reinforcements of either money or journal publication. During the course of the work Eric Amsel and Bonnie Leadbeater received support from Canada Council doctoral fellowships. Incidental expenses and the support of the senior author were provided by a small private foundation whose president showed unwavering confidence, for which the senior author will always remain grateful. The senior author's discovery of the powers of the microcomputer also played no small role in the production of this volume. Finally, we are grateful to those who read and commented on drafts of the manuscript; in particular we want to acknowledge the comments of Jonathan Baron, which extended well beyond the routine.

Deanna Kuhn
Eric Amsel
Michael O'Loughlin

I

INTRODUCTION

Deanna Kuhn

1

THE DEVELOPMENT
OF SCIENTIFIC THINKING

While the teaching of thinking skills has become a topic of widespread interest and concern, science educators have long been in agreement that a major goal of science education ought to be fostering skills of scientific thinking (Bredderman, 1985; Shymansky, Kyle, & Alport, 1983). Implementation of this goal, however, has been constrained by the very limited body of research data identifying the specific nature of such skills. The purpose of the present work is to investigate the nature and development of some basic scientific thinking skills, specifically the thinking skills involved in the coordination of theories and evidence. A central premise underlying science is that scientific theories stand in relation to actual or potential bodies of evidence, against which they can be evaluated. Reciprocally, scientific "facts" stand in relation to one or more actual or potential theories that offer a vehicle for their organization and interpretation. While we would not want to make the claim that they encompass all aspects of scientific thinking, skills in coordinating theories and evidence arguably are the most central, essential, and general skills that define scientific thinking. A high level of mastery of such skills is assumed not only in the conduct of formal scientific inquiry but in a wide range of other skilled endeavors, such as medical diagnosis (Elstein, Shulman, & Sprafka, 1978) or legal practice (Kassin & Wrightsman, 1985).

Skillful coordination of theory and evidence entails a complex interplay. While existing theories provide the basis for interpretation of new information, new information ideally is attended to and utilized as a basis for evaluating and revising theories. Skillful coordination of theory and evidence also entails a high degree of metacognitive function, that is, reflection on one's own cognition. The proficient scientific thinker presumably can say the following: "I am aware of and can reflect on the theory in terms of which I understand a phenomenon. I can

3

conceive of alternative theories that might explain the same phenomenon, and I understand that they differ from my theory. I can contemplate evidence, and I can evaluate how it bears on both my own and alternative theories, drawing on rules of inductive inference that I am aware of and able to apply. I can recognize and acknowledge discrepancies between theories and evidence, and, based on such discrepancies, I can contemplate revision of a theory." We make no claim here that an idealized portrayal such as this resembles the thinking of professional scientists in their day-to-day activities (Mahoney & Kimper, 1976). Yet if one were to ask any scientist to explain why he or she came to accept a particular theory and reject another purporting to account for the same set of phenomena, it is precisely the set of skills just listed that we would take for granted the scientist had mastery of and would utilize in fulfilling our request.

While the exercise of such skills clearly is cognitively demanding, is it not also true that very simple, common kinds of everyday cognition entail the coordination of theory and evidence? Even the simplest information requires some prior conceptual framework to enable it to be assimilated, which means that new information must in some manner be coordinated with existing theory. Is it possible, then, that at least rudimentary cognitive competencies of the sort indicated are in place early in childhood? Weighing on the side of a positive answer to this question is the growing evidence that beginning with the onset of representational cognition, children encode and represent reality in terms of naïve theories, or scripts, that specify how things work or how events happen. These theories exercise a powerful organizing influence on cognition. In interpreting causal phenomena, for example, young children may overlook violation of fundamental causal cues such as spatial contiguity if they conflict with the child's concept of the causal mechanism involved (Shultz, 1982). With experience, theories are elaborated and revised repeatedly, yielding a sequence of partially correct theories that some theorists have suggested is the heart of cognitive development (R. Glaser, 1984).

Though naïve and sophisticated representations, or theories, of phenomena have been the subject of considerable research attention in recent years (Gentner & Stevens, 1983), very little attention has been paid to the *process* of theory revision, in either adults or children. While children undoubtedly revise their theories as their experience increases, young children are notoriously weak in reflecting on their own thought, and it is unlikely that their theory revision is based on the kind of reflective cognitive processing portrayed above. How, then, does the ability to coordinate theory and evidence, an ability likely to be present among even very young children, develop into the sophisticated form characteristic of mature scientific thought?

Before turning to the research we have undertaken on this topic, it is worthwhile to make explicit several aspects of our methodological orientation, for it differs in two major respects from those currently most common in cognitive development research. A major focus of research effort in the field of cognitive development in the last decade has been identification of the developmental origins of cognitive competencies. If tasks are presented in familiar, facilitative contexts, stripped of extraneous demands, or if minimal training is provided, how early in life can particular cognitive competencies (notably those associated with Piaget's stage of concrete operations) be identified (Gelman & Baillargeon, 1983)? A second focus of research attention has been the role of a developing domain-specific knowledge base. The development of cognitive skills, it has been argued, is most profitably investigated within content-rich, domain-specific contexts (R. Glaser, 1984). At a minimum, the growing knowledge base interacts with skill development; more radically, it is proposed that cognitive development consists entirely of changes in domain-specific knowledge (Carey, 1985a; Keil, 1984), with the implication that attainments within a domain proceed to a large extent independently and show little or no generality across domains.

The present research departs from these two current research thrusts in the field of cognitive development—identifying the origins of cognitive competencies and the role of domain-specific knowledge—though in a way that we believe enriches rather than contradicts them. In the present work we undertake to identify and examine thinking skills assumed to be of some generality across a wide range of content (rather than tied to a specific knowledge domain). Assertions (for example by Keil, 1984) that there presently exists no conclusive evidence documenting the existence of general cognitive skills are probably fair. At the same time, it is also fair to say that existing research is not adequate to decide the matter and that it would be premature to foreclose the possibility that cognitive skills of some generality can be identified. The issue of generality versus domain-specificity of thinking skills is in fact a complex, rather than an either-or, one (Baron, 1985; Levin, 1986). It is very unlikely that thinking skills are either entirely general or entirely domain specific. Moreover, the question can be posed in at least three different forms, one developmental, one conceptual/analytic, and one instructional: (a) To what extent does the acquisition of thinking skills take place in a general versus domain-specific manner? (b) Once skills are acquired, even if in highly domain-specific contexts, are these skills identifiable in more general or only in their domain-specific forms? (c) Should instruction in thinking skills be undertaken in domain-specific or more general form? The working hypothesis adopted in the present research is that most thinking skills emerge and develop in specific contexts and content domains but may nevertheless be identifiable in more general form across domains, even though those using such skills may quite likely themselves be unaware of them in any general form.

The issue of generality/specificity is further complicated by the likelihood that degree of generality versus domain-specificity depends to a considerable extent on the kinds of thinking skills and contexts being investigated. If one investigates thinking in an academic discipline characterized by a highly elaborate knowledge base—for example, physics—then the conclusion is likely to be very compelling that any developments in thinking strategy that may occur are heavily dependent on (or even are tantamount to) changes in the student's representation of the particular knowledge entailed in the domain. In contrast, in the present research we undertake to investigate skills in coordinating theory and evidence in very simple contexts that evoke everyday knowledge but in which a minimal formal knowledge base is required. It is reasonable to assume that the sorts of skills we examine would be applied, and therefore identifiable, in a wide variety of such simple contexts. Identifying them in such contexts could well make it possible to determine how they might contribute to thinking in highly knowledge-rich domains, such as physics, where the complexity and the central role of a specific knowledge base may make them less readily observable.

Nothing in our approach, it should be emphasized, negates or diminishes the importance of domain-specific knowledge in reasoning. To the contrary, its primary focus is on how prior knowledge or belief that a subject brings to a setting is reconciled, or coordinated, with new information that is encountered. The assumptions we make are simply that (a) this prior knowledge takes the form of naïve theories that undergo successive revision in the face of new information and experience; (b) there is at least some generality to the processes in terms of which this revision, or theory/evidence coordination, takes place; that is, the revision process is not completely unique within content domains; and (c) the nature of the revision or coordination process is likely to undergo developmental change. We should mention also at this point that the term *skill* used throughout the book to refer to the cognitive abilities and competencies that we investigate is intended to be taken in a theoretically neutral way. We regarded this term as more neutral than alternatives, and its use carries no implications regarding generality versus specificity of skills nor their mechanisms of development.

The second feature of our approach that is worthy of note is its focus on later developing, metacognitive aspects of skill acquisition rather than on the developmental origins of skills. In its broadest sense, the term *metacognition* has been used to describe a very general "executive" function that selects, controls, and monitors the use of cognitive strategies, though it is often left unclear whether this function entails conscious awareness. In the present work we follow Vygotsky (1962) in regarding "reflective awareness" and "deliberate control" as the dual aspects of metacognitive functioning. The two can be regarded as describing the subjective (or phenomenological) and the objective (or behavioral) aspects of the same phenomenon. Persons aware of their own mental acts are able to reflect on those acts as objects of cognition and are also likely to be able to access and apply them in a manner under their voluntary control, such that control of a function is the counterpart of consciousness of it.

Most studies of metacognition are studies of cognition about how to learn and remember or studies of the cognition involved in choosing and monitoring strategies to solve problems. Yet there remains a whole, relatively unstudied and very significant realm of metacognition consisting of cognition about what one knows and how one knows it (though not in any formal, epistemological sense). It entails thinking explicitly about a theory one holds (rather than only thinking with it) and about its relation to evidence that might or might not support it and provide a basis for one's belief in it. It is this aspect of metacognition to which the present study is addressed.

Interest in metacognition has grown in recent years, and it is being awarded an increasingly prominent place in theories of cognition and intelligence (Sternberg, 1985). At the same time, the focus on identifying the origins of cognitive competencies mentioned earlier has fostered a research orientation that does not lend itself to investigation of metacognitive processes. To use an example that figures prominently in the present work, researchers in several studies have traced acquisition of a covariation strategy to an early age (Shultz & Mendelson, 1975; Siegler, 1975): Quite young children will attribute an outcome to an antecedent that covaries with the outcome over one that does not. At most, such evidence reveals the emergence of a covariation principle, or strategy, in its most rudimentary form. Claiming that such performance reflects a covariation strategy may constitute no more than a descriptive labeling from the perspective of the observer; it is not clear what if any psychological reality the strategy has from the perspective of the subject. In any case, considerable development clearly must take place before such a subject could be regarded as having metacognitive control of this strategy, in our sense of entailing reflective awareness and control.

The focus of the present work, then, is on the attainment of metacognitive control of the skills involved in the coordination of theory and evidence, not on the developmental origins of these skills. Certainly, from a very early age children modify their primitive theories in the face of evidence. Paralleling Vygotsky's (1962) example of grammar, which young children use correctly but have not yet become aware of, our interest is in examining how children develop the ability to access and apply such skills explicitly and reflectively, in other words, how they come to know that this is what they are doing and to be in control of the process. Also of interest is whether the quality or sophistication of the skills themselves increases in relation to conscious control by the subject.

We would maintain that it is the conscious control of such skills that is most significant in the development of scientific thinking. While nonconscious, associative processes may play a role in a scientist's generation of ideas, it is through use of established principles of inference over which the scientist exercises conscious control that he or she reconciles those ideas with evidence that bears on them. Also, interestingly, the development of explicit, consciously controlled thinking skills has always been taken for granted as primary in importance by educators. In particular, skills having to do with the coordination of theory and evidence, such as the ability to draw on evidence to substantiate and justify one's judgments, are seen as central goals of the educational process. In stark contrast, a number of psychologists in recent years have tended to regard such skills as epiphenomena, irrelevant to, or at least not particularly revealing of, the "real" mental processes that produce a judgment, with only the latter worthy of investigation.

Having described the present work in terms of its broad features, let us turn now to its more specific characteristics. We examine the simplest, most fundamental theory in scientific thinking: a theory asserting a relationship between one category of phenomena and another. Among the most elemental forms of cognition are those that organize phenomena into categories based on relations of similarity and difference. Further organization of reality is achieved by inferring relations among the categories themselves. Though not always, the relations inferred are very often interpreted in causal terms. A generative mechanism is conceived whereby phenomena in the antecedent category produce the phenomena in an outcome category.

Our investigation focuses on two basic inferences, likewise fundamental to scientific reasoning, that (after Inhelder & Piaget, 1958) we refer to as *inclusion* and *exclusion*. Inclusion is the inference that a body of evidence indicates a relationship (usually interpreted in causal terms) between one of a number of potential antecedent variables and an outcome variable. Exclusion is the inference that the evidence indicates no relationship between an antecedent and an outcome variable. Though it has received relatively little investigation as a cognitive skill, exclusion ranks at least as high as inclusion in its importance in scientific reasoning. Through its correct usage one can eliminate variables, declaring them to have no bearing on the phenomenon of interest and therefore to require no further consideration. Without the ability to dismiss factors as irrelevant, scientific thinking about a topic could scarcely proceed. In making both inclusion and exclusion inferences, one must coordinate prior theories (regarding these relationships) with newly available evidence of some greater or lesser degree of consistency with these theories. What skills are entailed in such a process? How does the character of this coordination process change developmentally?

To give the reader some preview of what lies ahead, in the following chapters we present data that suggest that less mature forms of coordination are characterized by a lack of differentiation between theory and evidence. Neither "theory" nor "evidence" really exists in the strict sense of these terms, for two reasons. First, the possibility of the theory's being false and of the existence of alternative theories is not conceived. Second, relevant data are regarded not as evidence but rather as *instances* that simultaneously (a) can be explained by the theory and (b) serve to illustrate the theory. In other words, there is no concept of evidence standing apart from the theory and bearing on it. In sum, the person uses theories as a means of organizing experience and thinking about the world, but does not think about the theory itself; nor does the individual contemplate evidence as such, differentiated from a theory and capable of bearing on it. If enough discrepant evidence is registered, a theory may be revised, but neither discrepancy nor revision is explicitly acknowledged. Because theory and evidence are not differentiated, the two must be in accordance with one another; the person cannot acknowledge them as discrepant. Any adjustments that reduce discrepancy thus are likely to take place outside of the person's conscious control.

If these assertions are correct, a major development in scientific reasoning skill is the differentiation of theory and evidence and the elevation of the process of theory/evidence interaction to the level of conscious control. Awareness of and differentiation between theory and evidence paves the way for contemplation of *relations* between them. Ideal coordination of these relations minimizes distortion in the influence of theory on evidence evaluation or the influence of evidence on theory modification. The evaluation of a piece of evidence in relation to multiple theories is not altered by which theory one favors. Conversely, multiple pieces of evidence relevant to a theory are given comparable consideration irrespective of their compatibility with the theory; that is, those inconsistent with the theory are not slighted in favor of those consistent with the theory. In the absence of such ideal coordination, distorting effects of one's own theoretical preferences on the evaluation of evidence can be predicted.

The development from lack of differentiation between theory and evidence to their full differentiation and coordination reflects mastery of a wide range of skills and subskills in scientific thinking that most likely develop gradually through exercise, that develop incompletely in most people, and that may be amenable to instruction. The object of the present work is to gain insight into the nature of such skills and how they develop.

In the next chapter, we place our work in the broader context of existing research. In the following chapter, we begin the report of our own research. In the initial set of studies, reported in Part II (Chapters 3–6), we examine subjects' coordination of theory and evidence as manifested in their ability to evaluate newly presented evidence that bears on a theory that they have espoused. To accomplish this, the subject must be able to represent and reflect on the theory as an object of cognition, encode and represent the presented evidence as an entity distinct from the theory, and mentally construct relations between the two. The initial indicator we examine of subjects' ability in this respect is whether a subject references any aspect of the presented evidence in response to a request to evaluate the bearing of the evidence on the theory. Sometimes, in responding to this request a subject may make no reference to the evidence and refer only to the theory itself. It does not follow that the presented evidence had no influence on a subject's thinking in such cases, and we examine data that address this issue. Our focus does not entail a denial of the possibility that, from an objective frame of reference, factors to which people do not have conscious access influence their inferences. But it is the conscious awareness and control of processes in which evidence influences inference that is the focus of our interest and, as we argued above, most significant in understanding the development of scientific thinking skills.

Given some subjects' failure to do so in the initial study, in two studies subsidiary to the initial one we further explore the ability of subjects to relate evidence to a theory. The particular questions we ask are: (a) Does explicit instruction enhance this skill? (b) Does salience of the theory weaken this skill, by detracting from attention to evidence? (c) Are implicit evidence evaluation skills discernible in subjects who fail to evaluate the evidence explicity? In each of these studies, we go on to examine how subjects do evaluate the evidence when they do so. Do they have concepts of how evidence of the particular forms presented bears on a theory? What forms of evidence are regarded as sufficient to warrant inferences of inclusion and exclusion? We then examine how subjects reconcile their initial theories with evidence that is discrepant from them. This investigation includes an assessment of the extent to which evaluation of evidence is distorted by commitment to a theory, reflecting limitations in the coordination of theory and evidence. In the final chapter in Part II, we examine how subjects represent theory and evidence, as reflected in their reconstructions of them following evaluation of the evidence.

In the work reported in Part III, we first replicate the initial research, this time using real (rather than symbolic) objects, which the subject is able to examine and manipulate. We then go on to examine some aspects of skills in the coordination of theory and evidence that are broader than the simple kinds of evidence evaluation examined in the initial studies. Subjects are asked to coordinate theory and evidence in the case of multiple sets of evidence and multiple theories that sometimes do and sometimes do not reflect the subjects' own views. A major focus of the investigation continues to be on the evaluation of evidence, but we present subjects with more varied and complex kinds of evidence than are presented in the initial studies—in particular, cases in which evidence provides only partial or mixed support for a theory. In each case, the subject is asked to relate evidence to multiple theories rather than just a single theory. A second focus of the investigation is on the reciprocal aspect of theory/evidence coordination: Rather than evaluating existing evidence relative to a theory, the subject is asked to take the theory as the starting point and generate sets of evidence that would both support and refute that theory.

Chapter 11, the final chapter in Part III, addresses the question of mechanism and reports on changes that occur in subjects' skills when the subjects undergo practice over a period of months, engaging in problems that require them to coordinate theory and evidence. In the single chapter in Part IV, subjects' broader conceptions regarding the nature of scientific inquiry are explored. Finally, in Part V, we summarize the findings and their implications with respect to the identification and development of thinking skills, the development of causal and inductive inference, the development of metacognitive skill, the development and teaching of scientific thinking, and the relations between scientific and everyday thinking.

2

RELATED WORK

What is scientific thinking? While this question has long occupied philosophers of science, their debate has tended not to be influenced by psychological data. Within the psychology literature, answers are to be found reflecting a broad spectrum of views. At one end of that spectrum is the view that scientific thinking is a mode of exploring and coming to know the world that is within the competence of even very young children. At the other end is the view that proficient scientific thinking makes cognitive demands that even professional scientists are unable to fulfill. In this chapter, we consider each of these views, a number of intermediate ones, and the empirical evidence related to each. In so doing, we contemplate relations between scientific thinking and other kinds of thinking. To what extent is scientific thinking synonymous with logical thinking? To what extent is it similar to everyday thinking? To what extent does it undergo development?

Answers to these questions are to a large degree shaped by broad underlying psychological theories, or metaphors, regarding the nature of human beings. In the case of developmental psychology, metaphors of the child exert powerful influences on the way that development is conceived. The child as "unfolding flower" and "lump of clay"—metaphors that reflect maturationist and empiricist views of development—have shaped the history of the study of child development (Kuhn, in press). They and the other metaphors we consider—the child as scientist, as philosopher, as logician, as computer—continue to exert a broad influence on the research questions asked and the conclusions reached.

The topic of scientific thinking bears potential connections to a number of research literatures in psychology. We do not attempt in this chapter to present comprehensive reviews of each of them. Instead, we identify and describe each in broad terms and indicate how it is related both to the general topic of scientific thinking and to the research presented in this volume.

SCIENTIFIC THINKING AND SCIENTIFIC KNOWLEDGE

The very use of the term *scientific thinking* in fact implies a point of view, by suggesting that scientific thinking is to be distinguished from scientific knowledge. The major advance in the field of science education in the past few decades has been the recognition that the task of science instruction is not simply to supply previously lacking information about the nature of the world. Research by both cognitive psychologists and science educators has revealed that both children and adults hold a variety of naïve, intuitive conceptions, usually misconceptions, about how the world works (Carey, 1985a, 1985b, 1986; Champagne & Klopfer, 1984; DiSessa, 1983; Gentner & Gentner, 1983; Larkin, 1983; McCloskey, 1983; West & Pines, 1985). These conceptions, though wrong, have been shown to be powerful and remarkably resistant to instruction, such that the science educator must conceive of his or her task as making contact with these incorrect conceptions and working to change them, rather than superimposing new, correct concepts on them.

These mental models, as cognitive scientists refer to them, are more than the scripts (of event sequences) that Nelson (1985) and her colleagues have investigated, for they contain at least some element of *explanation* of how the phenomena operate. Yet, they are less than systematic, comprehensive theories. Multiple, inconsistent models of the same phenomenon are likely to coexist within an individual and be activated in different contexts (Williams, Hollan, & Stevens, 1983). An implication of this mental model view of scientific thinking is that the development of scientific understanding consists of a succession of incorrect theories within individual conceptual domains, theories that replace one another and only gradually come to approximate the correct one. It is this developmental process to which the science educator must be attuned. Such conceptual change, it is stressed, is likely to consist not only of changes in the relations among terms in the domain but in the very meaning of the core terms themselves, rendering successive theories not directly comparable with one another (Carey, 1985b, 1986). A number of researchers have identified sequences of this sort for particular scientific concepts (Carey, 1985b; Kaiser, McCloskey, & Proffitt, 1986; Krupa, Selman, & Jacquette, 1985; Strauss & Stavy, 1982).

The research presented in this volume falls within the boundaries of this new wave of work on the development of scientific understanding in one respect but not in another. The respect in which it is directly connected to this work is in its attention to the child's own theories as the starting point for examination of the child's thinking processes, a characteristic that distinguishes the present work from most research literature on the development of thinking skills. In another respect, however, our research is asking a very different set of questions than does the work on scientific understanding described above. That work reveals a great deal about the child's and adult's understandings of various scientific phenomena and the multiple forms they may take. It has little to say, however, about how these understandings are transformed from one form to another or, indeed, how they arose in the first place, in other words, about the process in terms of which the child constructs and revises theories as a way of learning about the world.

In justifying her approach, Carey (1985b) rightly points out that the task of identifying and describing such sequences of understandings logically precedes any investigation of mechanism. Carey goes on to argue, however, that many of the changes that previous researchers have identified in the child's cognitive functioning—the child's *ways of knowing* the world—were mistakenly identified as such and can in fact be explained in terms of the succession of conceptual changes within particular domains that her work and that of the others cited above investigates. While not denying the possibility that such changes in the child's "cognitive machinery," as she terms it, occur, Carey (1985a, 1985b) claims that there at present exists no firm evidence for such changes, changes that cannot more readily be accounted for in terms of conceptual change within content domains. Keil (1984) expresses a similar view.

Aligned with the view that cognitive development consists largely or entirely of domain-specific changes in conceptual understanding of the phenomena in the world is the metaphor of "child as scientist." Thomas Kuhn's (1962) ideas regarding the history of science as a progression of paradigms that replace one another have been very influential in fostering the child-as-scientist metaphor. As scientists through history have labored to understand the world around them and in so doing have constructed a succession of gradually more comprehensive and more correct theories, so the young child labors to understand his or her world and constructs the same (or at least the same type of) succession of theories (Carey, 1985b; Gruber, 1973; Piaget & Garcia, 1974). The power of the child-as-scientist metaphor lies in its implication that the child possesses the same conceptual apparatus for going about his or her task as does the scientist, an assumption to which Carey (1985b), Keil (1984), and many of the other researchers studying domain-specific conceptual change are sympathetic.

In the present work, in contrast, we present data to suggest that the conceptual tools used by the child, the lay adult, and the scientist are significantly different—that each goes about the task of understanding the world in significantly different ways. Framed in the terms we introduced in Chapter 1, the manner in which existing theories are coordinated with new evidence may not be the same in the child as it is in the adult or the scientist. It is in this sense, then— the *process* of coming to know about the world—that our research explores the nature of scientific thinking. It is not about the development of scientific thinking in the sense of developing concepts of scientific phenomena.

As a result, our work draws less directly on the work of Carey (1985a, 1985b,

1986) and the other researchers referred to above than it does on work addressed to questions of the nature of thinking and reasoning processes themselves and how they develop, a quite different and wide-ranging literature. If the scientific thinking that the child engages in is not that of the mature adult or the professional scientist, then what is its nature and in what ways does it develop, either naturally or through instruction, to resemble that of the scientist? The question is a critical one for the science educator. The idea that science educators ought to be teaching methods of scientific thinking, rather than merely scientific knowledge or concepts, has become increasingly popular, as we noted in Chapter 1, but in order for this prescription to be meaningful, it is necessary to have very explicit ideas as to what scientific thinking consists of. Curiously perhaps, the major place that science educators turned in seeking such definitions was not to science, but to logic, primarily the logical model of formal operations proposed by Piaget (Lawson, 1983).

SCIENTIFIC THINKING AS LOGICAL THINKING

On the face of it, logic would appear to be a fairly good model for scientific thinking. If we would ask anything of scientists, it would be to reason logically, to consider the information available and determine the conclusions that follow. Two different logical systems have been suggested as models of scientific thinking. One is the standard logic of deductive argument, reasoning from premises to conclusion (Braine & Rumain, 1983; O'Brien, 1987). The other is the combinatorial logic proposed by Inhelder and Piaget (1958) as characterizing the structure of the cognitive stage of formal operations.

In their 1958 volume *The Growth of Logical Thinking from Childhood to Adolescence,* Inhelder and Piaget presented the stage of formal operations as the culminating stage in the sequence of stages of cognitive development described in their earlier work. At the core of their definition of formal operations is the concept of second-order "operations on operations." In other words, with the advent of formal operations the adolescent becomes able to reflect, or "operate," on the concrete operations of classification and relation used during the middle childhood years as a means of organizing experience. These second-order operations, Inhelder and Piaget claimed, are organized into a "structured whole" which has the form of a logical system having properties based on a combinatorial and an INRC group structure. This logical structure manifests itself in the form of a number of broad cognitive strategies, the two most important among them being isolation, or control, of variables and systematic combination.

Inhelder and Piaget's theory of formal operations has been criticized on two major grounds, logical and empirical. The logical model itself has been alleged to contain serious inconsistencies and anomalies (Braine & Rumain, 1983;

Ennis, 1975, 1976; Parsons, 1960). At the empirical level, a good deal of research has indicated that not only do the individual cognitive strategies alleged to be manifestations of the formal operational structure not emerge in close conjunction with one another, but a single strategy itself may be exhibited in some contexts or content domains and not in others (see Keating, 1980, for review of literature). Seemingly minor and irrelevant changes in mode of assessment often produce major changes in performance. The import of these findings was to bring into question the structured-whole concept of formal operational thought as a unitary entity.

It is the second of these criticisms that is actually the more serious. If Inhelder and Piaget perhaps got their logic wrong, the obvious possibility remains that it can be corrected, that there is *some* logical structure that underlies the set of cognitive competencies observed. If these competencies appeared in people's behavior as a tightly linked whole, the claim that they were manifestations of a logical system would have plausibility, and it would remain to identify the precise nature of this system. But the fact that these competencies are not closely tied empirically makes matters more difficult. Because they by and large do not appear to be tightly linked, the question can be raised as to whether the behaviors are in fact manifestations of *any* underlying logical system. Is it logic that ties together the set of cognitive competencies that Inhelder and Piaget observed to be absent before adolescence?

A positive answer is made even more uncertain by the fact that the cognitive skills alleged to be the manifestation of the formal operational logical structure are not, on the face of it at least, primarily skills in logic. In the experiments on which Inhelder and Piaget's theory is based, subjects are asked to experiment with physical phenomena and to draw inferences regarding the causal relations that obtain among the variables examined. The skills being assessed appear on the surface at least to be skills in scientific thinking, or perhaps more narrowly in multivariable causal inference (though research on causal inference, which we come to shortly, has tended not to be connected to research on formal operations). Arguments can certainly be made that an underlying logical competence is at stake but that various performance variables moderate its expression (O'Brien, 1987; Overton, 1985; Overton & Newman, 1983). But the point is that such arguments need to be constructed—that the connection between logic and performance is not apparent on the surface, as it would be, for example, if subjects were being asked to evaluate syllogisms. The ambiguity surrounding formal operational reasoning is reflected in the fact that while Piaget characterized formal operations as the final stage in his system and the end point of cognitive development, the underlying metaphor that characterizes this attainment is subject to interpretation and has been variously identified by authors writing about Piaget. Is the "epistemic subject" Piaget described a developing logician, a developing philosopher, or a developing scientist?

Interestingly, Piaget himself exhibited ambivalence regarding formal logic as a model of human thought, proposing near the end of his career that a "logic of meanings" might be better (Beilin, 1984).

It is also worth noting in this respect that while science educators concerned with teaching scientific thinking skills have turned primarily to Piaget and formal operations (Lawson, 1983), they have not focused on the theory as a model of logical competence. Rather than undertaking to induce some broad logical structure, they have focused by and large on the individual cognitive strategies (notably control of variables) and attempted to devise ways to induce those.

The situation is similar in the case of standard deductive logic as a model of scientific thinking. If it is a logical system equivalent to standard deductive logic that underlies and produces a subject's reasoning performance, then problems that entail the same logical deductions ought to yield the same performance. In fact, problems that are equivalent from a logical point of view often produce very different types of performance. Arguments can always be made that other variables moderate the expression of logical competence, but again the question arises as to whether it is a system of deductive logic at all that underlies a subject's performance. The logical reasoning task that bears the strongest potential link to scientific reasoning is Wason's (1966) selection task. In the original version of the task, four cards are placed before the subject, one containing the letter A, one the letter B, one the numeral 4, and one the numeral 7. It is explained that each card contains a letter on one side and a numeral on the reverse side. The subject is asked to turn over the necessary cards to determine the validity of this rule: "If a card has an A on one side, then it has a 4 on the other." The question a subject is being asked in this task is thus "What set of evidence corresponds to the truth, and what set to the falsehood of this proposition?" While it is appropriate to regard the selection task as a problem in logical reasoning, it comes closer to the kind of reasoning that a scientist might engage in than do, for example, traditional syllogistic reasoning problems. When presented in the form just indicated, the selection task is solved correctly by only about 10% of college students. Instead of the correct choices, A and 7, subjects frequently choose A and 4, failing to see the relevance of the 7 (to insure that it does *not* have an A on the other side), and incorrectly regarding as relevant the 4 (which would not disconfirm the rule no matter which letter appeared on the reverse side). These results frequently have been interpreted as evidence for a confirmation bias, that is, a predisposition to search for evidence that will confirm a theory (Mynatt, Doherty, & Tweney, 1977; Wason, 1960; Wason & Johnson-Laird, 1968, 1972), a conclusion of direct relevance for scientific reasoning.

The problem with straightforward interpretation of these results as an indication of logical-reasoning competence, however, is that they have been found to vary dramatically when the form of the problem remains the same but different content is introduced. For example, when the rule to be evaluated was changed to "If a letter is sealed, then it has a 5d stamp on it," correct performance among college students rose to over 80% (Johnson-Laird, Legrenzi, & Legrenzi, 1972). Cheng and Holyoak (1985) make a convincing argument against interpretation of such so-called facilitation effects as due merely to the substitution of concrete in place of abstract content. They propose the view that reasoning of the sort examined is based not on a system of formal logic but on knowledge structures that are induced from ordinary experience. These "pragmatic reasoning schemas," such as permission, obligation, and causation, are defined in terms of classes of goals (such as taking desirable actions or predicting future events) and relationships to these goals (such as cause and effect or precondition and allowable action). Cheng and Holyoak (1985) found performance in the selection task highly likely to be correct if the rule to be evaluated mapped onto an existing pragmatic reasoning schema, for example, "If a person is to drink alcoholic beverages, s/he must be at least 18," which evokes the permission schema. Significantly, as long as the permission schema is activated, it is not necessary that the content be concrete. Cheng and Holyoak's subjects also did well when the rule to be evaluated was "If one is to take action A, then one must first satisfy precondition P." Additional studies they carried out established that what is critical to performance is not abstractness versus concreteness of the rule to be evaluated but that it have a plausible rationale, one either provided by the experimenter or already available to the subject. It is relevant to note that this same effect of providing a rationale has been observed in the case of formal operational reasoning strategies, particularly when subjects are nonacademic adults. Performance in generating systematic combinations, for example, can be improved significantly not just by substituting concrete materials (e.g., pizza ingredients) for abstract ones but, more important, by providing the subject a plausible rationale (e.g., preparing a menu and prices for a pizza shop) (Kuhn, Pennington, & Leadbeater, 1983).

Results of the sort cited have led Cheng and Holyoak and a number of their colleagues to reject formal logic as the basis of cognition (Cheng & Holyoak, 1985; Cheng, Holyoak, Nisbett, & Oliver, 1986). The formal material conditional that is at the heart of deductive logic, they claim, is too abstract to map well onto reality. As a result, it is both hard to understand and difficult to teach (Cheng et al., 1986). It should be emphasized that the issue is more than one of whether logic is or is not a good way to model cognition. The significance of a logical model lies in its claim that a general system of logic of one sort or another is in place as part of a person's cognitive apparatus and that (unless some moderating variable interferes) it is this system that produces the person's performance in reasoning tasks. Cheng and Holyoak, in contrast, posit an inductive apparatus that organizes the effects of experience and forms the basis of the person's knowledge of the world. Though they do not make this connection, the pragmatic reasoning schemas that Cheng and Holyoak posit might be regarded as highly generalized forms of the event scripts that Nelson (Nelson & Gruendel, 1981) has proposed are the "building blocks" of cognitive development. In any case, the essential claim is that what is critical to inferential behavior is the context and goals involved in the reasoning, not an abstract logical form it may resemble.

If thinking, and scientific thinking in particular, is more than logic, then what is it? To the extent that the rational thinking that humans display is not accounted for by a system of logic, then some alternative way to conceptualize that rationality must be proposed (Baron, 1985). Cheng and Holyoak (1985) offer one such alternative. We have more to say shortly about their pragmatic reasoning schemas and the general model of induction to which they are related. First, let us look at another model of scientific thinking.

SCIENTIFIC THINKING AS PROBLEM SOLVING

Analyses of scientific activity traditionally have divided it into three major phases: hypothesis generation, experimentation, and inference; investigations of scientific thinking are frequently organized around these divisions (Klahr & Dunbar, in press; Kuhn & Phelps, 1982; Mynatt, Doherty, & Tweney, 1977; Pitt, 1983). Simon (1977) proposed that this process can be characterized as a process of search through a problem space, similar to the one that occurs in any problem-solving task (Newell & Simon, 1972). Klahr and Dunbar (in press) have built on Simon's idea and proposed that scientific discovery consists of a coordinated search through two problem spaces, a space of hypotheses and a space of experiments. They criticize previous laboratory tasks that have been used to simulate scientific activity, for example, the rule discovery task first used by Wason (1960). Subjects in this task are given the series of numbers 2, 4, 6 and instructed to generate more such series in order to discover the rule of which these series are instances. In response to each series generated by the subject, the experimenter indicates only that it is or is not an instance of the rule; the experimenter also indicates whether any rules the subject proposes are correct or not. While the correct rule is simply "an increasing series," subjects in this task typically propose much more complicated rules. Klahr and Dunbar criticize this task as a poor simulation of scientific discovery, primarily on the grounds that it is essentially a guessing game in which all rules are arbitrary and hence equally plausible and on the grounds that experiments produce nothing more than binary outcomes. In their own research, Klahr and Dunbar present subjects with a device (a programmable computer-controlled robot called "BigTrak") and ask them to experiment with it to discover how certain of its features work. Subjects are asked to think aloud while experimenting and to report their conclusions.

This approach is similar to ones used in a study by Metz (1985), who also adopts the problem-space theoretical perspective, and in a series of studies by Kuhn and Phelps (1982) and Schauble and Kuhn (in progress) which we consider in more detail in Chapter 11.

Klahr and Dunbar (in press) interpret their results in the framework of subjects' coordination of movement through the problem space of hypotheses and the problem space of experiments (instances). This framework is presented as a model of "scientific discovery as dual search" (SDDS), which Klahr and Dunbar describe as an extension of the generalized rule inducer (GRI) proposed by Simon and Lea (1974). Search in the hypothesis space is guided both by prior knowledge and by experimental results, and search in the experiment space is guided by the type of hypothesis the subject is investigating and the results of prior experiments. The process of scientific discovery is portrayed as consisting of three components: *search hypothesis space, test hypothesis,* and *evaluate evidence*. The major connection between components that Klahr and Dunbar examine is the link between "*search hypothesis space*" and "*test hypothesis,*" that is, between hypothesis and experimentation. As in the Wason rule discovery task, subjects appear to generate experiments that will confirm their hypotheses: "If my hypothesis is correct, then the robot will do this." Klahr and Dunbar point out, however, that this strategy is not necessarily an inappropriate one. Whether it is or not depends on the probability of the hypothesis being correct. If the probability is high, this strategy will not provide any useful information. If it is low, however, the strategy can lead to disconfirmation of an incorrect hypothesis. Other authors have argued similarly that this so-called confirmation bias may not in fact reflect faulty reasoning (Baron, 1985; Greenwald, 1981; Klayman & Ha, 1987; Meehl, 1978).

Klahr and Dunbar devote less attention to the connection between the second and third components of their model and to the nature of the third component (*evaluate evidence*) itself. *Evaluate evidence,* they indicate, consists of two evaluations that are not further specified in the model. These evaluations determine whether the cumulative evidence about the current hypothesis and the experiments run under the hypothesis are sufficient to reject the current hypothesis or whether they are sufficient to accept the current hypothesis. If neither condition is met, a third branch is taken which loops back to the second component, *test hypothesis*.

Klahr and Dunbar's emphasis on the role of prior knowledge in guiding search through the hypothesis space and hence in shaping the process of scientific reasoning is consonant with the approach taken in the present work. As are we, they are concerned with how a subject coordinates existing theories with the generation of new evidence that will bear on them. In our case, however, a central concern is how the evidence itself is interpreted as bearing on the hypothesis or theory. As indicated above, Klahr and Dunbar's *evaluate evidence* phase contains little explanation of the nature of this inductive activity. Other approaches we shall examine, in contrast, focus on induction from evidence as the heart of scientific thinking. (Simon and Lea's [1974] GRI, on which Klahr and Dunbar's model is based, is in fact an example.) Before turning to these approaches, it is worthwhile to add that we see Klahr and Dunbar's work as an excellent effort to provide an explicit model of what a subject does in the process of self-directed experimentation and discovery. What is less apparent from their account is how a subject knows that this is what to do and where such knowledge comes from. These questions raise issues of both metacognition and development, topics to which we turn shortly.

SCIENTIFIC THINKING AS INDUCTION

How do humans in general, and scientists in particular, learn about the nature of the world? Clearly, some process of *induction* is involved. Associations, patterns, regularities are observed, and on this basis expectations or concepts regarding the way the world is organized are formed. Whether or not deductive logic plays a role in scientific thinking, inductive reasoning is clearly central to what scientists do. Inductive reasoning has been less amenable to study by psychologists than has deductive reasoning. A recent volume by Holland, Holyoak, Nisbett, and Thagard (1986) proposes a general theory of induction. It is significant as one of the first efforts to provide a systematic account of the process of induction, an account that is explicit as well as sufficiently broad to account for simple concept learning exhibited by animals and major scientific discoveries. The classic psychology literature on concept formation, in which subjects are asked to discover a concept consisting of an arbitrary combination of attributes by examining instances that are or are not examples of the concept (Bower & Trabasso, 1964; Bruner, Goodnow, & Austin, 1956; Hunt, 1962), can be regarded as dealing with induction. Holland et al. (1986), however, like Klahr and Dunbar (in press), are critical of that paradigm, and the work it generated, on the grounds of its providing too simplified and too restricted a picture of how humans reason inductively, one that fails to take into account the meaning of the material to the subject or the subject's goals.

Holland et al. (1986) regard their model as consistent with Simon and Lea's (1974) problem-solving model of cognition and see all inductive behavior as goal directed and contextual. They are also committed to a *computational* model of cognition, and they state explicitly that the processes they describe are meant to characterize any cognitive system, including artificial ones. The metaphor that underlies their model, and the terms in which it must be understood, is thus that of the child or adult as a computational system. The system they describe is like a standard production system, made up of condition-action rules (Newell, 1973;

Newell & Simon, 1972). These rules are organized on the basis of patterns that occur among them. The primary organizational entity Holland et al. refer to is a default hierarchy, which orders rules by default expectations based on subordinate/superordinate relations. For example, categorizing an object as a vegetable produces a set of default expectations about it, but if the object is also recognized as a turnip the more general default expectations may be overridden by more specific ones associated with the subordinate concept. Because the more specific rules override the more general ones in the hierarchy, imperfect default rules often fail to be disconfirmed. In other words, the individual generates exceptions to the rule rather than revises it. Rules compete with one another to represent the current state of affairs and to guide thinking and action. Together they give rise to a mental model which guides behavior and generate predictions, which, if not fulfilled, will lead to inductive change, that is, to revision of rules and generation of new ones.

To what extent does this model capture processes of scientific reasoning? The strength of the model lies in the combination of its detail and yet intended breadth. To attempt to conceptualize common elements in a category of behavior as broad as induction—elements that would apply equally well to the induction displayed by animals, scientists, and artificial cognitive systems—is clearly an ambitious and an important undertaking. Not surprisingly, what gets ignored in such an effort are the significant differences among inductive processes in these varying contexts. The approach taken in the research described in this volume in some sense complements the effort represented in the Holland et al. (1986) book, in that it is concerned with differences rather than commonalities in the inductive thinking of children, adults, and scientists. In addressing this concern, it incorporates two features that we see as absent in Holland et al.'s approach (and similarly claimed were missing in Klahr and Dunbar's work). The first is a developmental framework—the idea that the system itself may undergo development. Holland et al. portray their cognitive system as changing certainly, in the sense that the hierarchy of rules is continually undergoing revision; but the possibility that the processes of revision themselves may undergo modification is not addressed. The second, related aspect is that a major respect in which the system may itself develop is in the respect of becoming increasingly conscious of itself. Holland et al. make only one fleeting reference to such consciousness, in mentioning the possibility of a "model of the model." Human cognitive systems, they say, often have conscious awareness of their models, enabling them to bypass more local forms of rule revision by recognizing an incorrect rule and abandoning it. They do not go on, however, to explore the implications of the presence or absence of this conscious awareness, or model of the model, for the way in which the system functions. The research presented in the present volume suggests that the attainment of such consciousness is a central aspect of the development of scientific thinking and of cognitive development more generally.

An important implication of Holland et al.'s approach is the idea that scientific thinking is continuous with other forms of human thinking that involve induction. To the extent that this is so, then it is human thinking more broadly that needs to be investigated and understood, with scientific thinking regarded perhaps as a special case. The present work reflects this continuity view. Moreover, we believe that the developmental framework in terms of which our work is conceived suggests a way to conceptualize the continuity and the relation between scientific and everyday thinking. Before considering developmental issues, let us turn to the sizable research literature that relates to the everyday thinking of adults.

SCIENTIFIC THINKING AND EVERYDAY THINKING

In a volume that was to have a major impact on the field, Nisbett and Ross (1980) examined the layperson as an "intuitive scientist." They describe a wide range of research suggesting shortcomings in the inductive inference skills of adults. Much of the research they cite is from the pioneering work of Tversky and Kahneman and their colleagues (Kahneman, Slovic, & Tversky, 1982). Two inferential heuristics proposed by Tversky and Kahneman, the availability heuristic and the representativeness heuristic, carry much of the explanatory burden in accounting for subjects' inferential errors. The availability heuristic produces judgments of frequency based on availability in short-term memory. For example, subjects judge the letter r as more frequent in the first position of a word (though it is in fact most frequent in the third position) because words beginning with r are more available in their memory. The representativeness heuristic is defined as the judgment of likelihood of an event based on the extent to which the event resembles the parent population or generating process. For example, in coin tosses, the sequence H-T-H-T-T-H is considered more likely than the sequence H-H-H-T-T-T.

One phenomenon Tversky and Kahneman attribute to the representativeness heuristic is neglect of base rates. In a typical study, subjects were shown brief personality descriptions of several individuals allegedly sampled from a group of 100 professional engineers and lawyers. In each case they were asked to assess the probability that the individual described was an engineer versus a lawyer. Some subjects were told that the group consisted of 30 engineers and 70 lawyers, while others were told that the distribution was the reverse. Subjects' probability judgments were unaffected by this manipulation. Another example of nonuse of base rates is provided by the cab problem. A cab was involved in a hit-and-run accident at night. There are two cab companies operating in the city, Green and Blue, and 85% of cabs are Green and 15% Blue. The reliability of a witness who identified the cab as Blue was 80%. What is the probability that the cab was Blue rather than Green? Because the base rate is more extreme than the witness is credible, the cab is more likely to be Green than Blue. Yet subjects quite consistently give the response ".8," ignoring the base-rate information. A slight change in the problem, however, yields different results. Instead of being told merely that 85% of cabs are Green and 15% Blue, the subject is told, "Although the two companies are roughly equal in size, 85% of cab accidents in the city involve Green cabs and 15% involve Blue cabs." In this condition, attention to base rates is much greater, which can be explained by the fact that in this case the base rates are interpreted causally.

Nisbett and Ross (1980) examine the ways in which the availability and representativeness heuristics may operate in everyday life to produce faulty inductive inference. For example, evidence that is more vivid or otherwise more available in a person's memory is likely to achieve disproportionate weight. The lack of attention to base rates relates directly to the "fundamental attribution error" identified by social psychologists: the tendency to underestimate the impact of situational factors and to overestimate the role of dispositional factors in controlling behavior (Ross, 1977). Also, following Tversky and Kahneman, Nisbett and Ross stress the role of theories, notably causal theories, in directing people's inference, as the cab example in the preceding paragraph suggests. It is in this respect that their ideas are most directly relevant to the research reported in this volume. Theories, they suggest, play a disproportionate role in inference in two respects. First, they influence the way data are coded and interpreted. Second, they tend to persevere long after sufficient evidence has become available to discredit them.

How do theories influence the way in which data are perceived? Holland et al. (1986), whose ideas follow those of Nisbett and Ross (1980) in this respect, claim that in order for connections to become candidates for rules within default hierarchies, covarying properties need to be linked by a causal theory or at least a strong semantic association (or, in the case of animal conditioning, preparedness by virtue of past experience or perhaps genetic wiring). A similar idea is advanced by Murphy and Medin (1985). The implication is that covariation is not perceived unless the perceiver has expectations that it ought to be present. The classic research supporting this assertion is the work on illusory correlation by Chapman and Chapman (1967, 1969). In one of their studies, subjects were asked to study a set of cards each containing a verbal response to a Rorschach image and a stated psychological symptom. Some of these were homosexual "symptoms," for example, "has sexual feelings toward other men." The Rorschach responses that subjects reported to be correlated with homosexual symptoms were those that had some face valid association with homosexuality and not those that were in fact correlated with homosexual symptoms in the set of cards examined. Similar results were obtained in a study by Jennings, Amabile, and Ross (1982) and in several other more recent studies (Hamilton, Dugan, & Trolier, 1985; Spears, Van der Plight, & Eiser, 1985; Trolier &

Hamilton, 1986; Wright & Murphy, 1984). In the study by Jennings et al. (1982), subjects were presented a set of people's scores on a test of ability to delay gratification and a test of ability to resist temptation to cheat, and were asked to use these scores to estimate the relationship between these two variables. The majority of subjects greatly overestimated the strength of the relationship, presumably due to their belief that these two variables ought to be related. In contrast, when asked to estimate correlations between neutral variables, for example, pairs of numbers, subjects tended to greatly underestimate the true correlation, a result in accord with a great deal of earlier literature suggesting the limited ability of both adults and children to assess correlation (Alloy & Tabachnik, 1984; Arkes & Harkness, 1983; Crocker, 1981; Inhelder & Piaget, 1958; Jenkins & Ward; 1965; Shaklee & Mims, 1981; Shaklee & Paszek, 1985; Smedslund, 1963).

Other work reviewed by Nisbett and Ross suggests that theories bias the selection, not just the interpretation, of evidence. Snyder and Swann (1978), for example, instructed subjects to determine in an interview with another subject whether or not that subject was an extrovert. Subjects tended to ask questions to which a positive answer would support the theory that the person was an extrovert, while a negative answer would have provided, at most, weak evidence that the person was not an extrovert. In other words, subjects showed the same confirmation bias discussed earlier.

The other way in which Nisbett and Ross (1980) have suggested that theories play a disproportionate role in inference is in their tendency to persevere after sufficient evidence is available to discredit them. These so-called belief perseverance effects, also discussed by Baron (1985) and a number of others, are highlighted in a widely cited study by Lord, Ross, and Lepper (1979). Subjects whose responses on an attitude survey identified them as either proponents or opponents of capital punishment were presented, in a counterbalanced order, two purportedly authoritative studies, one supportive of and the other in opposition to capital punishment. Subjects showed a marked asymmetry in evaluation of this information. They regarded the information supportive of their position in a more accepting and less critical, scrutinizing manner than the information opposing their position and shifted their beliefs accordingly further in the direction of their initial position. The experience of examining mixed evidence thus had the effect of further polarization of initial beliefs.

Though the Lord et al. (1979) study has been widely cited as evidence for polarization effects, it does not provide clear evidence regarding the conditions that produce polarization. Perhaps, for example, it was not examination of the evidence itself that led subjects in their study to become more extreme in their beliefs but merely the opportunity to contemplate those beliefs. If so, the same polarization effect might have been produced by instructions to write an essay on the topic, with no presentation of evidence. In addition to no evidence, it would be important to know how the evaluation of either supportive or discrepant evidence alone, as well as mixed evidence, influence beliefs. In Chapter 6, we present some data that bear on these questions. A further broad issue raised by the Lord et al. study is the extent to which belief perseveration is irrational. How much evidence of what sort ideally should lead to belief revision? Debate continues as to whether normative models of human inference that could answer such questions are justified, as Baron (1985) and others claim, or whether it is impossible to define, for example, just how much belief perseveration is normative, as Nisbett and Ross (1980) suggest.

What are the implications of the research on the shortcomings of adults' performance as intuitive scientists with regard to the thinking processes of professional scientists? Are we to assume that they are equally flawed? Thomas Kuhn's (1962) account of scientific progress, though at a broader level than the individual thinker, suggests an affirmative answer in his view that normal science proceeds within theoretical paradigms that are resistant to disconfirmation and ultimately are replaced rather than disconfirmed. Investigations of the thinking processes of professional scientists support this view (Faust, 1984; Mahoney & Kimper, 1976). Scientists display confirmation bias, it has been claimed, when they persevere by revising procedures until obtaining a theory-predicted result (Greenwald, Pratkanis, Lèippe, & Baumgardner, 1986). Studies of the reasoning of medical doctors have shown less than optimal performance, with some of the same errors observed as those described above (Eddy, 1982; Elstein et al., 1978; Schwartz & Griffin, 1986). Chapman and Chapman (1969) obtained the same results as those described earlier when their subjects were professional clinical psychologists.

The question of the rationality of human thought, however, is far from resolved. So little is known about complex reasoning processes such as those used by a scientist that it is premature to label them faulty. The research reviewed by Nisbett and Ross (1980) and their conclusion that the layperson performs very poorly as an intuitive scientist have generated considerable debate and are subject to some significant criticisms. In a major critique, Cohen (1981) complains:

> The ordinary person is claimed to be prone to serious and systematic error in deductive reasoning, in judging probabilities, in correcting his biases, and in many other activities. Yet, from this apparently unpromising material—indeed, from the very same students who are the typical subjects of cognitive psychologists' experiments—sufficient cadres are recruited to maintain the sophisticated institutions of modern civilisation. (p. 317)

This paradox, Cohen maintains, reflects the irrationality of claims of human irrationality. His argument is based on the classic problem that arises in defining normatively correct reasoning and then using it as a standard against which other forms of reasoning can be evaluated (Goodman, 1965; Stitch & Nisbett, 1980). What is normative in the domain of inference has been defined on the grounds of intuitive reasonableness, or rationality. How then can one claim that human intuition departs from this standard of rationality?

Cohen's (1981) broad conclusion that "nothing in the existing literature on cognitive reasoning, or in any possible future results of human experimental enquiry, could have bleak implication for human rationality" (p. 330), and hence that the scientific investigation of mental processes is irrelevant to the revelation of their true nature, has been strongly refuted in a number of commentaries following his article. Yet the argument that the conclusions of Kahneman et al. (1982) and Nisbett and Ross (1980) and their colleagues are more sweeping than the limited available data warrant deserves attention. All of these researchers tend to portray the "intuitions" displayed by the subjects in their studies as revealing fundamental characteristics of the human mind: the basic way people are. Little attention is paid to characteristics of either subjects or context that might limit the generality of the inferences that are drawn.

A strong claim can be made that the experiential backgrounds of the college students who are the typical subjects in these studies and the nature of the experimental situations themselves are likely to place significant constraints on the behavior that is displayed in them. To the extent that interpreters of this behavior ignore such constraints, they themselves may be guilty of the earlier cited fundamental attribution error that psychologists rely on to explain their subjects' behavior (Becker & Kuhn, 1984). Years of schooling have ingrained in such subjects the attitude that in situations such as these, in which an examiner presents information and asks for a response, one should try to understand what the examiner has in mind. What might be a plausible purpose of the activity that the examiner and subject are engaging in, and how might the information that has been provided be put together to produce an answer in a way that accords with this purpose? In the case of the base rate problems described earlier, for example, if the interviewer provides personality descriptions of people and asks for a judgment regarding their occupations, is not the most plausible interpretation that the purpose of the activity is to assess the subject's ability to match occupations with personalities? If this is the way they construe the task, the probability estimates subjects give are likely to be judgments of degree of confidence that they have made the correct match (estimates to which base rates are irrelevant). In a very different, perhaps real-life context, imagine that the subject had a real need to determine whether John was a lawyer or an engineer (though it is difficult to imagine a situation in which this binary choice had to be made, especially with such impoverished knowledge about John). In this case, it is this goal that would dominate, rather than the goal of trying to behave intelligently with an examiner. Can we infer with any confidence that base rates would be ignored in this case?

And what if a subject's experiential background is entirely different from that of the typical college sophomore? Though Nisbett and Ross (1980) make passing reference to cross-cultural and individual differences, there is no real consideration of variability—individual, cultural, or developmental—in the research they review. In the research presented in this volume, it is developmental variation in particular that concerns us. We believe that developmental investigation provides a framework for conceptualizing skills in inductive inference and stands to inform debate about human rationality. In particular, we claim, developmental investigation suggests a framework in which to conceptualize the biasing effects of one's theoretical beliefs and the developmental progression that effects their decline. Let us turn, then, finally, to the matter of development.

THE DEVELOPMENT OF INDUCTIVE THINKING SKILLS

Two major lines of research have to do with the development of inductive thinking skills. They remain largely unconnected to one another, and each has a different set of limitations. One is research on the development of causal inference (Shultz & Kestenbaum, 1985) and the other is research on the formal operational reasoning strategies identified by Inhelder and Piaget (1958).

In light of the large body of research just described suggesting weaknesses in the inferential reasoning of adults, it is striking to observe that the research on children's causal inference is devoted almost entirely to demonstrations of early competence. In Chapter 1, we alluded to the methodological factors that might account for this paradox. The majority of studies of children's causal inference have focused on the traditional Humean principles, notably covariation, that might be relied on in situations in which two competing potential causes are present (Bullock, Gelman, & Baillergeon, 1982; Sedlak & Kurtz, 1981; Shultz, 1982). Studies of both children and adults carried out within the framework of attribution theory (Kelley, 1973) likewise follow the method of eliciting a choice between two competing causes. Those studies investigating covariation show some convergence in their findings that, in attributing causality, children, by school age, show a preference for a factor that consistently covaries with the effect over a factor that does not (Mendelson & Shultz, 1976; Shultz & Mendelson, 1975; Siegler, 1975, 1976). The conclusion commonly drawn from these studies is that school-age children "have" or "use" a covariation principle. In what sense is this conclusion warranted?

Bindra, Clarke, and Shultz (1980), in a slightly more complex design, undertook to assess children's understanding of two causal situations, one in which A or B was sufficient to cause an effect (sufficiency) and the other in which only A and B together produced the effect (necessity), by asking subjects to predict forward and backward, that is, to the effect when the antecedents were known and to antecedents when the effect was known. Subjects' predictions were scored in terms of their correctness in each of the two situations. For example, a subject was told that A and E (effect) had both occurred and asked whether or not B had occurred; in the conjunctive (necessity) case, the correct answer is yes (since E occurs only when both antecedents have occurred), while in the sufficiency case, the correct answer is maybe, since B may or may not have occurred. Thus, a subject who answers yes for both is scored as correct in the one problem and incorrect in the other. A significant proportion of answers to such questions were correct among 3- to 13-year-old subjects.

In fact, however, based on this method of analysis, we can conclude little about the strategy that a subject is using to generate his or her predictions. It is entirely possible, for example, that a considerably simpler strategy or principle than the necessity or sufficiency principles, comprehension of which Bindra et al. (1980) intended to assess, may have been the strategy subjects used to generate predictions. It is impossible to tell for certain from their published data since they indicate only whether a subject's prediction (yes, no, or maybe) was correct or incorrect and not what the prediction actually was, but, for all but the oldest subjects on one or two items, the prediction data presented are not inconsistent with usage of a very simple co-occurrence strategy (if antecedent positive, outcome positive; if antecedent negative, outcome negative, and conversely for predicting from outcome to antecedent). Nevertheless, the Bindra et al. study has been widely cited, usually with negligible qualification, for example by Brainerd (1979), as demonstrating the impressive competence of young children in comprehending the complex concepts of causal necessity and sufficiency.

The Bindra et al. procedure deviates from the more typical one of asking the subject to attribute an effect to one of two potential causes, but the general point is that such procedures do not permit strong inferences regarding the strategy generating the subject's responses. From the fact that the subject's response choice matches that of a sophisticated strategy or principle, it cannot be inferred that the subject is using the strategy or comprehends the principle. Describing the subject's behavior as reflecting the sophisiticated strategy may provide a convenient label for the behavior, but little more. Suppose, for example, that instead of asking the subjects in the studies by Siegler and by Shultz and Mendelson to choose which of two antecedents (one covarying and one not) caused an event, they were asked simply whether or not a causal inference was warranted with respect to the noncovarying factor? Data we present in subsequent chapters indicate that the response is likely to be yes, among many older as well as younger subjects. It is only in a limited sense, then, that such subjects can be said to have or use a covariation principle in making causal inferences.

While still focused on early competence, later work by Shultz (1982), Siegler (1983), Bullock (1985), and others investigating children's causal reasoning acknowledges that causal inferences are likely to be based on a variety of different, sometimes conflicting, cues and that context may be an important determinant of which cues are attended to (Einhorn & Hogarth, 1986; Koslowski

& Okagaki, 1986; Mackie, 1974). Shultz (1982), for example, undertook to show the importance of the child's understanding of the mechanism by means of which a cause produces an effect—what we refer to as causal theories in the present work and what Shultz termed concepts of "generative transmission" (from cause to effect). Shultz contrasted these cues to causality with those provided by the traditional Humean principles such as contiguity and covariation. Significantly, Shultz's results revealed no developmental differences: Children aged 2–13 consistently chose as cause of an effect that factor consistent with their understanding of the mechanism involved over a factor that was inconsistent with their understanding of the mechanism but (unlike the first factor) consistent with Humean principles. For example, it was always the lamp that was turned on (rather than off) that was attributed as causing a spot of light to shine on the wall; similarly, if one lamp's path between itself and the wall was blocked by a mirror, causality was not attributed to that lamp, despite the fact that in both cases conditions were such that Humean principles would have predicted the opposite choice.

Shultz's (1982) study is significant in indicating that rules for attributing causality do not operate in some general, context-free fashion, independent of the subject's theoretical understanding of the particular content involved. Indeed, this understanding can override clues that normally indicate causality. This "contextualization" of causal inference is consonant with the pragmatic reasoning schema approach of Cheng and Holyoak (1985) discussed earlier and with the approach taken in the present work. Unlike Cheng and Holyoak, however, and contradictory to Shultz's developmental data, we shall present data suggesting that the manner in which existing causal theories interact with the interpretation of new information undergoes developmental change. In addition, of course, the causal theories themselves, and the understanding of the physical world that they reflect, undergo developmental transformation, as both Piaget's work (Piaget & Garcia, 1974) and the more recent research on scientific concepts discussed earlier indicates.

Later work by Siegler has evolved in a similar direction by demonstrating that a child's causal theories determine which environmental cues are encoded and therefore eligible as candidates for causal attribution. Children who do not recognize distance from the fulcrum as a causal variable in the balance scale problem do not encode information about distance (Siegler, 1983; Siegler & Klahr, 1982). Kaiser et al. (1986) likewise have shown that causal theories determine the information that is attended to.

Following the general line of thought regarding the importance of context and multiple cues, especially the ideas of Einhorn and Hogarth (1986), we would argue that the most significant form in which to examine causal reasoning is not one in which a forced choice between two causes is required, but rather one in which a number of potential causes are present, any or all of which might be implicated as causal in connection with an observed event. It is this situation, it can be claimed, that best approximates the situations in which inductive reasoning occurs naturally. Surprisingly, however, few studies of this so-called multivariable causal inference exist. Those that do are restricted to college subjects, and the judgments that subjects are required to make are not straight-forward causal attributions, casting doubt on the extent to which the reasoning resembles that occurring in more natural contexts (Downing, Sternberg, & Ross, 1985; Schustack & Sternberg, 1981; Shaklee & Fischhoff, 1982). With the exception of our own earlier work (Kuhn & Brannock, 1977; Kuhn & Ho, 1980; Kuhn, Ho, & Adams, 1979; Kuhn & Phelps, 1982), there have been no developmental studies of multivariable causal inference.

In contrast, there has been a large volume of developmental research based on Inhelder and Piaget's (1958) studies of adolescents' experimentation with simple physical phenomena. These studies might well be regarded as studies of multivariable causal inference, as the subject's task is to experiment with the materials to determine what makes a difference to the outcome. Curiously, however, this work has been regarded as pertaining only to formal operational reasoning and has rarely been connected to the literature on causal inference. One reason may be that the focus of Inhelder and Piaget's attention was on the subject's experimentation strategies, in particular, ability to control variables, rather than on the inferences the subject made as a result of the experimentation. A further reason may be a dominating focus on the implications of these studies with respect to the validity of Inhelder and Piaget's theory of formal operations, as we discussed earlier. Only a few researchers have examined reasoning strategies related to the ones investigated by Inhelder and Piaget, outside of the context of the theory of formal operations (Case, 1978a, 1978b; Gholson, 1980; Tschirgi, 1980).

Independent of the correctness of their theory of formal operations, the empirical studies by Inhelder and Piaget (1958) and numerous replication studies have shown that before adolescence, skills in assessing the causal influences of physical variables on one another are deficient. The full implications of these findings, we believe, have not been explored, again probably because of the focus on their relation to the theory of formal operations. Though, for the reasons indicated above, we focus on inference rather than experimentation skills, the scientific thinking skills examined in the present volume relate very directly to those investigated by Inhelder and Piaget. Probably because of their role in the formal operational logical model, however, we believe that Inhelder and Piaget regarded these skills in too "formal" a way, that is, as completely generalized, abstract operations that function in a uniform way independent of the particular content about which a subject is reasoning. With the exception of some later work by Inhelder and her colleagues (Karmiloff-Smith & Inhelder, 1974), Inhelder and Piaget never regarded their subjects' particular theories about the phenomena they were exploring as directing or even affecting the experimentation process. It is this interaction that is central to the present work.

METACOGNITION AND DEVELOPMENT

There is a second respect in which the present research, though diverging from it in important ways, builds on Inhelder and Piaget's pioneering work on the development of scientific thinking. The defining core of formal operations, in their view, is the ability to reflect on one's own thought, that is, to "operate" on the concrete operations of classification and relation used during the childhood years as a means of organizing experience. Another major developmental theorist, Vygotsky (1962) similarly regarded the middle childhood years as a time when "the higher intellectual functions, whose main features are reflective awareness and deliberate control, come to the fore in the developmental process" (p. 90).

In the present work we likewise regard the ability to consciously reflect on one's own thinking as a key factor in the developmental change that we observe. The huge literature that has sprung up in the last decade on the topic of metacognition (Forrest-Pressley, MacKinnon, & Waller, 1985) is potentially relevant in this regard, and as we noted in Chapter 1, we see the present research as having to do with a central, though not frequently studied, aspect of metacognition. Moshman (1979), to our knowledge, is the only other developmentalist who has explored metacognition as reflection on one's own theories — as thinking about a theory rather than with it.

As virtually all reviewers of the metacognition literature have noted, the term has been employed in such broad and variable ways as to risk losing its explanatory value. A key aspect of the ambiguity that has surrounded use of the term, we believe, is whether or not metacognitive operations entail conscious awareness. Sternberg (1984) alleges that "metacognitive components" play a central role in the development and functioning of intelligence. Yet, the theory he proposes that describes the function of metacognitive and other components of intelligence suggests that metacognitive components operate in an automatic, unconscious manner. In sharp contrast, the above quote from Vygotsky (1962) makes it clear that Vygotsky regarded conscious awareness as the heart of metacognition, and it is in this respect that we regard the term in the present work.

The difference between an account in which metacognition in the sense we have just indicated figures prominently and one in which it does not is well illustrated by Case's (1978a, 1978b) reformulation of the development of Inhelder and Piaget's (1958) control-of-variables strategy in information processing terms (Kuhn, 1983). The strategy for controlling variables, Case (1978b) claims, is a relatively simple one. . . . All the subject must do is to identify an object with an extreme position value on the dimension to be tested (e.g., a long stick), then identify an object with an extreme negative value (e.g., a short stick), and then check to see if there is any other difference between these two objects that might affect the result of interest (e.g., bending). (p. 199)

It is hard to dispute Case's claim that the test he describes (of the effect of rod length on flexibility) is not a difficult one to execute, and Case (1974) demonstrates that it is possible to teach 7- and 8-year-olds to conduct such tests. However, as argued by Kuhn (1983), there is a more formidable challenge involved in this task, and attention to this aspect of the task is missing in Case's account. Case's analysis is an analysis of a subject's ability to execute the sequence of strategies that lead to success on the task. There is another equally if not more important aspect of a subject's competence in a psychological task, however, and that is the *knowledge that these are the appropriate strategies to apply* in order to execute this task successfully. What is involved in the case of the first aspect, or component, of competence typically is evident from the observable features of successful performance. What is involved in the case of the second component is less apparent and may be quite complex. It entails not just reflection on the correct strategy, to know what it "buys one," so to speak, in terms of solution attainment and efficiency, but also reflection on other potential strategies, to know why they do not work, or work as efficiently, and what errors they lead to. The distinction, in other words, is a distinction between executing a strategy and understanding the significance of it. It is this latter, metacognitive aspect of competence that Case fails to acknowledge. It is this same aspect that we claimed earlier was missing in Klahr and Dunbar's (in press) work and, indeed, is likely to be missing in most accounts founded on the metaphor of child as computer (Kuhn, 1983). As we explore further in Chapter 13, it is this aspect of development that determines not only when strategies are likely to develop in natural (noninstructed) contexts but also whether instructed strategies will transfer to new contexts. As a result, it has an important role to play with respect to the teaching of thinking skills.

THE PRESENT RESEARCH IN THE CONTEXT
OF EXISTING LITERATURE

In sum, the major objective of the research presented in this volume is to provide a developmental framework for conceptualizing skills involved in scientific, as well as everyday, thinking. Indeed, as we suggest in the concluding chapter, it is likely to be in the realm of everyday thinking rather than science that the failure of these skills to develop fully has the most far-reaching implications. In this respect, the present work is relevant to the large body of literature addressing the shortcomings of adults' inferential skills, literature that by and large has not adopted a developmental perspective. The present research suggests a framework in which to conceptualize phenomena such as the biasing effect of belief and the developmental progression that effects its decline.

Our research builds on earlier work on the development of causal inference and formal operational reasoning. As in Inhelder and Piaget's account of formal operations, the idea of reflection on one's own thinking, a form of metacognition, is central to the developmental course that we identify. However, we do not see the development of these thinking skills as deriving from an underlying competence in logic. Though the skills we examine are general in the sense of being definable across a wide range of content, we see them as emerging in specific, concrete contexts to which they are initially wedded. The resulting pragmatic, goal-related schemes, of the sort proposed by Cheng and Holyoak (1985), both provide an inductive apparatus through which new information is interpreted and themselves undergo development of a sort that our findings help to describe. Existing theories thus remain the starting point for the interpretation of new information, a point of view consonant with much of the recent work on the development of scientific understanding (Carey, 1986).

In contrast to Carey and some of the other researchers investigating the development of scientific concepts, however, we argue that it is not only these concepts themselves that undergo transformation. The results we present suggest that development occurs as well in ways of coming to know the world, or in the terms we use, in skills in the coordination of theories and evidence. The metaphor of child as scientist is thus correct in one sense but not in another. It is correct in the sense that T. Kuhn (1962) characterizes the development of scientific thinking as a succession of theories that replace one another. Our results suggest, however, that the child-as-scientist metaphor in the sense of the child as an intuitive scientist with the same conceptual skills as the accomplished scientist may be fundamentally misleading.

We have said little in this chapter or the preceding one regarding the broad issue of the mechanisms in terms of which cognitive development occurs (Sternberg, 1984), or on the related practical issue of how the skills that we examine might best be fostered. In this respect, a large volume of literature on teaching thinking skills (Baron & Sternberg, 1987; Nickerson, Perkins, & Smith, 1985) becomes relevant. Nor have we said anything about some of the literature on adult cognitive development that is relevant to the issue of the end point of the developmental progression that our results suggest. As we have already considered a large number of different topics and literatures in this chapter, we postpone considering these remaining topics until later: adult cognitive development in Chapter 12, mechanisms of cognitive development in Chapters 11 and 13, and the teaching of thinking skills in Chapter 13.

II

THE EVALUATION
OF EVIDENCE

Deanna Kuhn and Eric Amsel
with the assistance of Leona Schauble

3

THE EVALUATION OF EVIDENCE

In this chapter we describe the design and method of our initial studies and present those results having to do with subjects' ability to evaluate the bearing of evidence on a theory. The problem context was chosen as one likely to elicit an implicit "pragmatic reasoning schema" of the sort Cheng and Holyoak (1985) describe as guiding everyday reasoning, in particular a causal reasoning schema, which Cheng and Holyoak maintain invokes implicit expectations of covariation between cause and effect and temporal priority of cause. Subjects did in fact interpret the problem material presented to them in a causal framework, expressing a series of causal beliefs, or theories, connecting antecedents and outcomes. All subjects also expressed a number of noncausal beliefs, that is, beliefs that no causal relation existed between an antecedent and an outcome variable. We refer to these beliefs as causal and noncausal theories, respectively, without prejudging whether they have the characteristics of true theories as discussed in Chapter 1 and even though the content of these theories was in most cases very simplistic. The evidence presented to subjects was of two simple forms, one in which potential cause and effect covary perfectly with one another and the other in which there is a total absence of covariation (independence) between the two. As explained in Chapter 1, the focus is on subjects' explicit evaluation of the bearing of evidence on a theory; however, we consider as well what kinds of implicit evidence evaluation subjects may engage in.

STUDY 1a METHOD

Subjects

A total of 65 subjects participated in Study 1a. Sexes were equally represented. Of the 65, 20 came from a mixed fifth- and sixth-grade classroom in a lower-middle-class urban school system. For convenience, this group is referred to as the sixth-grade group. Their ages ranged from 10 years, 5 months to 12 years, 11 months, with a median age of 11 years, 8 months. Pretesting indicated subjects in this age group were the youngest with whom the Session 1 procedure could be employed successfully, although in subsequent studies subjects of younger ages are included. Another 20 subjects came from a ninth-grade classroom in a school in the same lower-middle-class neighborhood. Their ages ranged from 14 years, 0 months to 16 years, 2 months, with a median age of 14 years, 7 months. A third group of 20 subjects came from an unselected adult population and were solicited through personal contacts of the interviewers. Their age range was 19–60, with a median age of 29. They were employed mostly in sales or office occupations. All had graduated from high school, and 4 had two years or less of college experience. In order to get an indication of what the most advanced levels of performance might be on this kind of problem, an additional 5 adult subjects were included as a separate group. All 5 were advanced-level candidates for the Ph.D. degree in the department of philosophy at Columbia University. They are referred to as the philosophers.

Design

The problem was introduced to the subject as concerning a study some scientists have been conducting on how children's diets affect their susceptibility to colds. The following introductory explanation was given:

> Some scientists have been studying whether the kinds of foods children eat make any difference in whether or not they get lots of colds. The scientists decided to do their study at a boarding school, where children live. The children eat all their meals in the school dining room and they all eat the same food. They sit in the dining room at tables of six children each. The scientists wanted to see if what the children eat makes a difference in whether or not they get lots of colds. So for six months they asked the dining room workers to serve certain foods at certain tables. During that time, the school nurse kept careful records of children's colds. I'm going to ask you some questions about the foods the scientists studied and what they discovered.

Following an initial session devoted to eliciting the subject's theories, the second and main interview session was devoted to the subject's evaluation of evidence. Evidence was presented sequentially and cumulatively, and the subject's evaluation was elicited after each presentation. In each of the eight instances of evidence presented, information was given about the status of four binary variables and a binary outcome. In the case of two of the four variables, there was no covariation with outcome over the eight instances. The other two variables covaried perfectly with outcome. In the first case, we were interested in whether the subject was able to interpret the absence of covariation as evidence against a causal theory linking variable and outcome or, in other words, as evidence for an exclusion inference. In the second case, we were interested in whether the subject interpreted the covariation evidence as supporting but not conclusive evidence for a causal theory linking variable and outcome, in other words, as insufficient evidence for an inclusion inference because there are multiple covariates.

To permit an investigation of how theoretical belief affects the evaluation of evidence, the two variables with respect to which covariation evidence was presented were selected on the basis of their having been identified in Session 1 as a variable for which the subject held a causal theory and another variable for which the subject held a noncausal theory; in other words, the subject had indicated his or her belief that antecedent and outcome are causally related in one case and that antecedent and outcome are causally unrelated in the other case. Likewise, the two variables with respect to which noncovariation evidence was presented were selected on the basis of their having been identified as variables with respect to which the subject held one causal and one noncausal theory.

The four variables are referred to as A, B, C, and D. A and B are variables for which the subject holds causal theories. The evidence presented for A is covariation evidence, and the evidence presented for B is noncovariation evidence. C and D are variables for which the subject holds noncausal theories. Covariation evidence is presented for C and noncovariation evidence for D. The evidence is thus identical for A and C and is likewise identical for B and D, but the prior theories differ in each case. By comparing A to C and B to D, it is possible to examine how theoretical belief affects the interpretation of identical evidence. In the cases of A and D, prior theories are supported by the evidence; in the cases of B and C, prior theories are disconfirmed by the evidence. It is thus also possible to examine and compare subjects' evaluation of supporting versus disconfirming evidence, for both causal and noncausal theories.

An example of the evidence presented to the subject in the case of the variables fruit, cereal, potato, and cola is shown in Figure 1. Eight instances of evidence were presented one at a time, and the subject's evaluation was elicited after each presentation. Each instance was portrayed visually by sketches of the four foods and an outcome presented on a large board.

The two variables portrayed at the top of each instance (as shown in Figure 1), fruit and cereal, are the variables the subject believes to be related to colds (Variables A and B). The two at the bottom, potato and cola, are those the subject believes not to be related to colds (Variables C and D). As seen in Figure 1, the

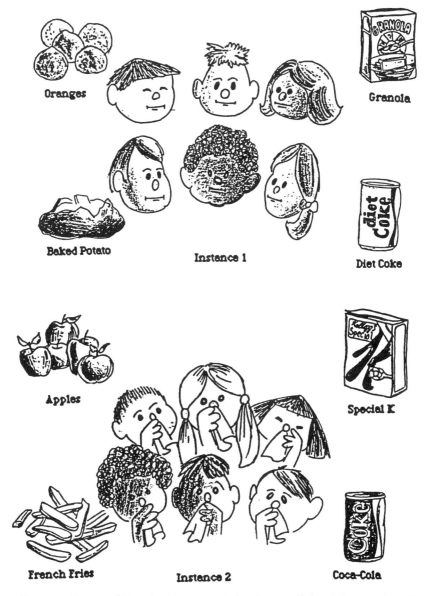

Figure 1. Example of Study 1 evidence presentation. Instances 5–8, not shown, maintain the same pattern of covariation and noncovariation.

Figure 1. (*Continued*)

two variables on the left, fruit and potato (A and C), covary perfectly with outcome, one the subject believes to be related to colds and one not. The two on the right, cereal and cola (B and D), are independent of outcome, again one the subject believes to be related to colds and one not. The remaining four instances (not shown in Figure 1) maintain this same pattern of covariation and independence. The evidence is thus identical for the two variables on the left, but the prior theories differ, enabling us to examine how theoretical belief affects the interpretation of identical evidence, and likewise for the two variables on the right.

Procedure

Session 1

Following the introductory explanation (presented above), the subject was presented a sequence of 35 types of foods the scientists were said to be studying. Each consisted of a type of food, that is, a variable, and two instances, or levels, of that variable. Each was portrayed on a card (13 × 19 cm) with a label of the type of food at the top and labels and accompanying colored drawings of the two levels on either side. For example, the card labeled "meats" at the top had the label "liver" and an appropriate sketch on one side and the label "pork" and an appropriate sketch on the other side. To assess subjects' theories, a scale consisting of a cardboard-covered wood strip (41 × 8 cm) was used. No numbers appeared on the scale, but it was divided into 21 equal units. A verbal anchor at the right end read, "Very sure the food makes a difference"; a verbal anchor at the midpoint read, "Don't know whether or not the food makes a difference"; and a verbal anchor at the left end read, "Very sure the food makes no difference." To explain use of the scale, the interviewer described hypothetical ratings given to three foods chosen to provide good examples of the anchor points. The following explanation was given:

> This is one kind of food the scientists studied. At one table the children have only orange juice as their drink (card displayed). At another table the children have only Coca-Cola. This is the scale we are going to use for you to tell me what you think about whether a food makes a difference in children getting colds. If you're very sure a kind of food makes a difference, you should put the marker all the way up here (right end point indicated). If you're very sure a kind of food makes no difference, you should put the marker all the way down here (left end point indicated). If you don't know whether a kind of food makes a difference or doesn't make a difference, you should put the marker here in the middle space (indicated).
>
> Here are some examples. Many people I've talked to feel very sure that which drink the children have, orange juice or Coca-Cola, makes a difference in whether or not children get colds. They think the children who drink Coca-Cola are more likely to get lots of colds and the children who drink orange juice are less likely to get lots of colds. So they put the marker all the way up here (right end point indicated).

Similar examples were given of hard-boiled versus soft-boiled eggs as likely to lead to choice of the opposite (left) end of the scale and of yellow versus green wugs, a new food from Canada, as likely to lead to choice of the midpoint. The following instructions were then given:

> Now I will ask you what you think about some other foods the scientists studied. In telling me what you think, you can put the marker in any of the spaces, not just the three I've shown

you. The more sure you are that a kind of food makes a difference, the higher up the line you should put the marker. Here you are a little sure; here you are even more sure; here you are as sure as you can be that the kind of food makes a difference (interviewer moves marker to illustrate). The more sure you are that a kind of food makes no difference, the lower down the line you should put the marker. Here you are a little sure; here you are even more sure; here you are as sure as you can be that the kind of food makes no difference (interviewer illustrates).

The subject was then presented with three other food variables, as trial items. The subject was asked to rate each as described above and after each rating to explain why that point on the scale had been chosen, in order to evaluate the subject's understanding of the rating question and use of the scale. If a subject's explanation was inconsistent with the rating given, an attempt was made to correct the misunderstanding. Such confusions were infrequent and misunderstandings easily corrected. The remaining 29 food variables were then presented without eliciting verbal explanations of the ratings.

Subjects selected to continue were those who rated at least two variables between $+2$ and $+8$ and at least two variables between -2 and -8 (the midpoint of the scale was designated 0). Of the subjects participating in Session 1, 85% met this criterion. Two of the variables a subject rated between $+2$ and $+8$ were chosen as Variables A and B (reflecting the subject's causal theories), and two of the variables a subject rated between -2 and -8 were chosen as Variables C and D (reflecting the subject's noncausal theories). No two subjects had an identical set of variables chosen as A, B, C, and D. An attempt was made to select variables rated as close as possible to $+5$ as A and B variables and variables rated as close as possible to -5 as C and D variables. The mean rating score across subjects for A was 5.02; for B 5.02; for C -5.12; and for D -4.98.

Following the ratings and the interviewer's selection of variables A–D, subjects were asked to explain their ratings for each of the four variables selected, that is, to describe the causal or noncausal theories underlying them, by means of the question: Why do you think that (*variable*) makes/doesn't make a difference?

Session 2

Session 2 took place approximately 1 week later. The interviewer began by repeating the introduction given at Session 1. The additional information was added that the nurse found that at some tables children had lots of colds and at other tables children had very few colds and that there weren't any cases that fell in between. The eight instances of evidence were presented on an upright display board (96×64 cm), made of heavy cardboard, onto which had been affixed eight pieces of Post-it tile (27×16 cm) that permit easy affixing and removal of paper. The tiles were arranged in two rows of three and a middle row of two. Each instance of evidence was arranged on one of these eight rectangular frames. A colored drawing of six children portrayed either as having colds (red, runny noses and tissues held to noses) or having no colds (clear noses and no tissues) illustrated the alternative outcomes and was affixed to the center of each rectangle. Four of the rectangles portrayed one outcome and four the other. Drawings of one or the other level of each variable, A–D, were placed in the four corners of each rectangle (see Figure 1). All eight instances were arranged on the board initially covered, and the covering was removed from each instance one by one.

The evidence was arranged such that A and C covaried perfectly both with outcome and with each other; in other words, the same level of each always occurred with one outcome and the other level with the other outcome. Which level occurred with which outcome was determined by the subject's Session 1 explanation of his or her causal theory for Variable A and was assigned so as to be consistent with the subject's theory; for example, if the subject's theory was that children were more likely to have colds if they drank orange juice than apple juice, orange juice always occurred with the colds outcome. The evidence for B and D was arranged such that each showed no covariation with outcome; nor did they covary with each other. Over the eight instances, two instances for B and two for D reflected violations of sufficiency (antecedent present, outcome absent); likewise two instances for B and two for D reflected violations of necessity (antecedent absent, outcome present).

After each instance was revealed, the interviewer summarized it verbally. The subject was then questioned about each of the four variables, in counterbalanced order across instances. Though our earlier work (Kuhn & Brannock, 1977) indicated that subjects even from college populations rarely consider interaction effects, in order to remove this as a possible source of variation in subjects' interpretation of the evidence, the interviewer made the following statement after presentation of the first instance: "I should mention one other thing we know for sure: Whether or not one kind of food makes a difference does not depend on what other foods are eaten." The initial question then asked about the first variable was the following:

> Does the kind of (*variable*) the children have make a difference in whether they get lots of colds or very few colds? You can answer the question by saying yes, no, or maybe. If you think the kind of (*variable*) makes a difference in whether children get lots of colds or very few colds, then answer yes. If you think the kind of (*variable*) makes no difference in whether children get lots of colds or very few colds, then answer no. If you can't say whether the kind of (*variable*) makes a difference or doesn't make a difference, then answer maybe. Okay, now here's the question again. Does the kind of (*variable*) the children have make a difference in whether they get lots of colds or very few colds—yes, no, or maybe?

The subject's response was followed by a probe to elicit its basis, either "How do you know that the kind of (*variable*) makes/doesn't make a difference?" if the response was *yes* or *no,* or "Why can't you tell if the kind of (*variable*) makes a difference?" if the response was *maybe*. The initial question deliberately did not contain an explicit direction to consider the evidence that had been presented or to base the response on this evidence, in order to obtain an indication of what subjects' own dispositions were in this respect: Do they spontaneously consider new evidence when it is available? If a subject's response to the initial probe included any reference to the presented evidence, the response was classified as an evidence-based response. If it did not, it was classified as a theory-based response (examples below).

If the response to the initial probe was classified as a theory-based response, it was followed by the *evidence-focus probe*, which was designed to direct the subject's attention to the presented evidence and to make it explicit that the response should be based on this evidence: "Now tell me, do the *findings of the scientists* (verbal emphasis) show that the kind of (*variable*) does make a difference, doesn't make a difference, or can't you tell what the scientists' findings show? (Subject responds.) How do you know?" The subject's response to the evidence-focus probe was likewise classified as either a theory-based or an evidence-based response.

If the response to either the initial probe or the evidence-focus probe was classified as an evidence-based response, it was followed by the *certainty probe:* "Do the scientists' findings tell you *for sure* (verbal emphasis) that (*variable*) does/doesn't make a difference? (Subject responds.) Why/Why not?" The certainty probe was omitted when the response was maybe or can't tell. This sequence of questioning was followed for each of the four variables (in counterbalanced order) following presentation of each of the eight instances.

Following this evidence evaluation phase, the subject's theories with respect to Variables A–D were reassessed in order to provide another, indirect indication of how the evidence had been evaluated. The same rating procedure described earlier was used. For purposes of comparison, subjects were also asked to rerate four other variables that had been rated originally (in the same -8 to -2 or $+2$ to $+8$ range) but for which no evidence had been presented. In addition, subjects were asked to recall their original ratings of the four variables. Finally, subjects were asked to recall the presented evidence, by reconstructing it on the display board. The four "colds" outcomes and the four "no-colds" outcomes were displayed on the board, and sets of duplicates of all of the various food types were supplied to the subject for affixing to the board.

STUDY 1a RESULTS AND DISCUSSION: EVIDENCE-BASED RESPONSES

Coding of Responses

Only those results are presented in this chapter that have to do with incidence of evidence-based versus theory-based responses. Those results that have to do with how subjects interpret the evidence when they do evaluate it are presented in Chapter 4. Evidence was evaluated for each of four variables at each of eight instances, yielding 32 overall evidence evaluation responses for each subject. If the subject's response to either the initial or the evidence-focus probe was classifed as evidence based, the subject's overall response for that variable and instance was classifed as an evidence-based response and was further classified into one of the categories in the coding scheme presented in Chapter 4. To assess reliability, half of all responses were coded by a second coder. Agreement between the two coders for classification of a response as evidence based was 97%.

Those responses that made no reference to the evidence (referred to as theory-based responses) were not formally coded into subcategories, but tended to be of four overlapping types. In one case the subject relied primarily on intuition ("Bread is just bread; the kind wouldn't make any difference"). In another, the subject appealed to authority ("The juice makes a difference because my mother says orange juice is better for you"). In a third, the subject referred to his or her own experience ("The liver makes you healthier, because when I eat pork, I get sick"). In a fourth, the subject articulated some mechanism connecting cause and effect ("Orange juice makes you healthier because it has lots of vitamins"). These examples make clear that (a) responses labeled theory based reflect very simplistic theories, with only one type of the four describing any connecting mechanism, and (b) the label "theory based" is not intended to imply that no past experience or knowledge has contributed to formation of the theory. Without question, various kinds of experience and acquired information (to which the label "evidence" might be applied) play a role in the formation of a theory. The issue investigated in the present work is subjects' ability to evaluate the bearing of newly presented evidence on an existing theory.

Spontaneous Evidence-Based Responses

The most basic question posed in Study 1a is whether subjects are able to coordinate theory and evidence in the very rudimentary sense of articulating how evidence of a certain form bears on a theory. The indication of their ability to do so is occurrence of an evidence-based response (which could be made to either the initial or the evidence-focus probe). We examine first evidence-based responses to the initial probe, reflecting subjects' disposition to take into account newly available evidence in making an inference, even when not explicitly instructed to consider this evidence. These we refer to as *spontaneous evidence-based responses*. Frequencies of spontaneous evidence-based responses by age group for covariation evidence (variables A and C) are shown in Table 1. Maximum score is 16 (eight instances for each of two variables). Statistical

Table 1

Frequencies of Spontaneous
Evidence-Based Responses
to Covariation Evidence

Group	Mean	Range
Sixth graders	4.85	0–12
Ninth graders	7.95	0–14
Adults	8.05	2–13
Philosophers	10.20	1–16

analysis showed the increasing frequency of evidence-based responses with age to be significant, $F(2, 57) = 4.31$, $p = .01$, and a Newman–Kuhls post hoc test showed the sixth graders' mean to be significantly lower than those of the ninth graders and adults, who did not differ. (This and all subsequent statistical analyses are based on the first three age groups only; results for the five philosophers are included in tables for purposes of comparison.) Sex differences were not significant.

The likelihood of spontaneous evidence-based responses increased as more evidence was presented. Across all age groups, for the first four instances only, 21% of responses to the initial probe were evidence based. For the latter four instances, this percentage rose to 66%. Thus, as the evidence presentation progressed, subjects came increasingly to regard the evidence as the appropriate basis for their responses. All adults and all but one ninth grader eventually made at least some spontaneous evidence-based responses. However, six sixth graders never did so. Performance of four of the five philosophers was comparable to that of the adult group, except for a tendency to shift slightly sooner from spontaneous theory-based to spontaneous evidence-based responses. The fifth made spontaneous theory-based responses in all but one case.

Results are comparable for noncovariation evidence (Variables B and D). Frequencies of spontaneous evidence-based responses by age group are shown in Table 2. The increasing frequency of evidence-based responses with age was significant, $F(2, 57) = 7.52$, $p = .001$, and post hoc analysis showed the sixth graders' mean to be significantly lower than those of the ninth graders and adults, who did not differ. A test for homogeneity of variance across the three groups, however, was statistically significant, Bartlett–Box $F = 3.44$, $p = .03$. Examination of individual responses confirmed the greater variability on the part of younger subjects: Adults always made at least some spontaneous evidence-based responses, while eight sixth graders and one ninth grader made none. Performance of the philosophers was comparable to that of the adult group except for a tendency to shift sooner to spontaneous evidence-based responses. Sex differences were not significant. As was the case for covariation evidence,

Table 2

Frequencies of Spontaneous
Evidence-Based Responses
to Noncovariation Evidence

Group	Mean	Range
Sixth graders	4.95	0–13
Ninth graders	8.10	0–13
Adults	9.60	5–13
Philosophers	12.00	11–14

spontaneous evidence-based responses increased as evidence was presented, from 25% for the first four instances to 68% for the latter four.

Elicited Evidence-Based Responses

Subjects were thus more likely to interpret the problem as requiring the evaluation of newly available evidence with increasing age and with increasing quantity of available evidence. More critical, however, is how subjects respond when they are asked explicitly to evaluate the bearing of evidence on a theory, in other words, when presented the evidence-focus probe: "Do *the findings of the scientists* show that the kind of (*variable*) does make a difference, doesn't make a difference, or can't you tell what the scientists' findings show?" Are subjects able to consider and evaluate the evidence?

Mean frequencies of evidence-based responses, whether these were elicited or spontaneous (that is, made to the initial or to the evidence-focus probe), are shown by age group for covariation evidence (Variables A and C) in Table 3. The increasing frequency of evidence-based responses with age approached significance, $F(2, 57) = 2.65$, $p = .08$. A test for homogeneity of variance, however, was significant, Bartlett–Box $F = 5.10$, $p = .006$. Examination of individual patterns confirmed the greater variability on the part of younger subjects: Adults,

Table 3

Frequencies of Elicited or
Spontaneous Evidence-Based Responses
to Covariation Evidence

Group	Mean	Range
Sixth graders	10.35	0–16
Ninth graders	12.30	0–16
Adults	13.30	7–16
Philosophers	16.00	16–16

with one exception, always showed a majority (eight or more) of evidence-based responses, while some younger subjects showed low frequencies of evidence-based responses. One sixth grader and one ninth grader showed no evidence-based responses, and two sixth graders showed only one evidence-based response. Two other sixth graders showed evidence-based responses only of the type in which the subject refers to the evidence but only to express an inability to interpret it (a response type we consider further in Chapter 4). Adults who made some theory-based responses were most likely to show a progression from theory-based to evidence-based responses, while younger subjects were more likely to vacillate between theory-based and evidence-based responses. Philosophers, as reflected in Table 3, always made evidence-based responses. Sex differences were not significant.

Results are comparable for noncovariation evidence (Variables B and D). Mean frequencies of evidence-based responses by age group are shown in Table 4. The increasing frequency of evidence-based responses with age approached significance, $F(2, 57) = 2.94$, $p = .06$. A test for homogeneity of variance was significant (Bartlett–Box $F = 3.92$, $p = .02$), with adults, but not younger subjects, almost always showing a majority of evidence-based responses. One sixth grader and one ninth grader showed no evidence-based responses; these were the same subjects who showed no evidence-based responses to covariation evidence. Three sixth graders either showed only one evidence-based response or showed evidence-based responses only of the type indicated above in which the subject refers to the evidence only to express an inability to interpret it. Adults were more likely to progress from theory-based to evidence-based responses, while younger subjects were more likely to vacillate between the two. Philosophers always made evidence-based responses. Sex differences were not significant.

Discussion

One interpretation of these results is that by sixth grade most children show some ability in explicit evaluation of how evidence bears on a theory; this ability

Table 4

Frequencies of Elicited or
Spontaneous Evidence-Based Responses
to Noncovariation Evidence

Group	Mean	Range
Sixth graders	9.75	0–16
Ninth graders	12.25	0–16
Adults	12.85	5–16
Philosophers	16.00	16–16

is nevertheless very limited among sixth graders. Though variability is high, with a few sixth graders showing performance comparable to that of adults, while others show no evidence-based responses, sixth graders frequently show a predominance of theory-based responses and a vacillation between theory-based and evidence-based responses, suggesting some confusion or lack of differentiation between theory and evidence. Ability increases modestly from sixth grade to adulthood but is by no means at a maximum level among average adults.

Before accepting this interpretation, however, other possibilities should be considered. One is that a subject's failure to give evidence-based responses to a request to evaluate evidence reflects only an inability to articulate verbally how evidence bears on a theory. The subject may understand that it does and how it does and draw on the evidence in making an inference. Such a lack of ability in verbal articulation would still be significant, but it is important to distinguish it from a more basic limitation in recognizing how evidence bears on a theory. One test of the correctness of the verbal articulation possibility can be made by examining the nature of subjects' theory-based responses. If it is correct and subjects are utilizing the evidence as a basis for an inference but are unable to refer to this use verbally, theory-based responses should more often involve a *yes* (variable makes a difference) response when the evidence presented is covariation evidence and a *no* (variable makes no difference) response when the evidence is noncovariation evidence. Examination of the Study 1a data did not support this prediction. The distributions of *yes, no,* and *maybe* (or *can't tell*) theory-based responses were comparable for covariation and noncovariation evidence. A similar prediction that can be derived from the verbal articulation interpretation is that subjects failing to make evidence-based responses to the request to evaluate evidence should nevertheless be able to make correct prediction judgments regarding outcomes of new variable combinations, based on this evidence. This prediction was tested in Study 2.

Another possibility is that subjects are able to recognize how evidence bears on a theory but are distracted by their real-world knowledge and beliefs regarding the theories, which interfere with their ability to see the relation between a given set of evidence and a theory. If evidence were presented with respect to "neutral" theories about which subjects had no prior knowledge or belief, ability to evaluate the bearing of evidence on theory might improve. Though it to some extent takes us away from the central focus of the present research—how people coordinate new evidence with the theories they do hold—this possibility also was examined as part of Study 2.

Still another possibility is that subjects do have greater ability to recognize how evidence bears on a theory than was displayed in Study 1a and that their less than optimal performance is attributable to a failure of the evidence-focus probe ("Do the *findings of the scientists* show that the kind of (*variable*) does make a difference . . . ?") to communicate effectively that what was being asked was how these particular findings *alone* bear on the theory, apart from any other knowledge or belief the subject might have with respect to the theory. In other words, the problem is not with subjects' ability to bracket this other knowledge temporarily but with their understanding that that is what they are to do. This possibility was investigated in Study 1b.

STUDY 1b METHOD

Subjects

Subjects were 15 fifth/sixth graders and 15 ninth graders from the same school population described in Study 1a. Age ranges, medians, and sex distribution were comparable to those in Study 1a. As in Study 1a, the fifth/sixth graders are referred to as sixth graders for convenience. An adult sample was not included pending the outcome for younger subjects.

Procedure

The procedure was identical to that used in Study 1a except for the following additional instruction inserted after the Session 2 introductory material:

Last time, you told me your ideas about different foods. Today, however, suppose you yourself don't have any idea if the different foods make a difference or don't make a difference in whether or not the children get colds. Suppose the only information you have is the information the scientists collected. I'm going to ask you some questions about the foods the scientists studied and what they discovered. In order to decide if the scientists' information shows that different foods do make a difference or don't make a difference, I want you to consider only the information that the scientists collected. Suppose you yourself don't have any idea if the different foods do or don't make a difference and you have to use only this information in making your decision.

Just before the subject's response to the specific question posed regarding each variable for each instance, a reminder of this instruction was given: "Remember to answer the question not from what you know about foods, but based only on the scientists' findings."

STUDY 1b RESULTS AND DISCUSSION: EVIDENCE-BASED RESPONSES

Mean frequencies of evidence-based responses, whether elicited or spontaneous (whether made to the initial or to the evidence-focus probe), for covariation evidence (Variables A and C) were 11.33 for sixth graders, compared to 10.35

in Study 1a, and 11.87 for ninth graders, compared to 12.30 in Study 1a. The instruction condition thus resulted in a very slight improvement in performance for sixth graders but not for ninth graders. Subjects from the two age groups in the two studies were combined for the purpose of a two-way (age by condition) analysis of variance (ANOVA); neither condition nor age showed a significant effect. Results were comparable for noncovariation evidence. Mean frequencies of evidence-based responses for Variables B and D were 11.07 for sixth graders, compared to 9.75 in Study 1a, and 12.13 for ninth graders, compared to 12.25 in Study 1a. Neither condition nor age reached significance in a two-way ANOVA, though age approached significance, $F(1, 66) = 3.00$, $p = .08$. Only one subject, a sixth grader, showed no evidence-based responses to either type of evidence. Results for spontaneous evidence-based responses (responses to the initial probe) also were comparable. The instruction condition produced a slight but statistically nonsignificant improvement for sixth graders and had no effect for ninth graders.

These results indicate that while explicit instruction to evaluate the presented evidence and to base an inference on that evidence appeared to be of slight help to sixth graders in producing evidence-based responses, a failure to convey adequately what it was they were being asked to do cannot be regarded as a major source of subjects' failure to make evidence-based responses. Even with explicit instruction in this regard, subjects did not consistently refer to the presented evidence when asked to evaluate its bearing on a theory.

STUDY 2 METHOD

Design

Study 2 focused on two issues. One is the extent to which subjects are able to make prediction judgments based on implicit evaluation of evidence. The other is the extent to which a rich set of knowledge and beliefs regarding a theory may make it more difficult for subjects to see the relation between a given set of evidence and the theory. To examine the second issue, performance on two parallel problems was compared. One was like the foods problem used in the preceding studies; the other was devised with the aim of minimizing any prior belief or knowledge the subject could bring to bear on the problem.

Subjects

A total of 100 subjects participated, 20 in each of five groups. The first three groups were third, sixth, and ninth graders from an urban public school system of mixed socioeconomic status. Subjects in the fourth group were adults, predominantly in their 20s, enrolled at a commercial business school studying general office systems and procedures. All but two were high school graduates, and four had some community college experience. Subjects in the fifth group were graduate students in education. Sexes were equally represented.

Procedure

The two problems were abbreviated versions of the foods problem used in Studies 1a and 1b. As two problems were to be administered, it was necessary to reduce the total length of the questioning for each. Only five evidence instances were presented, and the subject was questioned about only two of the four variables for each instance. The evidence-focus and certainty probes were omitted, as the major purpose was to compare the two problems rather than attempt to maximize subjects' performance. The Session 1 procedure from Studies 1a and 1b, in which prior beliefs were assessed as a basis for selection of particular experimental variables, was not germane to the purposes of Study 2 and was not included. These simplifications of procedure made it feasible to include a third grade group. The two problems were presented on separate occasions several days apart, in counterbalanced order across subjects.

The stains problem, the problem intended to minimize prior knowledge or belief, was introduced as follows:

> Some scientists in a lab have been working on figuring out how to make the best stain remover. They've been trying out different ways of doing it. To make a stain remover, they start with a liquid. Sometimes they use a liquid that looks like this (interviewer indicates a bottle of clear liquid from the display of materials before the subject), and other times they use a liquid that looks like this (interviewer indicates a bottle of cloudy liquid). The next thing they do to make a stain remover is to mix powder into one of the liquids, and as you see they've been trying two different kinds of powders, this one that's coarse and flaky and this one that's very fine (interviewer indicates two containers of powder).
>
> Also they sometimes add other things. Sometimes they add some of this benzen cream (interviewer indicates bottle of white creamy substance, labeled "benzen cream"). And sometimes they add a corizen tablet (interviewer indicates bottle of tablets, labeled "corizen tablets"). Then when everything is added, they mix it very well.
>
> For example, this is how they tried it once. They used the cloudy liquid, the flaky powder, and they added both the benzen cream and a corizen tablet. (Interviewer assembles the appropriate indredients together in a group.) After mixing it, they tried it on one of these test cloths. (Interviewer indicates a pile of 10-cm squares of white fabric, each with a dark stain in the center.) And this is how it turned out. (Interviewer produces another square of fabric, without a stain, and places it next to the collection of ingredients.) You see, the stain came completely out.

Each instance was similarly described and displayed, with previous instances remaining in view, and the absence of interaction effects was indicated as in Studies 1a and 1b. The questions about the variables that were asked after each instance had been presented and the response options were as in Studies 1a and

1b. A and C covaried with outcome, while B and D did not. Contrary to Studies 1a and 1b, the final instance served to unconfound variables A and C by showing that the positive outcome, up to then always associated with the positive levels (arbitrarily designated) of A and C, failed to occur when A, B, and D were negative and C positive.

Three prediction questions were also included, one after the fourth instance and two after the final instance. In the first, the subject was shown the combination of the negative level of A and the positive level of the other three variables and asked to predict whether the stain would be removed and to explain the basis for the prediction. The second consisted of the same combination presented following presentation of the final evidence instance, which made a determinate prediction possible. The third consisted of the positive level of A and negative levels of the other three variables, also allowing a determinate prediction.

The second problem, the plant problem, was identical in form. It dealt with the effect of different kinds of care on the health of house plants. The four variables were tap versus mineral water, two types of plant food, and presence versus absence of vitamins and leaf cream.

STUDY 2 RESULTS AND DISCUSSION: EVIDENCE-BASED RESPONSES

Only those results are presented in this chapter that have to do with incidence of evidence-based versus theory-based responses. Those aspects of both Studies 1a and 1b and Study 2 results that have to do with how subjects interpret the evidence when they do evaluate it are presented in Chapter 4.

The most notable outcome of Study 2 is the fact that the stains problem did not serve to eliminate theory-based responding. Though the problem content provided little basis for theorizing as to which of the four variables would or would not make a difference, subjects often alleged one variable to make a difference and another not, based on reasoning such as "The kind of liquid makes no difference because it's just for mixing it," or "The white liquid would be better because it can cover the stain." Nevertheless, as anticipated, there was, overall, more evidence-based responding in the stains problem than in the plant problem. This effect, however, varied by age group and was statistically significant only in interaction with age group, $F(4, 95) = 3.65$, $p = .01$. The youngest group, which showed a preponderance of theory-based responses, an average of 60% versus 56% in the plant and stains problems respectively, was unaffected by problem type, as was the graduate student group, which showed virtually no theory-based responding on either problem. Percentages for the middle three groups, in contrast, were higher on the plant than on the stains problem: 45%

versus 33% among sixth graders, 26% versus 13% among ninth graders, and 39% versus 0% among adults. Thus, the youngest subjects rely heavily on their theories in either case, and the graduate students focus on the evidence in either case. The middle groups, however, are less able to evaluate newly presented evidence when they have a set of beliefs readily available regarding the phenomena on which the evidence bears.

Overall effects of age were consistent with those found in Studies 1a and 1b. The overall effect was significant, $F(4, 95) = 4.23$, $p = .003$, and post hoc comparisons of adjacent groups showed significant differences between sixth and ninth graders and between the nonacademic adult and graduate student groups for each problem. No sex differences appeared.

Subjects were categorized according to the predominant type of response exhibited, as explained in fuller detail in Chapter 4. Among those subjects categorized as showing predominantly theory-based responses or a mixture of theory-based and evidence-based responses, correct responses on the prediction questions did not exceed the chance level. Furthermore, these subjects were no more likely to respond *yes* to the evidence evaluation questions when the evidence reflected covariation or to respond *no* when the evidence reflected independence. These two findings thus provide no evidence of implicit evidence evaluation skills on the part of these subjects that exceeded their explicit skills in evaluating evidence.

GENERAL DISCUSSION

If failure to make evidence-based responses reflects more than lack of ability in verbal expression or failure to understand the question, a number of factors could still be responsible for this failure. Research referred to in Chapters 1 and 2 has demonstrated that quite young children make judgments of causality based on covariation information. From an early age, children thus have at least implicit knowledge that covariation can serve as a cue for causality. In contrast, when a subject views evidence reflecting absence of covariation, it is possible that the subject sees only confusion and has no implicit or explicit understanding of the meaning of such evidence. In this case, then, lack of interpretability of the evidence could be a factor leading the subject to disregard the evidence and make a theory-based response (instead of referring to the evidence and indicating an inability to interpret it, as some subjects did). The extent to which this possibility may account for the absence of evidence-based responses, and the difference between covariation and noncovariation evidence in this respect, are considered in Chapter 4, when we examine the nature of subjects' interpretations of the two kinds of evidence.

A further possibility is that availability of a theory regarding the phenomena on which the evidence bears affects disposition to evaluate evidence, as the Study

2 results suggest. In particular, people may resist acknowledging and interpreting evidence if it conflicts with their theoretical beliefs and be inclined to disregard the evidence and base a response instead on their own theoretical views. The extent to which this possibility accounts for absence of evidence-based responses is further examined in Chapter 5, in which we examine the influence of theory on the evaluation of evidence.

Most sixth graders, we found, do have the competence to explicitly evaluate the bearing of evidence on a theory (even though, as we see in Chapter 4, they do not necessarily evaluate this evidence correctly). Yet, an average of one fourth of the responses made by sixth graders through adults to the request to evaluate the bearing of evidence on a theory were theory-based responses in which no reference was made to the presented evidence. This figure of one fourth is of course an average; some subjects, notably the younger ones, made a majority of theory-based responses while others never made them. This gap between competence and performance is suggestive of the possibility referred to above, that the conflict of evidence with theoretical beliefs diminished the subject's inclination to explicitly acknowledge and evaluate this evidence (though in such a case the evidence obviously had to have been processed by the subject at some level of awareness). However, as the comparisons of responses to theory-supporting versus theory-disconfirming evidence will show, failure to make evidence-based responses occurred more frequently in, but was not confined to, cases in which the evidence was theory disconfirming. Thus, some other, more basic limitations must have played a role in such failures. In Chapter 5, we consider further what they might be.

4

THE INTERPRETATION
OF COVARIATION
AND NONCOVARIATION
EVIDENCE

Chapter 3 dealt only with whether subjects did or did not make use of the evidence in justifying their inferences. In Chapter 4, we examine how subjects interpreted the evidence when they did do so. For this purpose all evidence-based responses (whether spontaneous or elicited) were classified into one of the categories listed in Table 5, based on the nature of the subject's justification for the inference made. Agreement between two coders for classification of evidence-based responses into one of these categories was 92%.

Table 5 is organized into three main categories (Types I–III), based on whether the inference is one of inclusion ("makes a difference"), exclusion ("doesn't make a difference"), or uncertainty ("can't tell" or "maybe"), as the justifications for these three types of inferences naturally were quite different. Exclusion and uncertainty inferences are divided based on whether justifications are valid or invalid. Valid justification for an exclusion inference consists of reference to noncovariation between antecedent and outcome, in either a single instance (Types IIb1 and IIb2) or multiple instances (Types IIb3 and IIb4). Valid justification for an uncertainty inference consists of recognition of other covariates as potential causes (Type IIIb2), or, when only the first instance of evidence has been presented, recognition of lack of variation of the antecedent variable (Type IIIb1). If sufficient evidence for exclusion is present (Instances 3–8 for Variables B and D), then no valid justification for an uncertainty inference is possible and justifications are of one of the three invalid types indicated in Table 5. No valid justification for an inclusion inference is possible

Table 5

Classification of Evidence-Based Responses (Studies 1a and 1b)

Type	Example
I. Inclusion (always invalid for Studies 1a and 1b evidence)	
a. Co-occurrence (single instance)	"Yes, because here they had potato salad and are healthy."
b. Covariation (multiple instances)	"Yes, because when they had brown rice they were healthy and when they had white rice they got colds."
c. Other	"It makes a difference because some children had one kind and some children had another."
II. Exclusion	
a. Invalid	
1. Discounting	"The kind of milk makes no difference because it's the fruit that matters."
2. Other	"The kind of sandwich makes no difference because not all the children had the same kind."
b. Valid	
1. Constant antecedent, variable outcome	"No, because the tomato soup is with healthy children here and sick children here."
2. Variable antecedent, constant outcome	"Some children with colds had tap water and some had bottled water, so it makes no difference."
3. Violation of sufficiency	"No, because here they had it and still got sick."
4. Violation of necessity	"No, because here they didn't have it and were healthy."
III. Uncertainty	
a. Invalid	
1. Evidence uninterpretable	"I can't tell what the findings show; it's confusing."
2. Noncovariation	"I can't say about the juice because sometimes apple juice gives them colds and sometimes it doesn't."
3. Other	"I can't say if the soup makes a difference because here they had tomato soup and got colds."
b. Valid	
1. Lack of variation (Instance 1 only)	"I can't say because we don't know what would happen if they got the other kind of bread."
2. Recognition of other potential variables	"I can't tell because it could have been the rice or the fruit that is making the difference."

based on the evidence presented; invalid justifications are of the three types indicated in Table 5.

STUDIES 1a AND 1b RESULTS AND DISCUSSION: INTERPRETATION OF COVARIATION EVIDENCE

The most common, though incorrect, evidence-based response all subjects except philosophers made to covariation evidence was an inference of inclusion. Justifications for virtually all of these responses made reference to either the co-occurrence (single instance) or covariation (multiple instances) of antecedent and outcome, though subjects occasionally drew on the evidence in an anomalous way to justify an inclusion inference (Type Ic, Table 5). Most responses made reference to multiple instances (Type Ib) once they were available. Of particular interest, however, are single-instance inclusion inferences made after only the first instance was presented. Such inferences signify a subject's willingness to infer a causal relation between antecedent and outcome based only on a single co-occurrence. A total of 27% of Study 1a subjects and 20% of Study 1b subjects (evenly distributed across age groups) made single-instance inclusion inferences for Variable A and/or C after presentation of the first instance. Roughly one fourth of all subjects, then, interpreted a single co-occurrence of antecedent and outcome as sufficient evidence to justify an inference of causality.

Mean frequencies of inclusion inferences in response to covariation evidence (Variables A and C) by age group are shown in Table 6. In this and subsequent tables, Study 1b subjects are shown separately, as the Study 1b condition tended to reduce the difference between sixth and ninth graders. Statistical analysis was done separately for age group effects in Study 1a and for effects of age in combination with condition for sixth and ninth graders in Study 1a and in Study 1b; the latter results are reported only if they differ from the Study 1a results. As in Chapter 3, philosophers are excluded from statistical analyses. No sex differences appeared in any of the analyses reported in this chapter. In the

Table 6

Frequencies of Inclusion Inferences in Response
to Covariation Evidence

Group	Mean	Range
1a Sixth graders	7.90	0–15
1b Sixth graders	9.13	0–13
1a Ninth graders	10.40	0–15
1b Ninth graders	10.87	1–15
Adults	9.75	0–15
Philosophers	1.80	0–6

case of the Table 6 data, the age-by-condition analysis for the two younger age groups resulted in a significant effect only for age, $F(1, 66) = 4.47$, $p = .05$. The age effect did not reach significance, however, for the three age groups in Study 1a, reflecting the fact that the frequency of inclusion inferences *increases* from sixth to ninth grade but then decreases between ninth grade and adulthood.

Subjects not only made many inclusion inferences, as reflected in Table 6; they also tended to respond affirmatively to the certainty probe, "Do the scientists' findings tell you *for sure* that (*variable*) does make a difference?" Percentages of Study 1a subjects responding affirmatively were 78% among sixth graders, 83% among ninth graders, and 77% among adults. Only the philosophers, as reflected in Table 6, tended not to succumb to an inference of causality based on covariation evidence. Three of the five never did so, and one did so only briefly, early in the evidence presentation, before recognizing his error. The fifth, however, showed the more typical adult pattern of succumbing to the inference of causality toward the end of the evidence presentation, as the covariation evidence mounted.

Mean frequencies of uncertainty inferences in response to covariation evidence by age group are shown in Table 7. Uncertainty inferences were infrequent except among philosophers, who almost always made them. No age group differences were found among the remaining subjects. Age differences do emerge, however, if one examines subjects' basis for the uncertainty. Younger subjects' uncertainty inferences tended to be of the invalid type, in particular Type IIIa1 (evidence referred to but declared uninterpretable). In contrast, only 4% of adults' uncertainty inferences were of the invalid type.

Of the 17 Study 1a subjects (other than the philosophers) who made *valid* uncertainty inferences, 14 made them all during the first half of the evidence presentation. As more covariation evidence accumulated, uncertainty inferences gave way to inclusion inferences. Only two adults and four of the philosophers maintained their valid uncertainty inferences through the final instance of evidence. One sixth grader made a valid uncertainty inference only of Type IIIb1

Table 7

Frequencies of Uncertainty Inferences in Response
to Covariation Evidence

Group	Mean	Range	Percentage valid
1a Sixth graders	1.90	0–13	29
1b Sixth graders	1.93	0–9	41
1a Ninth graders	1.50	0–9	33
1b Ninth graders	0.67	0–3	10
Adults	2.75	0–16	96
Philosophers	14.20	10–16	100

(lack of variation, based on first instance), which were infrequent overall. The remaining 16 subjects who made valid uncertainty inferences made at least some of Type IIIb2, in which the potential influence of other variables is recognized. Of these 16 subjects, 10 were adults, versus only 3 sixth graders and 3 ninth graders, $\chi^2(2) = 7.06$, $p = .03$.

Thus, younger subjects infrequently showed any recognition of the indeterminacy of the presented evidence. They were willing to infer that a variable played a causal role in an outcome based on evidence of its covariation with that outcome, even though other covariates (and thus potential causes) were clearly evident, and they usually claimed to be certain about such inferences. In contrast, half of the adult group recognized the indeterminacy early in the evidence presentation, but only two adults, and four of the five philosophers, maintained this awareness through presentation of all of the evidence. As the covariation evidence accumulated, most adults followed the path of the younger subjects and inferred a causal relation based on evidence of covariation.

Of additional interest are the relatively infrequent but nonnegligible number of occurrences of exclusion inferences based on covariation evidence. Eight Study 1a sixth graders, four ninth graders, and six adults made one or more exclusion inferences for Variables A or C. (Study 1b frequencies are comparable.) These frequencies are surprising, as the covariation evidence provides no basis whatsoever for an inference of exclusion. Exclusion inferences tended to occur early in the evidence presentation, often after the first instance; only two subjects made them during the second half, when there was considerable evidence of covariation. These inferences of course all fell into the invalid category. Adults' invalid exclusion inferences tended to be more frequently of the discounting type (Type IIa1), while younger subjects tended more to draw on the covariation evidence in an anomalous way to justify an exclusion inference (Type IIa2), often by distorting the evidence or by attending to only part of the evidence and ignoring the rest. Such invalid interpretations of evidence are of course of particular interest. In Chapter 5 we explore the possibility that a subject's theoretical belief that a variable made no difference motivated these instances of invalid interpretation of covariation evidence.

STUDIES 1a AND 1b RESULTS AND DISCUSSION: INTERPRETATION OF NONCOVARIATION EVIDENCE

Subjects did not always utilize evidence of noncovariation as a basis for drawing inferences of exclusion regarding Variables B and D. Mean frequencies of exclusion inferences in response to noncovariation evidence (Variables B and D) by age group are shown in Table 8. These frequencies are based on Instances 3–8 only, as the evidence of noncovariation for B and D does not occur until

Table 8

Frequencies of Exclusion Inferences in Response
to Noncovariation Evidence

Group	Mean	Range	Percentage showing some exclusion	Percentage showing final exclusion
1a Sixth graders	4.85	0–12	70	50
1b Sixth graders	3.73	0–11	67	27
1a Ninth graders	7.25	0–12	95	60
1b Ninth graders	6.40	0–12	87	67
Adults	8.75	3–12	95	70
Philosophers	7.40	2–12	100	80

Instance 3. Maximum frequency is therefore 12. The age effect for Study 1a data was significant, $F(2, 57) = 4.69$, $p = .013$, with post hoc comparisons showing sixth graders differing significantly from ninth graders and ninth graders differing significantly from adults. Exclusion inferences based on noncovariation evidence were almost always categorized as valid (i.e., the subject made reference to the noncovariation as the basis for the inference) and were predominantly of Types IIb1 and IIb2, in which reference is made to multiple instances (ranging from 91% for sixth graders to 100% for philosophers). Subjects also tended to respond affirmatively to the certainty probe, that is, to claim that the findings "tell you for sure" that the variable makes no difference (80% or more of exclusion inferences to noncovariation evidence at each age level).

Also shown in Table 8 are the percentages of subjects at each age level who made any valid exclusion inferences. A significant number of sixth graders showed no ability to utilize evidence of noncovariation as a basis for drawing an inference of exclusion. Nor did these sixth graders make invalid exclusion inferences; instead they interpreted noncovariation evidence as a basis for inferences of uncertainty or inclusion. Ninth graders were comparable to adults in showing some valid exclusion. Adults, however, were able to interpret the evidence correctly sooner than ninth graders: When evidence of noncovariation was first presented in Instance 3, only 35% of ninth graders, but 65% of adults, made an exclusion inference.

The final column in Table 8 shows the percentages of subjects at each age level who made exclusion inferences for B and D following presentation of all the evidence. Among no age group did 100% of subjects claim that B and D made no difference to the outcome, and among sixth graders no more than half did. How did such subjects interpret noncovariation evidence if not as a basis for exclusion? Most nonexclusion inferences based on noncovariation evidence were uncertainty inferences of Types IIIa1 and IIIa2. (Type IIIa3 occurred rarely.)

Type IIIa1 inferences, in which the noncovariation is not acknowledged, were concentrated among the sixth graders. Subjects making Type IIIa2 inferences recognized the noncovariation but interpreted it as a basis for uncertainty rather than exclusion. These responses occurred at all age levels. Of the 23 Study 1a subjects who made them, 21 also made some valid exclusion inferences, indicating that subjects who showed explicit recognition of the noncovariation but were uncertain how to interpret it came at some point to regard it as evidence for exclusion. Subjects tended, however, not to show an orderly progression from interpreting noncovariation as a basis for uncertainty to interpreting it as a basis for exclusion, and they often vacillated between the two interpretations.

Three of the five philosophers made uncertainty inferences in response to the noncovariation evidence. Two made them only in a few instances, while one made them a majority of the time. These uncertainty inferences (classified as Type IIIa3) were of a qualitatively different nature, however, from those made by any other subjects. Each of the three philosophers claimed that despite the evidence of noncovariation, no conclusive inference can be made because of the possibility of other, external (nonfood) uncontrolled variables. Technically this argument is invalid if one accepts the assumption that uncontrolled variables randomly, rather than systematically, influence outcomes. It nonetheless reflects a sophisticated and critical evaluation of the evidence.

Not all of the nonexclusion responses to noncovariation evidence were uncertainty inferences, however. Six Study 1a sixth graders, eight ninth graders, and two adults made inclusion inferences based on noncovariation evidence. (Study 1b frequencies are comparable.) Although a few such inferences were justified in an anomalous way (Type Ic), for the most part subjects justified their inclusion inferences by referring either to a single co-occurrence (about 50% of the cases) or a limited covariation (remaining 50%) of antecedent and outcome, ignoring that portion of the evidence reflecting noncovariation. In Chapter 5 we examine the extent to which a subject's theoretical belief that a variable made a difference motivated these instances of invalid interpretation of noncovariation evidence.

STUDY 2 RESULTS AND DISCUSSION: INTERPRETATION OF AND PREDICTIONS BASED ON COVARIATION AND NONCOVARIATION EVIDENCE

When Study 2 subjects did make evidence-based responses, their interpretation of covariation and noncovariation evidence was similar to that of Study 1a and 1b subjects. Performance of third graders did not differ significantly from that of sixth graders, with a significant proportion of both groups failing to show exclusion. No third or sixth graders and only one ninth grader and one nonacademic adult recognized the indeterminacy of the covariation evidence, while 70% of the graduate students did so. We omit parallel detailed analyses for Study 2 subjects and focus instead on an analysis of these subjects' prediction performance, as a function of the ways in which they interpreted the covariation and noncovariation evidence.

To examine prediction performance as a function of manner in which the evidence was explicitly evaluated, it was necessary first to classify subjects globally with respect to the latter. For this purpose, four broad evidence evaluation strategies were defined. The first, Type 0, consists of exclusive theory-based responding, without any reference to the evidence. Type 1, labeled a co-occurrence strategy, is defined by absence of exclusion inferences and by occurrence of inclusion inferences when either a single co-occurrence of antecedent and outcome, or evidence of (multiple instance) covariation between antecedent and outcome, is present. Type 2, a covariation strategy, is defined by occurrence of inclusion inferences when covariation evidence is present, exclusion inferences when noncovariation evidence is present, and uncertainty inferences in response to a single co-occurrence. Type 3, a covariation-without-covariates strategy, is like Type 2 except that inclusion inferences are limited to cases of covariation in which no other covariates are present. Additional, mixed types (0/1, 1/2, 2/3) were included to characterize subjects who on some responses showed the characteristics of one type and on others the characteristics of an adjacent type. All subjects but two, whose performance showed no consistent pattern, could be categorized into one of these types. Categorization was done separately for the two problems, and the higher of the two categorizations was used in further analyses. Percentages of subjects classified as each type were as follows: 0, 22%; 0/1, 29%; 1, 10%; 1/2, 18%; 2, 4%; 2/3, 5%; 3, 11%. (Age group differences occurred, but these analyses are not presented as they largely duplicate findings for Studies 1a and 1b.)

Figure 2 shows mean number of correct answers (*yes, no,* or *can't tell*) to the six prediction questions (three for the plant problem and three for the stains problem). Correctness is at no greater than chance levels for 0 and 0/1 subjects and increases as a function of strategy type thereafter, $F(6, 88) = 17.66$, $p = .01$, with Type 3 subjects achieving near perfect correctness. (Omitted from the analysis are the two unclassifiable subjects and three graduate students who were unwilling to make any predictions, maintaining that it was impossible to do so because of the possibility of uncontrolled influences on the outcome.)

Do subjects who show poor prediction performance fail to utilize the available evidence as a basis for predictions, or is their failure to make correct predictions the result of faulty analysis of the evidence? An analysis of subjects' justifications for their predictions sheds light on this question. Only a minority of

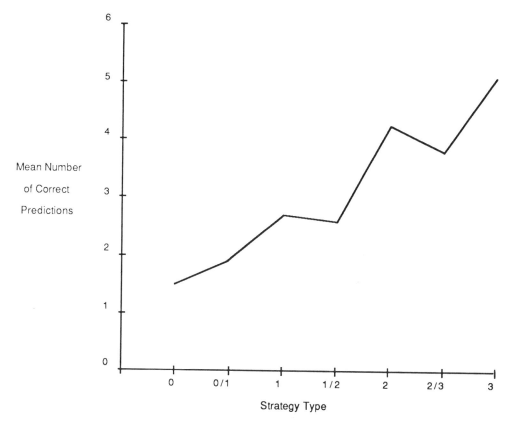

Figure 2. Prediction performance as a function of strategy.

subjects' justifications made no reference to the evidence as a basis for the predictions, ranging from 10% for 0 and 0/1 subjects to 3% for Type 3 subjects. Most subjects thus demonstrated some processing of the evidence. A number of the subjects who did make reference to the evidence in justifying their predictions, however, made no reference to an analysis of the effects of individual variables as a basis for making a prediction about a new variable combination. Instead, they justified the prediction using what we term a *matching* strategy. A subject using the matching strategy analyzes the evidence at the level of the entire set of variables and the associated outcome, treated as a whole. Predictions are based on a matching of the instance to be predicted to one of the instances presented as evidence. To the extent the variable levels involved in each are similar, the subject predicts a similar outcome and justifies this prediction by indicating this similarity: "It will come out good, because it has almost the same things as this one that came out good." Alternatively, to the extent the variable levels are dissimilar, the opposite outcome is predicted and justified by reference to this dissimilarity. Predictions justified by a matching strategy, not surprisingly, were correct at no greater than a chance level. The strategy was used primarily by 0 and 0/1 subjects (16–21% of their responses) and only occasionally by other subjects. Thus, even when 0 and 0/1 subjects did base their predictions on evidence, they often did not even attempt the analysis of individual variable effects that would have provided the basis for correct predictions.

As suggested in previous chapters, the argument can be made that ability to engage in explicit evaluation of evidence may reflect a cognitive skill worth examining (and perhaps even worth fostering) but nevertheless constitute no more than an epiphenomenon in relation to implicit evidence evaluation skills subjects could be shown to possess. The results presented above, however, show that subjects who have limited explicit evidence evaluation skills are also limited in their ability to make correct predictions based on presented evidence (a task that has no verbal production requirements at all). Furthermore, subjects who differ in the criteria they use for inferring causality or noncausality from evidence show corresponding differences in the prediction task, suggesting that some similar cognitive operations are involved whether the evaluation of evidence takes place explicitly or implicitly. Again, as indicated in Chapter 3, we cannot assume that Type 0 subjects, who show no evidence-based responses, engage in no processing whatsoever of the presented evidence. Their failure to make predictions of greater than a chance level of correctness, however, does set upper limits on the nature of the processing they could be hypothesized to engage in. Whatever implicit skills, not reflected in the explicit evidence evaluation task, Type 0 subjects might be hypothesized to have, they were not sufficient to enable the subject to predict new outcomes correctly on the basis of simple covariation and noncovariation evidence.

GENERAL DISCUSSION

All of the subjects in the studies we have described recognize covariation and noncovariation and respond to it differentially or they would not be able to function effectively in their daily lives. Yet, the results of these studies document that most of these subjects are a long way from being able to draw on explicit understanding of the implications of covariation and noncovariation evidence in order to relate such evidence to theories, using explicit reasoning strategies over which they have full and flexible control. One might say, then, that their metacognitive skills in thinking about their own thinking are not well developed.

The results presented in this chapter also indicate that when subjects do engage in explicit evaluation of the bearing of evidence on a theory, the criteria they use are far from rigorous. Both absence of exclusion inferences when the evidence is present to support them and presence of inclusion inferences when the evidence is not present to support them are frequent at all age levels. All subjects except the philosophers were willing at least some of the time to interpret covariation evidence as indicative of causality in the presence of multiple covariates. In contrast, in response to noncovariation evidence, one third of sixth graders were unable to draw *any* conclusions, and ninth graders did so only as noncovariation evidence mounted. Following presentation of all of the evidence, half of the sixth graders and a third of older subjects failed to conclude that the two variables for which noncovariation evidence was presented were noncausal. In making their inferences, no subjects attempted a controlled comparison by looking for two instances in which all foods but one were identical.

Inability to infer noncausality from noncovariation evidence leaves this evidence open either (a) to being ignored and hence left uninterpreted or (b) to a variety of incorrect interpretations, in particular, false inclusion based on a single co-occurrence or limited covariation (ignoring the conflicting portion of the evidence). Failure to correctly interpret noncovariation as indicating noncausality, coupled with lax criteria for inferring causality, is a particularly lethal combination, leaving the subject extremely prone to fallacious inference. Only a minority of subjects inferred causality based on the initial instance of co-occurrence of Variables A and C and outcome or based on a limited portion of the noncovariation evidence for Variables B and D. Almost all subjects, however, succumbed to false inclusion when consistent covariation evidence was present.

It is unlikely that subjects' false inclusion can be attributed to reluctance to make uncertainty responses. While this factor has been noted as a source of error in young children's performance in logical reasoning tasks (Braine & Rumain, 1983), the youngest subjects in these studies were above the age at which this factor has been noted as a problem, and recent research has shown that even quite young children do not have difficulty with the *undecidable* concept when responses are elicited in a facilitative context (Fabricius, Sophian, & Wellman, 1987). Moreover, in the case of the present work, none of our subjects exhibited any difficulty in making uncertainty responses in the practice items.

The weaknesses in inductive reasoning skills described in this chapter are significant not only in and of themselves but also from the perspective of the coordination of evidence and theory. To the extent the individual fails to employ strict criteria for interpreting evidence, the opportunity for theoretical beliefs to influence the interpretation of evidence becomes greater. To take the most extreme example, the very lax co-occurrence criterion, according to which any single co-occurrence of antecedent and outcome is treated as sufficient evidence for an inference of causality, makes it possible to identify evidence supportive of just about any causal theory. Stricter criteria for interpreting evidence as demonstrating causality limit opportunities for theoretical belief to distort the evaluation of evidence. In the next chapter we examine in detail how theoretical beliefs interact with criteria for evaluating covariation and noncovariation evidence.

The results reported in this chapter also have implications for the literature on hypothesis-testing strategies and formal operations referred to in Chapter 2. This literature has attributed children's limitations in inferring relations among variables to absence of adequate strategies for testing hypotheses, in particular ability to control variables. Implicit in this literature has been the assumption that if adequate hypothesis-testing strategies were employed, appropriate inferences based on the resulting data would follow automatically. The weaknesses in interpretation of evidence identified in the present work suggest that not all of the limitations in inferential reasoning prior to adolescence are attributable to absence of a set of strategies for testing hypotheses. In particular, absence of exclusion, that is, inability to draw an appropriate inference from evidence of noncovariation, suggests the role of equally fundamental limitations in interpreting evidence once it has been generated. We explore this possibility further in subsequent chapters.

5

THE INFLUENCE
OF THEORY ON
EVALUATION OF EVIDENCE

The design of Studies 1a and 1b allows us to observe whether a subject interprets identical evidence differently when the theories the subject holds relevant to the evidence differ from one another. The argument can be made that it is perfectly rational, or correct, to evaluate the same evidence differently when it confirms versus disconfirms a theory. Evidence has meaning only in the context of a theory, and thus, one might claim, it is quite natural to treat identical evidence differently in the context of different theoretical beliefs. Indeed, it could be argued that doing so reflects the rational model of Bayesian statistics, in which prior probabilities condition the evaluation of evidence.

The Bayesian model, however, carries the assumption that such adjustments are made at a level of highly conscious, rational awareness: The implications of the evidence must be ascertained and then adjusted in a precise manner as a function of prior probabilities. In the terminology we used earlier, the evidence must first be encoded and represented as an entity distinct from the theory, and its evaluation then adjusted as a function of the theory. If we were to ask Bayesian statisticians if and how such adjustments were being made, they would be able to tell us, and if we were to ask them to judge the evidence independent of prior probabilities, they could readily do so. In sharp contrast, as we shall illustrate in this chapter, the theoretical beliefs of many of our subjects appeared to influence their evaluation of evidence in ways quite out of their conscious control.

SUBJECT SELECTION

Each of the analyses presented in this chapter focuses on a subset of subjects selected from Studies 1a and 1b. The aim in the design of these studies was to identify for each subject two variables with respect to which the subject held a causal theory with moderate certainty and two variables with respect to which the subject held a noncausal theory with moderate certainty (operationalized as ratings between $+2$ and $+8$ or between -2 and -8 on the "sureness" scale from -10 to $+10$ described in Chapter 3). We chose these "moderately held" theories for investigation, as they seemed the ones for which it was most likely that an interesting interaction with evidence would be observed. Subjects rating a causal theory as $+10$ or a noncausal theory as -10 were likely to have a strong conviction about the theory that could make them very resistant to considering new evidence. A less desirable feature of "moderately held" theories, however, for research purposes, is that they are less likely to be stable, a fact confirmed both by pilot data we collected and by an examination of subjects' reratings of the four variables for which no evidence had been presented. Both initial causal ($+2$ to $+8$) and initial noncausal (-2 to -8) theories showed some regression when rerated a week later: Noncausal theory ratings rose an average of 3 points, and causal theory ratings dropped an average of 4 points, both thus much closer to the midpoint though still significantly different from one another. This instability is not at all surprising if a subject's theory is regarded not as a unidimensional entity but as a collection of concepts and concept fragments on a continuum from ill-formed to well-formed, some complementary and others contradictory to one another. A subject's response to a request for a unidimensional numerical ranking, then, will depend heavily on what subset of these concepts are accessed at the time of the rating.

Our desire in the present studies was to focus on those theories that were moderately, rather than strongly, held but that were nevertheless held consistent-ly, that is, the subject had a stable belief about the effect of the variable but was only moderately certain about its correctness. The fact that a very high proportion of responses to the very first evidence evaluation question posed at the beginning of the second session (following presentation of the first instance of evidence, prior to the evidence-focus probe) was theory based provided a convenient way to assess theory consistency. Causal theories judged inconsistent were those for which the initial evidence evaluation response was a theory-based *no* (variable makes no difference) response. Noncausal theories judged inconsistent were those for which the initial evidence evaluation response was a theory-based *yes* (variable makes a difference) response. The analyses presented in this chapter are based only on those theories judged consistent according to this criterion. (This criterion for classification as consistent could be regarded as an overly conser-vative one, since it conceivably could have been the influence of the initial instance of evidence that led to the inconsistency, even though the subject's response was theory based. We nevertheless chose to err in this conservative direction.)

Subjects who did not show consistency for all four theories typically did show consistency for two or three, in which case the subject was included in the analysis for those variables. Overall figures showed that older subjects' theories were slightly more likely to be consistent: Among sixth graders, a total of 70% of theories were consistent, according to the criterion stated above; among ninth graders this percentage was 79%; and among adults it was 85%. Numbers of subjects in the analyses by variable presented in this chapter are 65 for Variables A and B, 79 for Variable C, and 67 for Variable D (Studies 1a and 1b combined). As these numbers reflect, subjects' noncausal theories (C and D) were slightly more likely to be consistent. Philosophers showed no influences of theoretical belief on their evaluation of evidence and are not included in these analyses.

HYPOTHESES

Our core hypothesis was that a subject's theoretical belief regarding the relationship of a given variable to outcome will affect the subject's evaluation of evidence pertaining to the relationship. Such effects might take a number of forms, which can be identified as subhypotheses:

1. A subject will be more likely to evaluate the evidence, that is, to make evidence-based responses, if the evidence is consistent with the subject's prior theory and less likely to do so if the evidence is inconsistent with the theory.

2. Identical evidence will be interpreted differently as a function of its consistency with prior theory.

The latter form of bias could take the following particular forms:

2a. A subject will more readily interpret the evidence for Variable A as indicating inclusion (consistent with theory) than she or he will interpret the same evidence for Variable C as indicating inclusion (inconsistent with theory).

2b. A subject will more readily interpret the evidence for Variable D as indicating exclusion (consistent with theory) than she or he will interpret the same evidence for Variable B as indicating exclusion (inconsistent with theory).

2c. A subject may incorrectly interpret evidence for Variable C as indicating exclusion (consistent with theory) but will not interpret the same evidence for Variable A in this way.

2d. A subject may incorrectly interpret evidence for Variable B as indicating inclusion (consistent with theory) but will not interpret the same evidence for Variable D in this way.

BIASED EVALUATION OF COVARIATION EVIDENCE

We begin with several illustrations of these biases from the protocols of subjects who exhibited them, to make it clear what they are like, and then go on to present group data regarding their prevalence. Jake (not his real name), a ninth grader, showed both Biases 1 and 2a in his interpretation of covariation evidence. Variable A (causal theory and covariation evidence) was sandwiches, with cheese always co-occurring with the positive outcome (no colds) and peanut butter with the negative (colds). Variable C (noncausal theory and covariation evidence) was breakfast roll, with bran muffin co-occurring with the positive outcome and donut with the negative. Instances 1, 4, 5, and 8 always have positive outcomes, and Instances 2, 3, 6, and 7 always have negative outcomes.

In response to the initial question (Does the kind of [*variable*] the children have make a difference in whether they get lots of colds or very few colds?) and probe (How do you know?) following presentation of Instance 1, Jake made theory-based responses for both Variables A and C, claiming that the kind of sandwich makes a difference because cheese has fewer ingredients and hence is "more natural" but that the kind of breakfast roll makes no difference because "breakfast rolls are breakfast rolls." When the evidence-focus probe (Do the *findings of the scientists* show that the kind of [*variable*] does make a difference, doesn't make a difference, or can't you tell what the scientists' findings show?) was presented after each of these initial responses, however, the responses diverged sharply. For Variable A, Jake interpreted the single co-occurrence of cheese sandwiches and no colds as indicating the causal role of the kind of sandwich (despite the presence of B, C, and D, which also co-occur with the outcome):

> Yes [the kind of sandwich makes a difference], because there aren't so many kids with colds [pictured in Instance 1].

For C, he noted the identical co-occurrence of bran muffin and no colds but in this case claimed to be unable to interpret it:

> I don't know. (Why not?) Because, you know, scientists they discover their things and people think other things. And breakfast rolls I'm not too high on, so I won't understand too much about it.

Following presentation of Instance 2, Jake gave an initial evidence-based response for A (though invoking his theory to explain the evidence):

> (Does the kind of sandwich make a difference . . . ?) Yes. (How do you know?) Because in Table [Instance] 1, they had cheese sandwiches [and got no colds]. See, so it was more natural; they didn't have as much things [ingredients] as they do over here with the peanut butter sandwiches [Instance 2].

For C, in contrast, he reverted to totally theory-based responding, making no reference to the identical evidence, even in response to the evidence-focus probe:

> (Does the kind of breakfast roll make a difference . . . ?) No. They are the same, like before. They are only supposed to "pick you up." (Do the *findings of the scientists* show that the kind of breakfast roll does make a difference, doesn't make a difference, or can't you tell what the scientists' findings show?) It doesn't make a difference. (How do you know?) Because breakfast rolls are breakfast rolls.

Jake's response following Instance 3 showed a similar divergence in the interpretation of identical evidence for the two variables:

> (Does the kind of sandwich make a difference . . . ?) I say it makes a difference in the way that the kids who had cheese sandwiches didn't get so many colds. You see that the peanut butter shows up again and people have many colds. So I say it is pretty much the cause.
>
> (Does the kind of breakfast roll make a difference . . . ?) No, because the breakfast rolls are pretty much the same thing. The only thing, they taste differently, but they are made the same way, they have the same thing—dough; they have to mix. See, they got pretty much the same things inside. They just taste different. (Do the *findings of the scientists* show . . . ?) It doesn't make a difference. See, because to me they are the same things. Because they had bran muffin here [Instance 1] and donut here [Instance 2]. Here they have many colds [Instance 2] . . . (pause) . . . but the thing is . . . (pause) . . . they can have many colds if they mix their food. But the breakfast roll to me don't cause so much colds because they have pretty much the same thing.

Jake's responses following Instances 4 and 5 were similar: The by-now-considerable evidence of covariation of A and C with outcome was ignored in the case of C and used as the basis for an inclusion inference in the case of A.

Though Jake noted some of the evidence with respect to C in his response following Instance 3, he turned away from it abruptly without making any interpretation. Other subjects, in contrast, evaluated theory-inconsistent covariation evidence but interpreted it as indicating exclusion, while never interpreting theory-consistent covariation evidence in this way (Hypothesis 2c). For example, Kim, a ninth grader, following Instance 5 interpreted the covariation evidence as indicating causality for the variable she believed causal, Variable A:

> Yes [it makes a difference]. (How do you know?) These three they had bottled water and they are all healthy, so it should make a difference. (Do the scientists' findings tell you *for sure* that the kind of water makes a difference?) Yes.

For C, however, kind of breakfast roll, which she believed noncausal, she interpreted the identical evidence thusly:

> No [it doesn't make a difference]. (How do you know?) Because at Tables [Instances] 2 and 3, they're sick. (. . . *for sure?*) No.

Following presentation of Instance 6, Kim similarly interpreted the evidence as indicating causality for A. For C, her response was as follows:

No [it doesn't make a difference]. (How do you know?) Because they're sick here [Instance 5], and here [6] they were healthy. So it really doesn't make a difference. (. . . *for sure?*) Yes.

The breakfast roll variable of course covaried with sickness and health in the same way as the kind of water did, but instead of using this covariation as a basis for inferring causality as she did in the case of the water, Kim focused only on the outcomes, ignored their covariation with the breakfast roll variable, and interpreted this evidence as a basis for claiming that kind of breakfast roll made no difference.

Occasionally, unlike Kim, a subject implicitly acknowledged the covariation and its seeming implication of causality but nevertheless refused to accept this implication and interpreted the evidence as indicating exclusion (Hypothesis 2c). The following, for example, is the response of Duane, also a ninth grader, for Variable C (noncausal theory with covariation evidence) following Instance 4 (an inclusion inference was made for A):

It didn't make a difference. At Tables 1 and 4 they had potato salad, and they're not sick. At Tables 2 and 3 they had fruit salad, but they are sick. I think they got sick from something else.

Quantitative Analysis

The hypotheses presented earlier were tested statistically by comparing responses of all subjects for the two relevant variables (A and C or B and D) in a within-subjects analysis. In cases in which the subject's data had been excluded for one of the variables due to inconsistency of theory (as explained in the initial section of this chapter), the response for the other variable was substituted, making the two responses identical and thus working against the hypothesis of a difference in response between the two. Exclusion of these subjects thus provided no advantage in terms of yielding statistically significant differences between the variables. Their exclusion is important, however, for the more qualitative analyses presented later in this chapter, in which the processes by which a subject reconciles a theory with discrepant evidence are examined.

Two separate statistical analyses were performed for each comparison. One was a theory (causal versus noncausal) by condition (Study 1a or 1b) by age group (sixth or ninth grade) analysis (an adult group, recall, was not included in Study 1b). The other was a theory by age group (sixth, ninth, adult) analysis for Study 1a subjects alone. As no effects of condition or age group appeared, and the two analyses yielded very similar findings regarding the effect of theory, only the latter statistical analysis is reported here, and only the means for the entire group (age groups and conditions combined) are presented. As noted earlier, no biases of any of the forms hypothesized occurred on the part of the five philosophers, and they are not included in any analyses.

Hypothesis 1 was that subjects would be more likely to evaluate the evidence, that is, would make more evidence-based responses, if the evidence was consistent with their theory than they would if the evidence was inconsistent with their theory. In the case of covariation evidence, test of this hypothesis entails a comparison between theory-consistent Variable A and theory-inconsistent Variable C. Mean number of evidence-based responses (of eight possible) for Variable A was 6.23. For Variable C, it was 5.81. This difference was significant, $F(1, 57) = 4.69$, $p = .035$ (F value based on analysis for Study 1a subjects only). Hypothesis 2a was that subjects would make more inclusion inferences for Variable A than for Variable C. Mean number of inclusion inferences (whether spontaneous or elicited) for Variable A was 5.05. For Variable C, it was 4.58. This difference was significant, $F(1, 57) = 7.64$, $p = .008$ (F value based on analysis for Study 1a subjects only).

Exclusion responses to covariation evidence of course occurred much less frequently than inclusion responses, and the testing of Hypothesis 2c therefore required a more qualitative analysis. No subject made exclusion responses to both A and C, and subjects rarely made more than one exclusion response overall. Their occurrence, however, was much more frequent for Variable C than it was for Variable A, as predicted by Hypothesis 2c: For A, 4 subjects (6%) made one or more exclusion responses, while 17 (22%) made one or more exclusion responses for C. Subjects making exclusion responses for A were mostly sixth graders (3 of the 4, with the 4th a ninth grader). Exclusion responses for C, in contrast, were made by comparable proportions of subjects (20–25%) of all age groups.

Overall, 42% of subjects exhibited one or more of the three possible forms of bias (Hypotheses 1, 2a, and 2c) in their interpretation of covariation evidence. This percentage decreased only slightly with age: 47% for sixth graders, 41% for ninth graders, and 35% for adults. Male and female subjects were equally likely to exhibit bias.

BIASED EVALUATION
OF NONCOVARIATION EVIDENCE

Hypothesis 1 biases (more evidence-based responses for theory-consistent evidence) were infrequent in the case of noncovariation evidence. Subjects tended to evaluate the evidence to an equal extent for the two variables, B (for which the theory was causal) and D (for which the theory was noncausal). In their interpretation of the evidence, however, bias occurred of the forms predicted by Hypotheses 2b and 2d. The more prevalent bias was to interpret the evidence for D as indicating exclusion but fail to interpret the same evidence for B as indicating exclusion (2b). Dean is an example of a ninth-grade subject who showed this form of bias. After presentation of Instance 4, for Variable B (causal theory), he made this response:

(Does the kind of water make a difference . . . ?) The water? I'm not too sure because when they drink the tap water they get a cold and sometimes they don't get a cold.

For Variable D (noncausal theory), in contrast, he made this response:

> (Does the kind of vegetable make a difference . . . ?) No, I don't think so. (How do you
> know?) Because with the beans sometimes they get colds and sometimes they don't. (. . . *for*
> *sure?*) Yeah.

This case is notable as Dean explicitly recognized the lack of covariation in both
cases (which not all subjects did) but only recognized its implication in one.

Laura, also a ninth grader, is an example of a subject who recognized the lack
of covariation and made an inference of exclusion for Variable D (noncausal
theory) but in the case of Variable B (causal theory) drew on only part of the
evidence as a basis for an inference of inclusion (thus illustrating Hypothesis 2d
bias, as well as 2b). After all eight instances had been presented, Laura made this
response for Variable B:

> (Does the kind of relish make a difference . . . ?) Yes. Mostly likely all the time you get a cold
> with the mustard. Like there you did [Instance 2], and there you did [Instance 7]. (. . . *for*
> *sure?*) Yes.

In fact, of course, mustard co-occurred with no-colds as often as it co-occurred
with colds, but Laura made no acknowledgment of the discrepant cases. With
respect to Variable D, in contrast, she interpreted the identical evidence as
follows:

> (Does the kind of candy make a difference . . . ?) With the Mars Bar you get a cold off and
> on because here's one they got colds and over here they didn't. So it depends on what you got
> around it, so it really doesn't matter. (So the kind of candy makes no difference?) No.
> (. . . *for sure?*) Yes.

Quantitative Analysis

In contrast to evaluation of covariation evidence, subjects' evaluation of
noncovariation evidence did not conform to Hypothesis 1: Mean number of
evidence-based responses was not significantly different for Variable D (noncausal theory) than for Variable B (causal theory). While subjects thus evaluated
the evidence for B and D to a comparable extent, they nevertheless were more
likely to make exclusion inferences for D than for B (Hypothesis 2b). Mean
number of exclusion inferences of a possible 6 (Instances 3–8 only, as evidence
of noncovariation does not occur until Instance 3) was 3.33 for D and 3.05 for
B. This difference was significant, $F(1, 57) = 4.30$, $p = .018$, for Study 1a
subjects but only approached significance for Study 1b subjects. Though effects
of neither age group nor age in interaction with theory (B versus D) reached
statistical significance, it is worth noting that the differential occurrence of
exclusion inferences for B versus D did not appear among sixth graders, which
could be attributable to the overall lower frequencies of exclusion among sixth
graders, compared to older subjects (Chapter 4). Mean number of exclusions

was in fact fractionally higher for B than for D among sixth graders. Ninth graders showed some difference in favor of D (mean of 3.65 for D, versus 3.35 for B), but the differential occurrence of exclusion inferences was most pronounced among adults (mean of 4.75 for D, versus 3.95 for B). (Failure of the difference to reach statistical significance among Study 1b subjects is thus attributable to the fact that no adult group was included.)

Inclusion responses to noncovariation evidence of course occurred much less frequently than exclusion responses, and the testing of Hypothesis 2d therefore required a more qualitative analysis. Almost the same number of subjects made inclusion responses to noncovariation evidence as made exclusion responses to covariation evidence (reported earlier). However, while the latter subjects tended to make only a single exclusion inference, subjects making inclusion inferences in response to noncovariation evidence tended to make several, typically two or three. Occurrence of inclusion inferences was more likely for Variable B than it was for Variable D, as predicted by Hypothesis 2d: Inclusion inferences only for D were made by 4 subjects (6%), while 11 (17%) made them only for B; an additional 4 subjects made inclusion inferences for both B and D, with 2 of the 4 making more for B than D and the other 2 making an equal number for B and D. A total of 13 subjects (19%) thus favored B over D in making inclusion inferences, while 4 (6%) favored D and 2 (3%) showed no difference.

In contrast to exclusion responses to covariation evidence, inclusion responses to noncovariation evidence, for both B and D, were concentrated among younger subjects. Only two adults made inclusion responses to noncovariation evidence (Variable B only in both cases), while nine sixth graders and eight ninth graders did so. Adults, then, were more likely than younger subjects to deal with the discrepancy between a causal theory and noncovariation evidence by failing to infer exclusion (as reported above), but they were unlikely to distort the evidence to infer inclusion, as younger subjects often did.

Overall, 52% of subjects exhibited one or more of the three possible forms of bias (Hypotheses 1, 2b, and 2d) in their interpretation of noncovariation evidence, a slightly higher proportion than showed such bias in the interpretation of covariation evidence. Moreover, this percentage showed no tendency to decline with age; percentages by age group were 48% for sixth graders, 55% for ninth graders, and 56% for adults. Male and female subjects were equally likely to exhibit bias.

THE RECONCILIATION OF THEORY
AND DISCREPANT EVIDENCE

The illustrations presented in the preceding sections document the ways in which subjects' theories biased their interpretation of evidence. Such illustrations do not tell the whole story, however, for they do not reveal how the subject's reasoning evolved over the sequence of evidence presentation, as more discrepant evidence accumulated. In what way did the subject resolve the conflict and reconcile his or her theory with the discrepant evidence that he or she had been asked to evaluate?

The term *conflict* should really be in quotes, as a "conflict" in fact existed only if the subject chose to construe the discrepancy thusly. The stance a subject might quite reasonably take, and the one taken by all five philosophers, is the following: "This is my theory [regarding the relationship between variable and outcome] and what I take to be true. This is the evidence you have presented to me, which I recognize to be inconsistent with the theory I hold and consistent with an opposing theory. This evidence is thus wrong or my theory is wrong, but I needn't decide which." A subject taking this stance might make a theory-based response to the initial question, but he or she would always make an evidence-based response to the evidence-focus probe. Such a subject could continue to note the discrepancy between theory and evidence by juxtaposing what his or her theory implies (in response to the initial question) with what the evidence implies (in response to the evidence-focus probe). Or the subject might give only evidence-based responses, in effect setting aside any statement of the theory or of the fact that it is not in accord with this evidence.

In fact, very few subjects other than the philosophers took such a stance. The study of individual protocols, examining how the subject dealt with the discrepant evidence as it accumulated over the eight instances, revealed strategies of one sort or another to bring theory and evidence into alignment with one another. A major, and anticipated, strategy, of course, was biased evaluation of the evidence, to reduce its inconsistency with theory, though it was a strategy that was hard to maintain as the discrepant evidence mounted.

Another strategy, that we had not anticipated, was the adjustment of theory to reduce its inconsistency with the evidence. Most noteworthy about this strategy were the indications that it occurred without the subject's conscious awareness. Before looking at individual examples of how subjects reconciled theory and discrepant evidence, however, we examine how subjects' responses evolved over the eight instances of evidence presentation when theory and evidence were not discrepant, for these cases turned out to be equally informative.

Sequential Response Patterns When Theory and Evidence Are Not Discrepant

Peter, a sixth grader, serves as a typical example. For Variable A (causal theory with covariation evidence), he first made a theory-based response:

It makes a difference. Carrot cake has . . . is made with carrots, and chocolate cake is made with a lot of sugar. But this [carrot cake] is made with some sugar too, but it's made with less sugar.

In response to the evidence-focus probe, however, he made no reference to the evidence and merely elaborated the theory:

(Do the *findings of the scientists* show . . . ?) Less sugar means you don't . . . your blood pressure doesn't go up. It makes a difference.

After the second instance of evidence was presented, Peter reiterated the theory but then, in response to the evidence-focus probe, made his first evaluation of the evidence:

(Do the *findings of the scientists* show . . . ?) Yes. Because these [Instance 2] are like "*ugghh*" with tissues [the children held to their noses], and Table 1 has no tissues. (. . . *for sure?*) Yes.

One might suppose that having recognized and interpreted the fact that the evidence reflected covariation, Peter would continue to refer to the presented evidence, at least in his responses to the evidence-focus probe. After presentation of the third instance, however, he initially reiterated the theory and then, in response to the evidence-focus probe, simply repeated the theory again:

(Do the *findings of the scientists* show . . . ?) Yes [it makes a difference], because it [chocolate cake] has a lot of sugar and a lot of bad stuff in it.

After presentation of the fourth instance, Peter initially reiterated the theory but then, in response to the evidence-focus probe, again referred to the evidence:

Yeah [it makes a difference]. Because they're smiling here [Instance 4] and here [1], and in 2 and 3 they're not smiling and they both had chocolate cake.

Peter's responses after presentation of the fifth and sixth instances were similar. After Instance 7, however, in response to the evidence-focus probe, he again substituted a reiteration of his theory for evaluation of the evidence. His response after the final instance was comparable to those after Instances 5 and 6.

Peter's theory regarding the relation between kind of cake and outcome was completely compatible with the evidence that he was asked to evaluate. Yet the sequence of his responses has a curious quality, one that rarely appeared in those of older subjects. Especially because they are compatible, perhaps, he appears not to distinguish theory and evidence clearly, responding to questions about the evidence with a statement of his theory, even after he has attended to and interpreted the evidence.

This difference between younger and older subjects was evident, at a group level of analysis, for both variables for which theory and evidence were consistent (A and D). Older subjects occasionally made theory-based responses to the evidence-focus probe early in the sequence of evidence presentation, when very little evidence was available, most likely because of their uncertainty as to how such a minimal amount of evidence could be interpreted. Once the subject acknowledged the evidence, however, even if only to indicate that he or she did not know how to interpret it (Type IIIa1, Table 5), the subject rarely reverted to ignoring the evidence (at least in response to the evidence-focus probe) after successive instances in the sequence. A tabulation was made, therefore, of whether a subject ever made a totally theory-based response (both initial and evidence-focus probe) once he or she had made an evidence-based response. For Variable A, 40% of sixth graders, 22% of ninth graders, and 6% of adults did so. For Variable D, 43% of sixth graders, 21% of ninth graders, and 13% of adults did so.

These differences support the interpretation that subjects, particularly younger ones, show limitations in their differentiation of theory and evidence. Theory and evidence fit together into a consistent representation of the phenomenon, and there appears to be a less than firm distinction with respect to the contribution made by each. What if theory and evidence are at odds with one another, however? Would not this discrepancy force subjects into a clearer differentiation between them? To address this question, let us turn now to an examination of how subjects attempted to reconcile their theories and discrepant evidence.

The Reconciliation of Theory
and Discrepant Covariation Evidence

We examine first how subjects dealt with accumulating evidence of covariation when their initial theoretical belief was that the variable made no difference to the outcome. As we emphasized earlier, a "conflict" existed only if the subject construed there to be one, and this is doubly true in the case of covariation evidence: Evidence of common covariation between two variables and an outcome is in fact totally compatible with the theory that one of the variables has no causal effect on the outcome. A subject could thus easily have avoided any conflict between evidence and theoretical belief by attributing the covariation of A and C with outcome to the causal role of A and regarding the covariation of the third variable, C, as incidental. Few subjects, however, as we saw in Chapter 4, recognized that covariation of two variables with an outcome does not implicate either as causal. Thus, most regarded the evidence of covariation of C and outcome as discrepant with their theory that C makes no difference. How, then, did subjects deal with this discrepancy?

Adjusting the Evidence to Fit the Theory

Few subjects, as we indicated, simply acknowledged the discrepancy between theory and evidence and never blurred the distinction between the two—other than the five philosophers, only one adult and one ninth grader did so. "This is what I think," these subjects tended to articulate early in the evidence presentation, "but this is what the evidence shows." As the questioning continued, they tended to omit mention of their theory and simply interpret the evidence. A large number of subjects, in contrast, resisted the implications of the evidence by means of one of the strategies we have already examined: Either they failed to evaluate the evidence regarding C (and made a theory-based response instead) or they evaluated it in a way biased by their theory. What we did not consider in our earlier examination of these biases, however, is how a subject who displayed them ultimately resolved the conflict as the covariation evidence accumulated and the subject continued to be questioned.

The examination of individual protocols revealed three different resolution modes, defined by the nature of the responses during the last one fourth of the evidence presentation (Instances 7 and 8) on the part of subjects who initially showed bias in their evaluation of the evidence for C. One of the three was to do what the philosophers had done from the start, to acknowledge the discrepancy between theory and evidence and as a result to abandon any attempt to distort or deny the implications of the evidence. A subject was classified as showing this resolution mode if no further bias (as defined in the hypotheses presented previously) occurred in the last quarter of the evidence presentation and if the response for C after at least one of the last two instances consisted of an initial *no* (doesn't make a difference) theory-based response followed by an evidence-based response that acknowledged the covariation of variable and outcome. (The latter could be the correct one of uncertainty or, more commonly, the incorrect one of inclusion.)

A second mode of resolution was simply to ignore or set aside the theory and interpret the evidence in a way that acknowledged the covariation of variable and outcome. A subject was classified as showing this resolution mode if no bias occurred in the last quarter and the responses for C after both of the last two instances were *initial* evidence-based responses (that is evidence-based to the initial probe) that acknowledged the covariation of variable and outcome.

A third mode was lack of resolution, exemplified by subjects who continued either to ignore the evidence or to interpret it in a biased way during the last quarter of the evidence presentation. Andrew, a sixth grader, provides an example of a subject who displayed this continued tension between theory and evidence. The variable was gum, and Andrew's theory, which he always expressed in response to the initial probe, was that the kind makes no difference because "gum is gum." As early as Instance 2, however, he acknowledged the evidence of covariation:

(Do the *findings of the scientists* show . . . ?) Yes, because this one with this gum they were sick and this one they were not sick. (. . . for sure?) Yeah.

Though this recognition came early, it was not maintained consistently. Over the remainder of the instances Andrew's responses to the evidence-focus probe vacillated between evidence-based and theory-based, with a theory-based response occurring as late as Instance 7, when the evidence of covariation was considerable:

> (Does the kind of gum make a difference . . . ?) Maybe. Gum could make a difference, but it wouldn't make you get a cold. (Do the *findings of the scientists* show . . . ?) No, it doesn't make a difference. Gum is gum.

Despite the initial suggestion of a softening of the theory (possibly in reaction to the evidence), in response to the request to evaluate the evidence Andrew decisively reiterated his original theory. At this late stage in the evidence presentation, the tension between conflicting theory and evidence clearly has not been resolved.

The vacillation between theory-based and evidence-based responses to the request to evaluate the evidence is of course the same vacillation illustrated earlier in the case in which theory and evidence were not discrepant. The fact that theory and evidence now dictate the opposite conclusions does not eliminate the fluid movement from one to another as the basis for a response. Its implication in this case, however, is that it allows the subject to avoid a resolution between discrepant theory and evidence that subjects showing the other modes of resolution described above sought and achieved. Instead of explicitly acknowledging the discrepancy or setting aside the theory to interpret the evidence, as those subjects did, the subject allows the theory to intrude into, even to take over, evaluation of the evidence.

This unresolved tension between opposing theory and evidence is illustrated most clearly by Andrew's response for Variable C after the third instance. He initially expressed his "gum is gum" theory but then, after the evidence-focus probe, interpreted the covariation evidence as indicating inclusion:

> (Do the *findings of the scientists* show . . . ?) It makes a difference. They're still sick over here and here they're not sick.

In response to the final probe, however, we see the intrusion of the theory into his evaluation of the evidence:

> (Do the scientists' findings tell you *for sure* that the kind of gum makes a difference?) No. Gum does not get you colds.

Adjusting the Theory to Fit the Evidence

Another major strategy for reconciling theory and discrepant evidence which appeared in the examination of individual protocols—one that we had not anticipated—was the adjustment of theory to reduce its inconsistency with the evidence. David, a ninth grader, provides an example of a subject who displayed this strategy. The variable was relish, and his initial response was as follows:

No [it doesn't make a difference]. Because it's the same thing. (Do the *findings of the scientists* show . . . ?) No, no difference. (How do you know?) Because catsup is good. But they [catsup and mustard] have, I think, the same vitamins.

David's responses after presentation of Instances 2 and 3 were virtually identical to this. After Instance 4, however, his theory changed abruptly:

Yes, it makes some difference. (How do you know?) Because it's more better. It's made out of the same thing but still it's better. I think more ingredients. (Which one?) This one [mustard]. (How do you know?) Because I think it has more ingredients than that one, the catsup. (Why do you think that?) Uh . . . it's good for the health. It's something that. . . . This kind of relish is usually gonna be cold [mustard]. This kind of relish is usually gonna be hot [catsup]. This one [mustard] you have to use it cold. (Do the *findings of the scientists* show . . . ?) Yes. (How do you know?) For the same reason.

After Instance 5, the same sort of theory was again voiced, with some modification. (Now catsup, rather than mustard, is limited to one food temperature):

Yes [it makes a difference]. Because this kind of relish, the mustard, is used in hot things or cold. Only the catsup is only used for hot things. (Do the *findings of the scientists* show . . . ?) Yes. For the same reason.

David's response after Instance 6 was identical. After Instance 7, however, he finally made reference to the evidence:

Yeah, it makes some difference. (How do you know?) That you put on hot things and that you put on hot and cold things. (Do the *findings of the scientists* show . . . ?) Yeah. Because that three kind of tables they don't have no colds and they eat mustard, but when they eat catsup they have a lot of colds. (. . . *for sure?*) Yeah.

After Instance 8, David dropped mention of the theory and simply interpreted the evidence in the same way as above.

What is notable about the protocols of David and a sizable number of subjects like him is not just their formulation of a new theory to fit the evidence but the fact that they formulate and voice the theory *before* they acknowledge the implications of the evidence. It appears almost as if they are not willing to acknowledge the implications of the evidence unless they have a compatible theory in place that can provide an explanation of this evidence. A few subjects articulated a new theory to fit the evidence *after* they had interpreted the evidence as indicating inclusion, and this pattern of course has a very different meaning. "Given this is what the evidence indicates," such subjects said in effect, "here is a theory that might make sense of it." Many more subjects, however, displayed the strategy shown by David, in which the new theory is articulated before the evidence is acknowledged. Roughly a quarter of the subjects who articulated new theories also displayed one of the biases in evidence evaluation described earlier. For the remaining subjects, articulation of a new theory appeared to be a substitute strategy employed instead of biased evidence evaluation.

Also notable about the new theories these subjects constructed is their implausibility and, as in David's case, their sometimes marginal coherence. David began by articulating the new theory that mustard would lead to fewer colds because it has more ingredients than catsup, but then he drifted into a concern—about the temperature of the foods they are eaten with—of unclear relevance to their cold-causing capacities. Terry, a ninth grader, provides another example. Terry initially expressed the more plausible view that gum has nothing to do with colds but then, after several instances of evidence had been presented (but not acknowledged by Terry), advanced the following theory:

> Yes [the kind of gum makes a difference], cause one kind got a lot of sugar and everything, get you all hyper. (Which one is that?) The Juicy Fruit. If you eat a lot of sugar, you get all hyper, and if it's cold out and you get all hyper, you can catch a cold. You get hot, and then something like a little cold breeze comes out and you get a cold automatically.

Some interesting variation was also evident in the modes of resolution displayed by subjects who constructed new theories. We might assume that articulation of a new theory compatible with the evidence would be a sufficient resolution to the conflict, and for about half the subjects who articulated new theories it was. For the other half, however, articulation of a new theory was not sufficient to eliminate the old theory, and what was observed was first a resurfacing of the original theory and then a vacillation between the two. Peter, the sixth grader whose response pattern for A was described earlier, provides an example. His initial response for C was as follows:

> (Does the kind of potato make a difference . . . ?) Not really. (How do you know?) Because potato is potato. [If] It's baked, it has the skin on it. Fried it doesn't. (Do the *findings of the scientists* show . . . ?) No. (How do you know?) Because, it's the same thing.

After Instance 2, his theory changed, but his lack of enthusiasm for the new theory is evident:

> It makes a little bit of difference, but not much. The skin is sometimes good for you in baked potato. (Do the *findings of the scientists* show . . . ?) Not really, but a little bit. (Should I say *yes, no,* or *maybe?*) Yes. (And tell me how you know?) Because these [baked potato] might be nonfrozen. These [french fries] might be [frozen].

With a new theory articulated, Peter now acknowledged the covariation evidence, after Instance 3, but again his ambivalence regarding this resolution is evident:

> Yes [it makes a difference], because look at this. First they're smiling and then with french fries they're not smiling. And with Table 3 they're not smiling. (. . . *for sure?*) Not really. Because they don't really have any evidence. (They don't really have any evidence?) Not really, but a little bit. A little bit, because one's smiling and one's not.

After Instance 4, the original theory resurfaced:

Not really. Baked potato and french fries are pretty much the same. (Do the *findings of the scientists* show . . . ?) No, because, ummmm . . . (long pause) . . . because french fries is the same thing as baked potato, except it's baked and still has the skin.

Peter's responses after the next two instances clearly reflect the tension between the original theory, which he preferred, and the new theory with the growing body of evidence supporting it:

No, it doesn't make a difference. (How do you know?) Same as before. (Do the *findings of the scientists* show . . . ?) No. It doesn't say that it makes a difference. (Why doesn't it say that?) It doesn't say, really, cause they're smiling there. (They're smiling over here, with the baked potato [instance 1]?) Yup, and . . . uh . . . wait a second, maybe it does. Because these two have the french fries and they're not smiling. So it might make a difference. I just noticed that. (Should I say *maybe* or *yes?*) Maybe.

After Instance 6, Peter responded:

Yes. I just changed my mind. (Okay, tell me why.) Because these two have french fries, and they're not too good. (. . . *for sure?*) For sure . . . well, not really for sure. (Why not?) Because it might and it might not. Because the french fries and the baked potatoes, as I said before, I said . . . wait, let me think . . . I said that french fries are the same as the baked potato.

Though Peter characterized himself as having "just changed [his] mind," he had of course acknowledged the covariation and made an inclusion inference as early as Instance 3. With Instance 7, we see how he resolves the conflict. When Instance 7 was first presented, he began to list the items he thought made a difference:

Chocolate cake, yes. It does make a difference. Frozen beans, no, because on Tables 2 and 4. . . . It doesn't make a difference. The . . . wait! The french fries does. I keep forgetting about that!

When specifically queried about the kind of potato, he then responded:

Yes [it makes a difference]. (How do you know?) Because these people [Instances 2 and 3] both have french fries, and they both do not like it [have colds], and Table 4 and 5 both have baked potatoes and they both like it. (. . . *for sure?*) Yes.

His response after Instance 8 was identical.

Peter thus ultimately resolved the conflict by setting aside the theory (both old and new) and simply interpreting the evidence. For Variable A, recall, in contrast he continued to refer to his compatible theory in conjunction with evaluating the evidence. Other subjects, however, whose original theory regarding Variable C resurfaced following articulation of a new theory, showed different resolution modes, and the same three modes described earlier with respect to subjects who did not articulate a new theory were evident.

Categorization of all subjects with respect to how they reconciled their theories regarding Variable C with the discrepant covariation evidence is shown in Figure 3. Included are 30 sixth graders, 32 ninth graders, 17 adults, and the 5 philosophers (a total of 84 subjects). Figures for sixth graders appear first, for ninth graders second, for adults third, and for the philosophers fourth. Since frequencies in the groups vary, percentages (relative to the immediately preceding division) are included beneath the simple frequencies.

As reflected in Figure 3, if no new theory is articulated, adults may initially show bias, but they are more likely than younger subjects ultimately to acknowledge the theory/evidence discrepancy. Sixth graders are most likely to leave the discrepancy unresolved, continuing to either ignore the evidence or evaluate it in a biased manner. The most common resolution overall, nevertheless, is simply to set aside, in other words ignore, the theory.

If a new theory is articulated (lower half of Figure 3), adults are more likely than ninth graders and ninth graders more likely than sixth graders to maintain the new theory and resolve the conflict in this manner. Among sixth graders, in contrast, the old theory is likely to resurface, and either no resolution is achieved or resolution ultimately is achieved by ignoring the theory.

The Reconciliation of Theory
and Discrepant Noncovariation Evidence

The same classification system as was used in the case of covariation evidence proved adequate to classify the ways in which subjects reconciled theories with discrepant noncovariation evidence. This categorization is shown in Figure 4. Included are 70 subjects: 25 sixth graders, 22 ninth graders, 18 adults, and the 5 philosophers.

Comparison of Figures 3 and 4 indicates that a new theory (in this case a theory reflecting the belief that the variable does not make a difference to the outcome) is less likely to be articulated in response to discrepant noncovariation evidence than it is in response to discrepant covariation evidence. Whether a new theory is articulated or not, very few subjects besides the philosophers acknowledge the theory/evidence discrepancy, and again the most common resolution is simply to ignore the theory. Ninth graders as well as sixth graders, however, are likely to leave the discrepancy unresolved. If a new theory is articulated, ninth graders and adults are most likely to maintain the new theory; among sixth graders the old theory is more likely to resurface, and either no resolution is achieved or resolution is achieved by ignoring the theory.

We conclude this section with a single example of a subject struggling to reconcile a causal theory with discrepant noncovariation evidence. The subject is Andrew, the same sixth grader whose similar struggle in the case of covariation evidence we examined earlier. His is a particularly interesting case as he has only

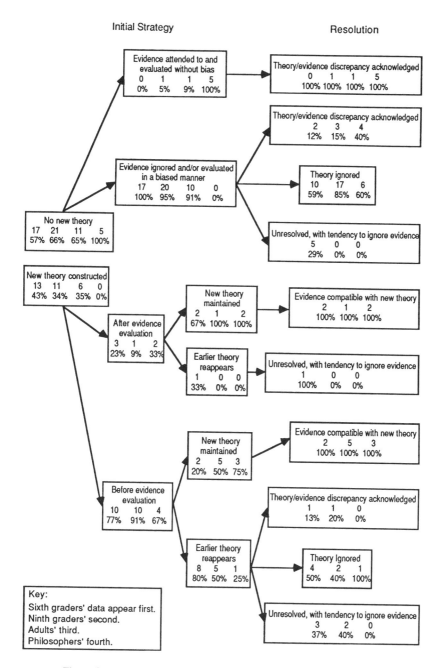

Figure 3. Patterns of theory/evidence reconciliation for covariation evidence.

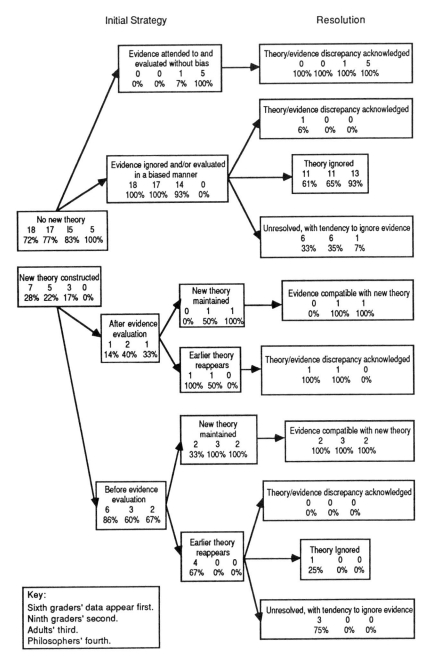

Figure 4.   Patterns of theory/evidence reconciliation for noncovariation evidence.

a very fleeting grasp of exclusion, and this contributes to the struggle. With respect to Variable B (in this case cheese, with cottage and cheddar the two types), Andrew initially expressed the "cold" theory of what causes colds (not unique to this subject):

> Maybe [it makes a difference], because some cheeses be in the refrigerator. Then they get real cold and give you a cold.

When the first evidence of noncovariation occurred (Instance 3), Andrew initially reiterated the above theory but then engaged in his first evaluation of the evidence:

> (Do the *findings of the scientists* show . . . ?) No [it makes no difference]. They're not sick over here [Instance 1] from it. (. . . *for sure?*) No. I don't know that much about cheese.

After presentation of Instance 4, Andrew initially reiterated his theory but then, despite his recognition of the noncovariation in his previous response, did not refer to the evidence:

> (Do the *findings of the scientists* show . . . ?) Can't tell. Because cheese is cheese, and the different kinds, I don't know that much about them.

In this response, however, we see the beginnings of a new theory, which is then crystallized after Instance 5:

> No [it makes no difference]. Cheese is cheese.

In response to the evidence-focus probe, however, we see the intrusion of his original theory:

> (Do the *findings of the scientists* show . . . ?) It makes a difference. They got sick [points to Instances 2 and 3] from the cold cheese. (Does it make a difference what *kind* of cheese the children had?) Table 3 got colds and Table 2 got colds. But they're not the same kind [of cheese]. (So, what do you think? Does the kind of cheese matter?) Yes. (. . . *for sure?*) No.

After Instance 6, Andrew's original ("cold") theory reappeared, followed by the same false inclusion evaluation of the evidence:

> Yes, it does [make a difference]. Cottage cheese is in the refrigerator. (Do the *findings of the scientists* show . . . ?) Yes [it makes a difference]. Table 2 had cottage cheese. (And what happened to them?) They got sick. (. . . *for sure?*) Yes.

After Instance 7, the original ("cold") theory again appeared, followed by this evaluation of the evidence:

> (Do the *findings of the scientists* show . . . ?) Yes . . . no. (Tell me why you said *no.*) Cause they got cottage cheese too [Instance 4] and they're not sick. (. . . *for sure?*) For sure.

Following the final instance, Andrew responded as follows:

No . . . yes. It makes a difference. They freeze cottage cheese. They put cottage cheese in the freezer. (Do the *findings of the scientists* show . . . ?) I don't know. Cause they got cheddar cheese and they were sick and they got cottage cheese and they're sick too. (Well, do you think that means the kind of cheese makes a difference, do you think it makes no difference, or can't you tell?) Makes a difference.

We thus see that for Andrew the new theory that was articulated after Instances 4 and 5 was not sufficient to resolve the conflict. The original "cold" theory reappeared and then vied with the increasing evidence of noncovariation (which Andrew had already recognized and correctly interpreted after Instance 3), leading to distortion of the evidence and false inclusion inferences after Instances 5 and 6. The discrepant theory also most likely contributed to the instability of his ability to interpret noncovariation correctly (Instances 7 and 8), and Andrew failed to achieve any resolution.

GENERAL DISCUSSION

The results presented in this chapter document the intrusion of theory into the evaluation of evidence in ways that appear to be outside the conscious control of the subject. When theory and evidence were compatible, one can sense, from the examples given, a melding of the two into a single representation of "the way things are." The pieces of evidence are regarded, not as independent of the theory and bearing on it, but more as *instances* of the theory that serve to illustrate it. The theory in turn is capable of *explaining* the evidence, of making sense of it. Articulating the theory is thus as good as analyzing the nature of the evidence itself in indicating what "the findings of the scientists show."

What are the skills that subjects who show this melding of theory and evidence lack? Ability to evaluate the bearing of evidence on a theory requires at a minimum that the evidence be encoded and represented separate from the theory. If new evidence is merely assimilated to a theory, as an instance of it, the possibility of constructing relations between the two, as separate entities, is lost. Or if the subject cannot represent the theory itself as an object of cognition, evidence cannot be evaluated in relation to it. Furthermore, and paradoxically perhaps, the ability to coordinate theory and evidence requires temporarily bracketing, or setting aside, one's acceptance of the theory, in order to assess what the evidence by itself would mean for the theory were it the only basis for making a judgment. Subjects who vacillated between theory and evidence as the basis for justifying inferences are, we hypothesize, weak in all three of these abilities: thinking *about* a theory, differentiating theory and evidence, and bracketing belief in the theory as a means of evaluating the relation of the evidence to it. The three abilities are of course linked, as one can neither "bracket" nor contemplate a theory to the extent it is undifferentiated from particular instances of evidence.

Ability to "bracket one's experience" or beliefs has been discussed by Scribner (1977) and others as a product of schooling. As a result, it has tended to be regarded as the discourse mode of those who follow academic paths—an ability to contemplate the purely hypothetical, divorced from practical thought and life. In contrast, the present results suggest, paradoxically perhaps, that this bracketing ability is essential to the very practical skill of evaluating new information that bears on one's existing beliefs. Only by bracketing one's belief in a theory and temporarily regarding it as an object of cognition can one assess the relation of the evidence to it and thereby effect conscious control over the interaction of theory and evidence.

Discrepancy between theory and evidence, we found, did *not* lead subjects to any clearer differentiation between the two. When theory and evidence were not compatible, we observed the variety of devices subjects used to attempt to bring them into alignment: either adjusting the theory, most often before acknowledging the evidence, or "adjusting" the evidence, by ignoring it, attending to it in a selective, distorting manner, or failing to acknowledge its implications. More notable even than these devices is the fact that the subject needed the two to be in alignment. Why did subjects like David or Terry need to discard their own very plausible theories that gum or relishes have nothing to do with getting colds, and formulate new, highly implausible and unstable theories about the relation of these variables to colds, before they were willing to acknowledge evidence showing a covariation between these variables and colds? Why were they unable simply to acknowledge that the evidence showed covariation, without needing first to explain why this is the outcome that one should expect? The answer, we propose, is that doing so would have left theory and evidence not in alignment with one another and therefore needing to be recognized as distinct entities.

The above characterization of course represents the extreme, reflected primarily in the protocols of some of the younger subjects. Younger subjects were less likely than older ones either to acknowledge the discrepancy between theory and evidence or, given they did experience a conflict, to resolve it by "setting aside" the theory or even by replacing it permanently with a new one compatible with the evidence. More notable than any developmental change, however, is the lack of it, as reflected in the presence of all of the characteristics just mentioned in the protocols of average adults and their marked difference from the protocols of the philosophers. We have more to say in later chapters about the issues of developmental change and the roles of expertise and education in the skills we have investigated.

The data presented in this chapter also have some implications regarding the evaluation of covariation evidence versus the evaluation of noncovariation evidence. We postpone a discussion of them until the next chapter, however, in which we report the final portion of the data from Studies 1a and 1b.

6

THE RECONSTRUCTION
OF THEORY AND EVIDENCE

In this chapter we report the results with respect to the three final tasks presented to subjects in Studies 1a and 1b, after they had completed evaluation of the evidence presented to them. First, the subject was asked to rerate each of the four variables, A–D, using the same rating procedure and scale used initially. As in the initial administration, the instructions were simply to "tell me what you think about whether a food makes a difference." No more specific instruction was given as to whether the evidence that had been presented should be taken into account, leaving the subject free to do so or not. For purposes of comparison, the subject was also asked to rerate 4 other variables from the set of 35 rated initially; these were selected to be ones whose initial ratings were in the same -2 to -8 or $+2$ to $+8$ range as the variables for which evidence had been presented. Next, the subject was asked to recall his or her original ratings for Variables A–D, for the purpose of assessing how subjects represented their original theories. Finally, as a measure of how subjects represented the evidence, the subject was asked to recall the evidence by reconstructing it on the display board. The four "colds" outcomes and the four "no-colds" outcomes were displayed on the board, and sets of duplicates of all of the various food types were supplied to the subject for affixing to the board.

REASSESSMENT OF THEORY

The major purpose of administering the rerating task, it should be emphasized, was to gain additional insight into how subjects evaluated the evidence, not to ascertain the extent to which the presentation of evidence led subjects to change their theories. Demand characteristics, which are likely to have been experienced to different degrees by different subjects, make problematic any interpretation of age or any other between-subjects differences in extent of accommodation to the evidence.

Of greater potential interest and interpretability are within-subject differences in the extent of theory change across the four variables. We might ask, for example, whether covariation evidence had more influence on a subject's theory when the theory was initially causal (A) or initially noncausal (C). Such comparisons, however, also are limited, due to varying ranges of possible movement. While covariation evidence did in fact lead subjects to become more certain regarding their causal theories (i.e., to give higher ratings on the -10 to $+10$ scale), these theories were already at a mean of $+5$ on this scale and therefore could move only an additional 5 points; noncausal theories, in contrast, were on the average at -5 and could move all the way to $+10$.

Two important comparisons that it is possible to make, however, are a comparison between the two theories that were supported by the evidence (A and D) and a comparison between the two theories that were not (B and C). The latter comparison of course is particularly significant: Does disconfirming evidence have a greater effect in disconfirming a theory that a causal relationship exists or in disconfirming a theory that no causal relationship exists? In examining the rerating data, we therefore first summarize other analyses briefly and then focus our attention on this question.

Two kinds of overall analyses were conducted. One was between the rerating scores for each variable and the rerating scores for the comparison variables for which no evidence had been presented (comparison variables initially rated in the -2 to -8 range for C and D and in the $+2$ to $+8$ range for A and B). For each of the four variables, A–D, the comparison of rerating scores for that variable versus the appropriate comparison variable was significant. Ratings for A and C were significantly higher, and ratings for B and D were significantly lower after the presentation of evidence than were ratings for the comparison variables, for which no evidence had been presented. A second kind of analysis was performed based on change scores from initial rating to rerating (as there was some variance in the initial ratings). Significant change occurred in the direction predicted based on the evidence that had been presented for each of the variables except D (a moderately held noncausal theory becoming more strongly noncausal following noncovariation evidence), which approached significance ($p = .066$). No age groups effects were statistically significant in any of these analyses.

Turning to the theoretically more interesting analyses, confirming evidence had greater influence on a causal than a noncausal theory. Mean change score was 3.17 for A (causal theory) versus -0.60 for D (noncausal theory),

$F(1, 52) = 12.72$, $p = .001$. Subjects thus became more certain about their causal theories after the evaluation of confirming evidence but became no more certain about their noncausal theories after the evaluation of confirming evidence.

Disconfirming evidence also differed significantly in the extent of its influence on a causal versus a noncausal theory. Before presenting this result, let us consider what some of the differences are between the two cases and what sort of differential influence might therefore be predicted. If a subject holds a theory that there is a causal connection between an antecedent and an outcome, it is likely that included as part of the representation of the theorized causal mechanism is an *expectation* that occurrence of the antecedent will be followed by occurrence of the outcome. In the case of noncovariation evidence, half of the instances evaluated will confirm such an expectation (and the other half will not). In other words, the subject's theory will be partially confirmed, and indeed we saw in the previous chapter examples of subjects' tendency to seize on this partial, confirming evidence and interpret it as confirming the theory, ignoring the nonconfirming portion of the evidence. In order to arrive at a correct interpretation of the noncovariation evidence, then, the subject must (a) overcome the expectation of co-occurrence, (b) overcome the partial confirmation of this expectation, (c) recognize the noncovariation, and (d) correctly interpret this noncovariation as indicating independence. As we saw in Chapter 5, subjects had difficulty with each of these.

Contrast the above to the case of a theory that there is no causal connection between an antecedent and outcome. Most likely, there is no representation of a mechanism (connecting, or not connecting, antecedent and outcome) and hence no expectation that data will be of a certain form. In fact, expressing a noncausal theory may be the subject's response to failure to access any representation of causal mechanism when the question of a causal connection is posed by the interviewer. Moreover, if the evidence the subject is asked to evaluate is covariation evidence, none of the evidence is supportive of the noncausal theory; the subject receives no partial confirmation of the noncausal theory. To interpret this evidence, the subject need only recognize and interpret the covariation, which, as we saw in Chapter 4, subjects overall found easier to do than to recognize and interpret noncovariation.

All of these differences, then, lead to the prediction that disconfirming evidence will have more of an influence on a noncausal theory than it will on a causal theory. Stated differently, disconfirming covariation evidence will have more of an influence than disconfirming noncovariation evidence, or stated in still another way, causal theories will be more resistant to modification than will noncausal theories. This prediction received some support from the data presented in Chapter 5. Articulation of a new theory as a means of resolving the theory/evidence discrepancy was less common in the case of an initial causal theory (B) than it was in the case of an initial noncausal theory (C). It is also supported by the fact that subjects differentially made reference to the evidence in the case of a noncausal theory (frequency of evidence-based responses to C, relative to A) but showed no such difference in the case of a causal theory (frequency of evidence-based responses to B, relative to D); subjects presumably were more willing to refer to the evidence for B because they found in it partial confirmation of their causal theory.

The prediction receives further support from the rerating data addressed in this chapter. Mean change score from initial to rerating for the disconfirmed noncausal theory (C) was 10.46, that is, from an initial mean of approximately -5 to a rerating mean of approximately $+5$. Mean change score for the disconfirmed causal theory (B) was -7.80, that is, from an initial mean of approximately $+5$ to a rerating mean between -2 and -3. Difference between the absolute values of these two change scores was significant, $F(1, 52) = 4.28$, $p = .04$. While age group effects did not reach statistical significance, the difference between B and C was more pronounced among younger subjects: Sixth graders showed a difference (between the absolute values of the change scores for B and C) of almost 4 points, ninth graders just over 2 points, and adults less than 1 point.

To get a better sense of what led to this difference in means, it is helpful to examine individual patterns of change. In the cases of both B and C, a majority of subjects did modify their theories to accord with the evidence, as defined by a rating in the causal ($+1$ to $+10$) zone in the case of C or in the noncausal (-1 to -10) zone in the case of B. However, a larger majority (81%) did so in the case of C than in the case of B (63%), leading to the significantly greater change score for C reported above. Also in accordance with the change score data reported above, it was the younger subjects who were more likely not to modify their original theories to accord with the evidence: In the case of B, for example, 48% of sixth graders, 36% of ninth graders, and 22% of adults did not do so. In virtually all of these cases, the subject retained his or her original theory (ratings in the $+2$ to $+8$ or -2 to -8 zones); only one or two subjects in each age group moved to a neutral position (ratings between -1 and $+1$) for either B or C.

These findings support the conclusion that disconfirming evidence is less likely to induce subjects to give up a causal theory and to begin to believe that there is no relation between variable and outcome than it is to induce subjects to give up a noncausal theory and to begin to believe that there is a relation between variable and outcome. As we saw in Chapter 5, subjects had little difficulty coming up with a causal theory to fit evidence that suggested a relation between variable and outcome (if they felt the need to do so). To abandon a causal theory already in existence, however, especially for younger subjects, is not so readily done. These differences have implications for how subjects are likely to remember their theories, the topic to which we now turn.

RECALL OF ORIGINAL THEORIES

The major purpose of investigating how subjects represented their original theories after the evaluation of evidence was to assess the possibility that evaluating evidence, particularly disconfirming evidence, would affect their ability to represent accurately what their original theory had been. Attempting to identify such effects is difficult, however, because so many other factors are likely to contribute to variance in subjects' recall ability. We did in fact find high variability in subjects' recall performance, both within and between subjects. Some subjects showed near perfect recall for their original ratings of all four variables, while others showed extreme differences between their original and recalled ratings for some variables but good recall for others; predictably, older subjects were, on the average, more accurate than younger ones.

Nevertheless, some interesting within-subject patterns were identified. Subjects' original ratings for Variables A and B, recall, averaged very near $+5$, and their original ratings for Variables C and D averaged very near -5. Recall also that when no evidence was presented and subjects were asked simply to rerate a set of four comparison variables they had originally rated a week earlier, the reratings showed an average of 3–4 points of regression toward the midpoint of 0. In contrast, when subjects were asked to recall their original ratings after the presentation of compatible evidence, this regression largely disappeared. Mean recall rating of Variable A was 4.28, and mean recall rating of Variable D was -4.21. Thus, the evaluation of compatible evidence enabled subjects to retain very accurate representations of their original theories (compared to representation of theories when no evidence was presented).

What happens, however, when discrepant evidence is presented? Our hypothesis was that evaluation of discrepant evidence might lead subjects to distort the recall of their original theories in the direction of the evidence, in which case we would predict a mean lower than 4.28 in the case of Variable B and a mean higher than -4.21 in the case of Variable C. Both of these predictions were borne out, though in the case of B the mean was only slightly lower: 3.72 for B (compared to 4.28 for A). In the case of C, the mean was -2.40 (compared to -4.21 for D). Given the very high variances, neither of these individual comparisons reached statistical significance. Especially because of this high variance, however, it is necessary to examine patterns of performance in a more qualitative way. Table 9 summarizes how each subject recalled each variable relative to the original rating given that variable. In the case of recall of noncausal theories (top half of Table 9), we see that the recall of only a third of the subjects is in the correct, moderately noncausal range, whether the evidence that has been presented is discrepant (Variable C) or compatible (D) with the theory. Direction of error, however, is different for C and D. If subjects have been presented covariation evidence, almost half fail to recall that their original theory was

Table 9

Percentages of Subjects Showing Various Forms of Recall of Original Theories

	Theory remembered as more strongly noncausal than it in fact was ($-9, +10$)	Theory accurately remembered as moderately non-causal (-1 to -8)	Failure to recall original theory as noncausal	
			Theory remembered as neutral (0)	Theory remembered as causal ($+1$ to $+10$)
Originally noncausal theories				
C	19%	35%	15%	30%
D	34%	31%	15%	19%

	Theory remembered as more strongly causal than it in fact was ($+9, +10$)	Theory accurately remembered as moderately causal ($+1$ to $+8$)	Failure to recall original theory as causal	
			Theory remembered as neutral (0)	Theory remembered as noncausal (-1 to -10)
Originally causal theories				
B	17%	62%	6%	15%
A	26%	55%	3%	15%

noncausal. If subjects have been presented noncovariation evidence, errors are more likely to be in the direction of remembering the original theory as more strongly noncausal than it actually was. Specifically, among subjects making errors, if covariation evidence has been presented, the error is most likely to be in the direction of failing to recall that the original theory was noncausal (36 versus 15 subjects). If noncovariation evidence has been presented, the error is equally likely to be in the direction of remembering the original theory as more strongly noncausal than it actually was, with this error almost twice as likely to occur in the case of noncovariation evidence (D) as it is in the case of covariation evidence (C). Errors of the predicted types were slightly more likely on the part of younger subjects but not enough so to justify a detailed breakdown by age group. Among sixth graders, for example, 63% failed to recall Variable C as noncausal (compared to the 45% for all subjects, reported in Table 9), but many adults did so as well.

In the case of recall of causal theories (bottom half of Table 9), subjects are much more likely to recall their theories correctly, whether the evidence is discrepant (Variable B) or compatible (Variable A), and errors are more evenly distributed. The difference between causal and noncausal theories in this respect is compatible with the smaller mean difference between A and B (relative to the difference between C and D) in memory ratings, reported above.

What these results suggest, then, is that once a theory is expressed that there exists a causal relationship between a variable and outcome, a subject is likely to retain an accurate representation of this causal theory and is unlikely to remember the theory as having been noncausal following the presentation of evidence of noncovariation. Consistent with this finding is the finding reported in the previous section that a significant number of subjects, particularly younger ones, do not modify their causal theories when evidence of noncovariation is presented. In contrast, when a theory is expressed that there exists no causal relationship between a variable and outcome and evidence is then presented showing covariation of the variable and outcome, a subject is likely not only to modify the theory in the direction of causality, as reported in the previous section, but to fail to recall that he or she had ever held a theory that the variable was not causally related to the outcome: Almost half of the total group and almost two thirds of sixth graders exhibited such a failure in their recall. Furthermore, if the evidence presented is noncovariation rather than covariation evidence, subjects may remember their noncausal theories as more strongly noncausal than they actually were.

RECONSTRUCTION OF THE EVIDENCE

The final task subjects in Studies 1a and 1b were asked to perform was to recall the evidence that had been presented by reconstructing it on the display board.

The four "colds" outcomes and the four "no colds" outcomes were displayed on the board, and sets of duplicates of the eight foods (two types for each of four variables) were supplied to the subject for affixing to the board. The purpose of the task was to gain some indication of how subjects represented the evidence (though reconstruction is of course an imperfect measure of representation). In particular, we thought that subjects might represent evidence discrepant from their theories as more congruent with the theory than it actually was. Doing so would constitute another mechanism for maintaining theory and evidence in alignment with one another, like the biased evaluation of evidence and the modification of theory examined in Chapter 5 and the biased recall of theory examined in the preceding section.

Necessary for such an analysis is an index of the extent to which the subject represented a variable as covarying with the outcome. Given the constraint imposed by the task of four positive outcomes and four negative outcomes, only a limited number of arrangements for each variable is possible. If the two variable levels and the two outcomes are regarded as arbitrary and therefore interchangeable (on the assumption that subjects will not represent covariation in the direction opposite to the actual evidence or their own theories), then representation of noncovariation, or independence, must take one of the following forms:

	$0+$	$0-$		$0+$	$0-$		$0+$	$0-$
$V+$	2	2	$V+$	4	4	$V+$	3	3
$V-$	2	2	$V-$	0	0	$V-$	1	1

A slight covariation can take one of these two forms:

	$0+$	$0-$		$0+$	$0-$
$V+$	3	4	$V+$	3	2
$V-$	1	0	$V-$	1	2

We assign the preceding degree of covariation an index of 2, computed as the difference between the sums of the diagonals. Based on this formula, the next strongest degree of covariation would have an index of 4 and could take one of these two forms:

	$0+$	$0-$		$0+$	$0-$
$V+$	2	4	$V+$	3	1
$V-$	2	0	$V-$	1	3

A stronger covariation could have an index of 6 and take this form:

	$0+$	$0-$
$V+$	1	4
$V-$	3	0

Or it could have an index of 8 and take this form:

$$
\begin{array}{ccc}
 & 0+ & 0- \\
V+ & 0 & 4 \\
V- & 4 & 0
\end{array}
$$

Each subject's reconstructed representation of each of the four variables was assigned one of these indices of strength of covariation (0, 2, 4, 6, or 8) based on which of the above patterns it matched. If one regards these indices as having interval scale properties, then degree of covariation in subjects' reconstructions of the evidence across subjects and variables can readily be compared, as shown in Table 10. Representation of covariation improved with age to a ceiling level of near perfect representation among adults, $F(2, 55) = 3.24$, $p = .047$. Variable C, however, which subjects originally theorized as noncausal, was represented as covarying less strongly with outcome than was Variable A, $F(1, 55) = 4.01$, $p = .05$. Variables B and D were represented as showing minimal covariation. Variable B, which subjects originally theorized as causal, was represented as covarying with outcome slightly *less* than Variable D. This difference, however, did not reach statistical significance.

Especially given the dubiousness of an interval scale assumption regarding these data, it is important to examine them in a more qualitative way. The focus of interest is on subjects who represent covariation evidence as other than highly covaried, which for the present purposes we define as an index of 4 or less, or who represent noncovariation evidence as highly covaried, which we define as an index of 6 or more. In the case of covariation evidence, 16 subjects (20%) represented Variable C with an index of 4 or less, while only 7 subjects (11%) represented Variable A with an index this low. In both cases, most of the subjects doing so were sixth graders—10 of the 16 and 4 of the 7. In the case of noncovariation evidence, only 4 subjects (6%) represented Variable B with an index of 6 or greater, and only 6 subjects (9%) represented Variable D with an index of 6 or greater. These subjects were evenly distributed across age groups.

The significant difference in means for A and C is thus accounted for by only a portion of subjects, mostly sixth graders, who showed the predicted misrepresentation of the relation between Variable C and outcome. Though only a third of sixth graders, and a smaller minority of the total group of subjects,

Table 10

Mean Reconstruction Scores by Variable and Age Group

Group	Variable A	Variable C	Variable B	Variable D
Sixth graders	6.50	5.90	1.60	2.35
Ninth graders	7.11	6.81	1.86	2.10
Adults	8.00	7.76	2.22	2.13

misrepresented covariation evidence in a way that brought it into closer alignment with their own originally noncausal theories, it is interesting that these subjects used this mechanism for bringing theory and evidence into alignment in conjunction with one or more of the other mechanisms we have examined, sometimes in ways that overcompensated one another.

Andrew, for example, the subject examined in Chapter 5 who struggled unsuccessfully to reconcile his theory that "gum is gum" (and therefore makes no difference) with the accumulating evidence of covariation of kind of gum with outcome, vacillated in his willingness to acknowledge the covariation, in some instances ignoring the evidence and simply reiterating the theory. In the reconstruction task, Andrew represented kind of gum as covarying only moderately with outcome (index of 4, compared to an index of 8 for Variable A). However, just before showing this reluctance to acknowledge the covariation in the reconstruction task, in the rerating task he modified his theory to reflect a causal relation between gum and outcome, while in the recall task he remembered his original theory regarding gum as having been causal!

A majority of subjects overall, in contrast, and almost all ninth graders and adults, demonstrated that they had constructed and maintained a fairly accurate representation of the evidence presented to them: an index of at least 6 in the case of covariation evidence and an index no greater than 4 in the case of noncovariation evidence. It should be noted, however, that only a minority of subjects (roughly a third, evenly distributed across age groups) represented noncovariation completely accurately, that is, an index of 0. To do so requires a sophisticated concept of noncovariation, or independence, and an effortful arrangement of the evidence to reflect this concept. More commonly, subjects appear to have represented noncovariation as a haphazard, or unconstrained, relation between variable and outcome, which in most cases yielded a covariation index of 2.

The fact that the evidence is accurately represented in the majority of cases suggests that, with the exception possibly of sixth graders, it is in the interpretation rather than the representation of evidence that bias is most likely to occur. In the case of covariation evidence, we saw that subjects very readily abandon their noncausal theories and moreover may not even recall ever having held them. The covariation evidence, then, is readily assimilated, indeed overassimilated, in the sense that few subjects recognize the causal indeterminacy associated with the common covariation of two variables and an outcome.

In the case of evidence of noncovariation, in contrast, we saw that many subjects show resistance to abandoning their causal theories and are unlikely to fail to remember them as causal despite the noncovariation evidence. Why, then, do such subjects not reconstruct the noncovariation evidence as showing strong covariation between variable and outcome? Subjects often evaluated noncovariation evidence (recall from Chapter 5) in biased ways when it conflicted with their causal theories, failing to acknowledge the noncovariation, failing to interpret it as indicating independence (exclusion), or focusing on a portion of the evidence as the basis for theory-compatible inferences of inclusion. This last tactic may provide an explanation for why they tended not to reconstruct noncovariation evidence as showing covariation: As we saw in Chapters 4 and 5, only very minimal evidence of covariation, often nothing more than a single co-occurrence of antecedent and outcome, may be regarded as adequate evidence for an inference of inclusion. Evidence of strong covariation, then, may not be necessary in order to be compatible with a causal theory; evidence of weak or minimal covariation may be regarded as just as satisfactory. When evidence of noncovariation was first presented in Instance 3 (in particular, evidence that the antecedent was not necessary for the outcome to occur) (recall from Chapter 3), almost all sixth graders, two thirds of ninth graders, and one third of adults failed to make an inference of exclusion.

Noncovariation evidence, then, may not be as strongly out of alignment with a causal theory as covariation evidence is out of alignment with a noncausal theory. Such an interpretation is consonant with the finding reported in the initial section of this chapter: Discrepant covariation evidence has a greater influence on a noncausal theory than discrepant noncovariation evidence has on a causal theory.

GENERAL DISCUSSION

The results presented in this chapter are secondary to the main purpose of Studies 1a and 1b, the assessment of skills in the evaluation of evidence. They nevertheless allow some refinement of the conclusions drawn from the main part of the study. The implications center in large part on the differences in subjects' reactions to covariation versus noncovariation forms of evidence, as discussed in each of the sections above. More broadly, the results presented in this chapter suggest that subjects' weaknesses in drawing inferences based on both of these forms of evidence have to do largely with how the evidence is interpreted, rather than with the representation of the evidence itself. Also, the errors subjects made in representation not just of the evidence but also of their original theories support the broad conclusion drawn from the results presented in the preceding chapters: Subjects, particularly younger ones, display a variety of mechanisms, which appear to be to a large degree outside their conscious control, for maintaining theory and evidence in alignment with one another.

If this conclusion is correct, what would happen if a subject were asked to contemplate more than one theory at a time, in particular two theories incompatible with one another, and to compare how a body of evidence bears on each of them? In this case, the same body of evidence could not readily be kept in alignment with both theories. Would such a situation elicit firmer differentiation between theories and evidence than we observed in the studies described thus far? Examination of this question is the major focus of Part III.

III

THE COORDINATION
OF THEORY
AND EVIDENCE

Deanna Kuhn and Michael O'Loughlin
with the assistance of William Yotive

7

REPLICATION:
THE EVALUATION
OF EVIDENCE

In the chapters in Part III, we report a series of studies based on a new set of materials, a set of sports balls that are physically present for the subject to examine and manipulate. The balls vary on four dimensions: size (large or small), color (light or dark), texture (rough or smooth), and ridges (present or absent), with each unique combination of dimensions represented by 1 ball in the set of 16 presented initially for the subject to examine. In each of the studies, the problem is presented as involving a sports company trying out different kinds of balls to use in a new game being developed. Some people at the company, it is explained, are investigating what features of the balls make a difference in the quality of a player's serve. After the subject's theories are elicited, evidence is presented by placing each of a particular subset of the balls in one of two baskets, labeled "Good serve" and "Bad serve" to indicate the outcome of a test serve with that ball. The problem structure is thus the same as that of the foods problem except that the four variables are embodied in a single object that is physically present for the subject to examine.

Use of these materials allows us to portray evidence in a more concrete, physically present way, minimizing any possibility that reasoning about evidence is hampered by difficulty in understanding the outcomes being depicted. In Study 4, presented in Chapters 8–10, we examined subjects' performance with these materials in more complex tasks in coordinating theory and evidence than the simple evaluation of covariation and noncovariation evidence examined in the studies in Part II. First, however, in Study 3, presented in this chapter, we replicated the study of these simple forms of evidence evaluation using the new materials, to ensure that the basic findings are comparable before going on to examine performance on more complex tasks.

Study 3 allowed us to investigate another question as well. Beyond the use of new materials, Study 3 differed in a further way from the studies presented in Part II. In those studies the subject's theories were selected to be ones the subject held with only moderate certainty. In Study 3, two (rather than four) theories for each subject were the focus of investigation: the theory regarding the variable the subject believed to be *most* important to the outcome and the theory regarding a variable the subject believed made no difference and was *least* important to the outcome. No effort, then, was made to identify theories a subject held with only moderate certainty. To the contrary, focusing on the variable the subject believed most important made it likely that the subject felt certain about its causal role, while inclusion of a highly implausible variable (color), which most subjects selected as the variable they believed least likely to make a difference, made it likely that the subject felt certain about its noncausal role. Furthermore, data we present in this chapter confirm that these theories were highly stable over time (in contrast to the theories in Studies 1a and 1b, which were only moderately stable).

Examination of theories the subject held with greater certainty, we anticipated, might cause the results to differ from those presented in Part II. Of particular interest was whether we would continue to see the phenomenon, exhibited by some subjects in the earlier studies, of theory change as a means of reconciling discrepant evidence with theories: Would subjects alter their theories or would they limit themselves to some different strategy for reconciling discrepant evidence with their theories, most likely failure to acknowledge, or biased interpretation of, evidence? Study 3 allowed us to answer this question.

Because the nature of the new materials made it feasible to incorporate a maximum of four potential variables and we wished to examine theories the subject felt fairly certain about, only the two variables the subject claimed to be most and least important were the focus of investigation for that subject. In the design of Study 3, type of evidence—covariation versus noncovariation—was therefore treated as a between-subject factor (rather than a within-subject factor as in Studies 1a and 1b). Half of the subjects were presented covariation evidence with respect to the two variables that were the focus of investigation, making it possible, as in Studies 1a and 1b, to examine how theoretical belief influences the evaluation of identical evidence. The remaining subjects were presented noncovariation evidence with respect to the two variables, permitting the same examination of the influence of theoretical belief. (For the remaining two variables for each subject, those not the focus of investigation, the opposite form of evidence was presented, for the sake of contrast, but the subject was not queried regarding these variables.) Except for this difference, the design of Study 3 is identical to that of Studies 1a and 1b.

Use of the new materials and other simplifications in the procedure (notably omission of the rating scale for assessment of theoretical beliefs) made it feasible to include a third-grade group in the studies reported in Part III.

STUDY 3 METHOD

Subjects

Subjects were 30 third graders, 30 sixth graders, 30 ninth graders, and 30 young adults. Sexes were equally represented in each group. The third through ninth graders were from several urban parochial schools of lower-middle to middle socioeconomic status. Median age of the third graders was 8 years, 11 months (range 8,1 to 10,2), of the sixth graders 11 years, 9 months (range 11,3 to 13,5), and of the ninth graders 14 years, 8 months (range 14,1 to 15,8). The adult subjects were recruited from a combined business training institute and beauty school. Students in this school were required to possess a high school diploma or to earn a certificate of equivalency concurrently with their vocational training. Median age of this group was 21 (range 18–26 years).

Procedure

Introduction

The subject was told that a sports company was conducting an investigation. A new game was being developed and different kinds of balls were being tried out to use in the game. All the rules of the game were not yet decided, but the game was to be played by two players, who hit a ball across a net to each other using a special kind of paddle. The interviewer also explained to the subject that the investigators at the company had tried lots of different balls and found that some resulted in good serves and some in poor serves and that there really were not any balls in between.

A box of 16 sample balls was then presented for the subject to examine. The four features of the balls, size (large or small), color (light or dark), texture (rough or smooth), and presence or absence of ridges (Figure 5), were then described verbally by the interviewer while he pointed to balls in the box to illustrate. The large balls were 18 cm in circumference and the small balls 13 cm.

Theory Assessment

Two baskets were then presented, one labeled "Good serve" and one labeled "Bad serve." The subject was asked to suppose that he or she had just tested each of the balls by serving it over the net using the special paddle. The subject was then asked, "What features of the balls do you think make a difference in how a person's serve comes out?" For each variable mentioned, the subject was asked to explain why he or she thought it made a difference. For each of the variables not mentioned by the subject, the interviewer asked, "Does (*variable*) make a

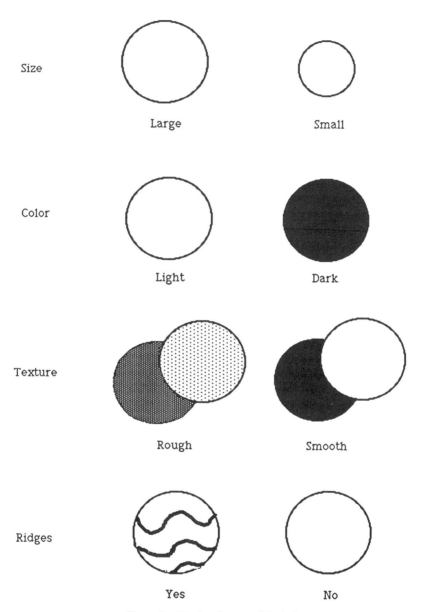

Figure 5.   The four features of the balls.

difference in how a person's serve comes out?'' Finally, an ordering of the four variables was elicited by asking the subject which one he or she thought made the most difference, the second most difference, and the least difference. Several subjects who claimed that no variables made a difference were excluded from the study. All subjects interviewed asserted that at least one variable did not make a difference.

Evidence Evaluation

The interviewer then proceeded to place a single ball at a time in one of the baskets and elicited the subject's evaluation of the evidence after each placement for the two variables that were the focus of investigation, the one the subject had indicated made the most difference and the one the subject had indicated made the least (and no) difference. The form of questioning and procedure was identical from this point to that used in Studies 1a and 1b, except that the subject was queried about only two variables, rather than four, after each presentation of evidence. For half the subjects in each age group, the evidence presented for the two variables of interest was covariation evidence; for the other half it was noncovariation evidence.

For 10 of the 30 subjects in each age group, the procedure varied slightly in that the theory assessment phase was administered twice, on two occasions approximately a week apart. The evidence evaluation phase followed the theory assessment phase only on the second occasion (and the second theory assessment was used as the basis for selection of the two variables that were to be the focus of attention in the evidence evaluation phase). The purpose of this additional procedure was to provide an assessment of the stability of subjects' theories.

STUDY 3 RESULTS AND DISCUSSION

The full set of results presented for Studies 1a and 1b are not presented for Study 3, and instead we focus only on those points of comparison of particular interest: the performance of third graders and the presence of theory change as a mode of resolving discrepant evidence with a theory. Other results not mentioned can be assumed to be in accordance with those obtained in Studies 1a and 1b. In addition, we examine the results regarding the stability of subjects' theories, based on data from those subjects to whom the theory assessment phase was administered on two separate occasions.

Stability of Theories

The stability of subjects' theories from first to second occasion was very high among all subjects except third graders.

Third Graders

Only 5 of the 10 third graders whose theories were assessed on two occasions ranked the same variable as the most important causal factor on both occasions. Of the remaining 5 subjects, 3 ranked the variable that had been judged causal and most important on the first occasion likewise causal on the second occasion but second in importance to another variable. The other 2 subjects changed their judgment regarding the variable judged causal and most important on the first occasion and judged this variable to be noncausal on the second occasion. Third graders' noncausal theories showed greater stability. Of the 10 subjects, 8 ranked the same variable as noncausal and least important on both occasions. One changed his judgment regarding the variable he had judged noncausal and least important on the first occasion and on the second occasion judged this variable to be causal (though not the most important causal variable). The final subject continued to rank the variable she had judged noncausal and least important on the first occasion as noncausal on the second occasion, but the second time she ranked it third rather than fourth in importance. This shift of course cannot be regarded as an error or instability, since all noncausal variables are presumably equally noncausal and cannot be ranked with respect to relative importance (or nonimportance).

Sixth Graders

In sharp contrast to the third graders, the 10 sixth graders whose theories were assessed on two occasions showed perfect stability across occasions with respect to both the variable judged causal and most important and the variable judged noncausal and least important. Some subjects did show change, however, in their judgments and/or ordering of the two intermediate variables.

Ninth Graders

Of the 10 ninth graders, 8 showed perfect stability across occasions with respect to both the variable judged causal and most important and the variable judged noncausal and least important. The 2 remaining subjects showed no change with respect to the variable judged noncausal and least important but changed their judgment with respect to the variable judged causal and most important on the first occasion. Both subjects continued to judge the variable causal on the second occasion but judged it second in importance to another variable now judged most important.

Adults

Performance of the adult subjects was similar to that of the ninth graders. Of the 10 adults, 7 showed perfect stability across occasions with respect to both the variable judged causal and most important and the variable judged noncausal and least important. The 3 remaining subjects showed no change with respect to the variable judged noncausal and least important but changed their judgment with respect to the variable judged causal and most important on the first occasion. All 3 continued on the second occasion to judge the variable causal but judged it lesser in importance to another variable, now judged most important, 2 of them judging it second in importance and the remaining subject judging it third.

These results on stability of theories are important in light of the only moderate stability observed in subjects' theories in Studies 1a and 1b. The theories examined in Studies 1a and 1b were selected deliberately as ones that the subject held with only moderate certainty. It was thus not surprising to observe that some instability over time occurred in these theories, in the absence of any presentation of evidence, as reported in Chapter 6. The results reported above confirm that our attempt in Study 3 to elicit theories that the subject held more firmly was successful (with the exception of third grade subjects), to the extent that such firmness can be inferred from evidence of stability. How, then, might this firmness influence the strategies subjects used to coordinate theory and evidence?

Reconciliation of Theory and Evidence

Results were analyzed in a manner following that used in Studies 1a and 1b, and subjects were classified in terms of the manner in which they dealt with the discrepancy between theory and evidence, using the classification scheme presented in Figures 3 (covariation evidence) and 4 (noncovariation evidence) in Chapter 5, for the Studies 1a and 1b data. These figures are not repeated for the present study, as their story can be very simply told. Virtually all Study 3 subjects fell into the top half of these figures, in which a new theory was not constructed as a means of maintaining theory and evidence in alignment. Instead, subjects tended to maintain their theories and to reconcile them with the evidence either by ignoring the implications of the evidence or by evaluating the evidence in a biased manner. By and large, the same strategies and forms of bias described in Chapter 5 were observed. Third graders were more similar to sixth graders than to any other age group, but they were more likely to make theory-based responses and showed biased evaluation of evidence more frequently than did sixth graders.

In the evaluation of covariation evidence, three subjects constructed new theories as a means of reconciling their original noncausal theories with the discrepant covariation evidence. One was a sixth grader, one a ninth grader, and one an adult subject. The sixth grader and adult both expressed the new theory *before* acknowledging the evidence. The ninth grader first acknowledged the covariation reflected in the evidence and then changed his theory to match the evidence. In the evaluation of noncovariation evidence (which, it should be recalled, was carried out by a different set of subjects, in a between-subjects design), two subjects constructed new theories as a means of reconciling their original causal theories with the discrepant noncovariation evidence. One was a sixth grader and one was an adult. Both expressed the new theory before acknowledging the evidence.

The results of the several studies we have presented thus far, taken together, suggest that not just the theory itself but the strength or certainty with which a subject holds the theory will influence the manner in which evidence bearing on the theory is evaluated. The results of Study 3 confirmed our expectation that theory change as a mechanism of reconciling theories and discrepant evidence becomes less likely as the firmness with which theories are held increases. This is an unsurprising result, perhaps, but an important one to confirm, both with respect to interpretation of our own results and more broadly. A good deal of evidence is available from the attitude change literature (McGuire, 1969) to indicate that weakly held beliefs are more likely to be influenced by new information than are strongly held ones. To the extent the present results are generalizable to everyday reasoning in natural contexts, they are important in their suggestion that the process whereby theories are modified to accord with new evidence may occur in a way over which individuals lack conscious control. The focus of the present work has been on the process of interaction between theories and evidence rather than on the nature of the theories themselves. We have no basis for saying here whether most theories that people hold resemble the weak ones examined in Studies 1a and 1b or the stronger ones examined in Study 3 and therefore how prevalent the theory change mechanism is likely to be, relative to the biased evaluation mechanism, as a means of maintaining theories and evidence in alignment. The most important point is that both mechanisms reflect the interaction of theory and evidence in the person's thinking in a manner over which the person lacks conscious control. Both suggest, therefore, significant deficiencies in skills in the coordination of theory and evidence.

8

THE INTERPRETATION
OF INSUFFICIENT
AND MIXED EVIDENCE

In the next three chapters, we report the results of Study 4. Study 4 employs the same set of sports balls employed in Study 3, but goes on to examine more complex skills in the coordination of theory and evidence than the very simple kinds of evidence evaluation that have been the subject of the preceding studies. In the present chapter (parallel to Chapter 4 in Part II), we describe subjects' inferential skills overall when asked to evaluate more complex forms of evidence than the simple covariation and noncovariation evidence presented in the preceding studies. In Chapter 9 (parallel to Chapter 5 in Part II), we examine the role of theory in evidence evaluation, in particular the coordination of evidence with multiple theories. In Chapter 10, we examine subjects' skills in generating their own evidence to evaluate theories.

STUDY 4 METHOD

Subjects

Subjects were 20 third graders, 20 sixth graders, 20 subjects from a mixed ninth/tenth grade classroom (referred to for convenience as the ninth grade group), 20 noncollege young adults, and 20 undergraduate college students. Sexes were equally represented in each group. The third through ninth graders came from one secondary and two elementary urban parochial schools in the same lower-middle to middle socioeconomic status neighborhood. Median age of the third graders was 8 years, 4 months (range 7, 9 to 8, 7), of the sixth graders 11 years, 7 months (range 10, 11 to 13, 3), and of the ninth graders 15 years, 6 months (range 14, 1 to 15, 9). The adult subjects were recruited from the same combined business training institute and beauty school Study 3 subjects attended. Students in this school were required to possess a high school diploma or to earn a certificate of equivalency concurrently with their vocational training. Median age of this group was 23 (range 18–25 years). Undergraduates were recruited from an introductory psychology class at an urban private liberal arts college. They participated in fulfillment of a course requirement.

Procedure

The two initial phases of the procedure, the introduction and theory assessment phases, were identical to those described in Chapter 7 (Study 3). The new game being developed by the sports company was explained, and the balls were presented and described verbally (Figure 5, Chapter 7). The subject's theories regarding which features of the balls affect a player's serve were then assessed. As in Study 3, subjects who did not identify at least one variable that made a difference and one that made no difference were excluded from the study and replaced (10 subjects, evenly distributed across subject groups).

Evidence Generation

In this phase of the procedure, the subject was asked to generate evidence for and against two theories, one stating that Variable X makes a difference ("subject's theory") and the other that Variable Y makes a difference ("other's theory"). Variable X was always the one the subject had claimed to be the one that made the most difference. Variable Y was always the one the subject had claimed to be the one least important of the four and one of those that made no difference. The subject was thus asked to generate four major sets of evidence: (1) for subject's theory, (2) against subject's theory, (3) for other's theory, and (4) against other's theory. In each case the subject was subsequently asked to generate the requested evidence using other balls, fewest balls, and two balls. The "for" evidence generation task always preceded the "against" task. The "subject's theory" and "other's theory" tasks, however, were counterbalanced, with half the subjects in each subject group receiving one first and half the other first. Further details of the evidence generation phase of the procedure are given in Chapter 10.

Evidence Evaluation

This phase of the procedure began after a short rest period or, in the case of the youngest subject group, the next day. After a brief review of the four features of the balls, the evidence evaluation problems were introduced as follows (assuming, for purposes of illustration, that "size makes a difference" is subject's theory and "color makes a difference" is other's theory):

> Now I'd like to ask you about other people's views on this. Suppose that two of the company's experts disagree on what features of the balls make a difference in how a serve comes out. For instances a Mr./Ms. S [for size] thinks that *size,* that is, whether the ball is large or small, is what makes a difference, while a Mr./Ms. C [for color] thinks that *color,* that is, whether the ball is light or dark, is what makes a difference. Here are some pictures that can help you keep in mind what Mr./Ms. S and Mr./Ms. C think. (A sketch depicting the variable and a stick figure saying "*Size* [or *Color*] makes a difference" is displayed for each variable.) To try to settle the argument they did some tests. Suppose this is what they found out. (Balls constituting the first evidence set are placed in the *Good* and *Bad* baskets by the interviewer.) Remember now that these are the results of some tests.

The following questions were then asked:

1. Do these results help more to show that one person is right rather than the other? In other words, do they help more to show that Mr./Ms. S is right that *size* makes a difference, or do they help more to show that Mr./Ms. C is right that *color* makes a difference, or is there no difference between them? Can you say why?

2. (For theory subject claims more right) Do the results prove that Mr./Ms. S(C) is right? (If yes) How do they prove it? (If no) Why not?

3. (If subject has made no mention of the alternative theory) What do these results have to say about the other person's view? (Probe, if necessary) Do they say nothing about it, do they show that it's wrong, or do they show that it's a little bit right but not as right as Mr./Ms. S(C)'s view?

Consecutive presentation of 15 problems of the above form followed. The specific evidence presented in each problem was tailored to each individual subject as a function of the particular theories (i.e., variables) designated as subject's theory and other's theory (based on that subject's responses during the theory assessment phase of the interview). The problems fall into four categories. Order of presentation was counterbalanced across subjects within categories, but the four categories were presented in constant order.

Category 1: Insufficient Evidence.   This category contains four problems. In each, the evidence presented is insufficient to bear on either theory, as no variation occurs in the two variables critical to the theories; for example, all the balls tested are large and light colored, and no information is given about outcomes for balls having the opposite characteristics (small or dark colored). Two of the problem presentations (Problems 1a and 1b) in fact consist of only a single such ball. The other two (1c and 1d) consist of six balls all of the same type with respect to the two critical variables (e.g., all large and light colored), four with one outcome and two with the other. (The remaining two, noncritical variables are varied but arranged so as to covary neither with the critical variables nor with outcome.)

Category 2: Equal Evidence.   The three problems in this category, Problems 2a–2c, likewise present evidence that is identical with respect to the two theories. All consist of 12 balls, 6 in the *Good* basket and 6 in the *Bad* basket, 6 always of one variable level (e.g., large) and 6 of the opposite level. Furthermore, the two critical variables always covary completely with each other (e.g., all the large balls are also light colored). In Problem 2a, which we term the 5/1 problem, 5 of the 6 balls of one variable level of each variable appear in the *Good* basket, and the remaining 1 in the *Bad* basket. (With respect to the variable involved in the subject's theory, the variable level is always the one the subject designated as associated with a positive outcome during the theory assessment phase of the interview, so that the direction of the association between variable and outcome is consistent with the subject's theory.) Conversely, 5 of the 6 balls of the opposite variable level of each variable appear in the *Bad* basket, and the remaining ball appears in the *Good* basket. For example, 5 of the 6 large, light balls appear in the *Good* basket, and the remaining 1 in the *Bad* basket, while 5 of the 6 small, dark balls appear in the *Bad* basket and the remaining 1 in the *Good* basket. The evidence presented is thus consistent with both subject's theory and with other's theory (for which the variable level associated with a positive outcome has not been articulated). As was the case for the covariation evidence presented in Studies 1a, 1b, and 3, however, the evidence remains indeterminate as there are multiple covariates, making it impossible to establish whether one variable, the other, or both are responsible for the outcome. (As in Category 1 problems, the remaining two, noncritical variables are varied but arranged so as to covary neither with the critical variables nor with outcome.)

Problem 2b, which we refer to as the 4/2 problem, is identical in all of the characteristics just described except that only 4, rather than 5, of the balls of one variable level appear in the *Good* basket, and the remaining 2 appear in the *Bad* basket, while 4 of the 6 balls of the opposite variable level appear in the *Bad* basket and the remaining 2 in the *Good* basket.

Problem 2c, which we refer to as the 3/3 problem, is identical except that 3 balls of one variable level appear in the *Good* basket and 3 in the *Bad*. This evidence thus reflects independence between both of the critical variables and outcome.

All three of the problems in Category 2 are regarded as mixed-evidence problems, in that in contrast to the covariation evidence presented in the previous studies, covariation between variable and outcome is never perfect.

Category 3: Unequal Evidence.   The four problems in this category present different evidence with respect to the two theories and consist of all possible adjacent combinations of the three basic types in Category 2. Problem 3a consists of the 5/1 pattern for the subject's-theory variable and the 4/2 pattern for the other's-theory variable, while Problem 3b consists of the 4/2 pattern for the subject's-theory variable and the 5/1 pattern for the other's-theory variable. Similarly, Problem 3c consists of the 4/2 pattern for one variable and the 3/3 pattern for the other, while Problem 3d consists of the reverse. In Category 3 problems, however, in contrast to those in Category 2, the evidence is carefully constructed in each case so as to show no covariation *between* the two critical variables, enabling the independent effects of each to be assessed. These effects are always independent, that is, the two variables show no interaction in their effect on outcome. (Noncritical variables continue to vary independently, as indicated above.)

Category 4: Asymmetric Evidence.   The four Category 4 problems also involve unequal evidence, but they are more complex than Category 3 problems in that frequencies of neither the two outcomes nor the two variable levels are fixed in a symmetrical 6/6 ratio. This is a critical difference, for removal of these two symmetries means that the only means of solving the problem is a direct comparison of the two ratios, that is, the ratio of good to bad outcomes at each variable level (or, alternatively, the ratio of the two variable levels at each outcome level). Two of the problems (4a and 4b) involve a comparison between a modest positive correlation between variable and outcome for one variable and a zero correlation between variable and outcome for the other variable. Exact frequencies used in these problems are as follows:

	0+	0−			0+	0−
V+	4	4		V+	6	3
V−	4	0		V−	2	1

The other two problems (4c and 4d) involve a comparison between two correlations of slightly different strengths:

	0+	0−			0+	0−
V+	6	4		V+	8	2
V−	6	0		V−	4	2

The frequencies were specifically chosen so that application of anything less than a comparison of the two ratios would yield an incorrect solution, for example, comparison of the frequencies in the upper-left-hand ("positive case") cells or comparison of the two first rows or two first columns. In each problem, one variable was the subject's-theory variable and one the other's-theory variable, and for the corresponding problem of the same form, the two were reversed, yielding four problems in all. Because of their difficulty and because of the overall length of the interview, Problems 4a–4d were omitted for the third-grade group.

Multiple-Evidence Problems

The final phase of the procedure departed from the preceding format in that only one theory, but multiple sets of evidence, were presented for evaluation. As the results for this final phase relate primarily to results for the evidence generation phase, a detailed description of the multiple-evidence problems is postponed until Chapter 10, which is devoted to evidence generation.

STUDY 4 RESULTS: INTERPRETATION
OF INSUFFICIENT AND MIXED EVIDENCE

Based on responses to the questions in the evidence evaluation segment of the procedure, the subject's evaluation of a set of evidence with respect to its bearing on each theory was classified first of all as either theory based or evidence based, as in the previous studies. The data presented in Table 11 enable us to assess the extent to which subjects in Study 4 made evidence-based responses, compared to subjects in Studies 1a and 1b. The evidence set in Study 4 most nearly comparable to the covariation evidence presented to subjects in Studies 1a and 1b is the set described above as 5/1 evidence, while the set described above as 3/3 evidence is equivalent to the noncovariation evidence presented in Studies 1a and 1b. Over the course of the evidence presentation, each Study 4 subject evaluated 5/1 evidence a total of four times and 3/3 evidence a total of four times. Shown in Table 11 are the mean frequencies of evidence-based responses for the two kinds of evidence (of a possible 4.00 in each case). Also included in Table 11, for completeness, are responses to the intermediate 4/2 evidence (for the first

Table 11

Mean Frequencies of Evidence-Based Responses (Study 4)

Group	Covariation (5/1) evidence	Intermediate (4/2) evidence	Noncovariation (3/3) evidence
Third graders	1.85	1.65	1.80
Sixth graders	3.65	3.50	3.65
Ninth graders	3.95	3.90	3.85
Noncollege adults	3.25	3.40	3.25
College adults	4.00	4.00	4.00

four of a total of six evaluations). These frequencies are high among all age groups except third graders, who failed to make evidence-based responses slightly more than half the time. Statistical analysis showed no effect of evidence type and a significant effect of age group on frequency of evidence-based responses, $F(4, 95) = 17.95$, $p \leq .001$, with only the third graders' mean differing from the others. No sex differences appeared in any of the Study 4 analyses.

Frequencies of evidence-based responses were comparable for the other evidence types (insufficient and asymmetric) presented to Study 4 subjects. These data thus confirm that the Study 4 procedure, in which the subject is asked to evaluate the evidence with respect to two conflicting theories, was successful in getting subjects to focus on the evidence a majority of the time, except in the case of third graders, who were likely not to base responses on the evidence even under this procedure. It should be noted, however, that all groups except college subjects showed lack of evidence-based responses at least on occasion. Among all subjects, such failure was more likely when the evidence was discrepant with the subject's theory, as we see in the next chapter.

How did subjects interpret the evidence that they did evaluate? In Table 12 appear the categories into which subjects' evidence-based responses were classified, with an example provided for each category, based on the variable of size. This table parallels Table 5 in Part II. The major categories of inclusion, exclusion, and uncertainty remain the same, but some differences in subcategories occur, arising from differences in the nature of the evidence evaluated in this study in contrast to Studies 1a and 1b. Percentage agreement between two coders for classification of responses into one of these categories was 91%.

The statement included in the earlier studies advising the subject that no interactions among variables were present was omitted in Study 4, to allow us to assess whether the possibility of interaction effects would in fact enter into subjects' thinking. The only subjects who made any statements to suggest that they considered the possibility of interaction effects were 3 of the 20 college subjects. Of these 3, 2 also indicated the desirability of a controlled comparison between two balls or sets of balls differing on only one dimension. Recognition of the possibility of interaction effects tended to take the form of statements about the outcome for a certain combination of variable levels, for example, large balls with ridges, though there was nothing in the evidence to suggest the presence of such interactions.

Interpretation of Insufficient Evidence

Two forms of insufficient evidence were presented in Problems 1a–1d, one consisting of a single ball and the other of six balls. The six balls were all of only one variable level with respect to the two critical variables (e.g., large and light

Table 12

Classification of Evidence-Based Responses (Study 4)

Type	Example
I. Inclusion	
a. Invalid	
1. Co-occurrence	"Size matters because this big ball came out good."
2. Qualified inclusion	"Size sometimes matters, because sometimes the big balls come out good and sometimes bad."
3. Other	"Size matters because a lot of balls are big."
b. Valid or invalid (depending on problem type)	
1. Covariation (multiple instances)	"Size matters because big balls usually come out good and small balls usually come out bad."
II. Exclusion	
a. Invalid	
1. Discounting	"Size doesn't matter because it's texture that's making them good."
2. Lack of variation (Problems 1a–1d only)	"Size makes no difference because all the balls are big."
3. Other	"Size doesn't matter because the small ones can be rough or smooth."
b. Valid	
1. Constant antecedent, variable outcome	"No, because some big balls came out good and some came out bad."
2. Variable antecedent, constant outcome	"No, because both big and small balls came out good."
3. Comparison of ratios	"No, because both baskets have the same number of big and small balls."
III. Uncertainty	
a. Invalid	
1. Evidence uninterpretable	"I don't know what it shows about size."
2. Noncovariation	"You can't tell because sometimes big balls come out good and sometimes bad."
3. Other	"I can't say if size makes a difference because this big ball came out bad."
b. Valid	
1. Lack of variation (Problems 1a–d only)	"You can't tell because all the balls are big."
2. Insufficient sample	"You can't tell with just these balls; you'd need more to be sure."
3. Recognition of other potential causes	" I can't tell if size makes a difference because the good ones are both smooth and large."

colored), with four of the six of one outcome and two of the other. Did subjects recognize that in neither of these cases was the evidence sufficient to permit an inference regarding the relation between variable and outcome? Shown in Table 13 are the mean frequencies by problem type of responses classified in the uncertainty category (the subject responded that the evidence presented did not allow one to conclude whether the variable in question did or did not make a difference to the outcome). Maximum frequency in each case is 4.00, as the subject was asked to make four different evaluations for each problem type, one with respect to subject's theory and one with respect to other's theory for each of the two one-ball problems and likewise one with respect to subject's theory and one with respect to other's theory for each of the two six-ball problems. For the one-ball problem, the number of subjects ever recognizing the indeterminacy (i.e., making an uncertainty response) ranged from a low of 0 for third graders to a high of 13 for college subjects. For the six-ball problem, the range was from 0 for third graders to 15 for college subjects. (Theory-based responses, it is relevant to note, never included a judgment of uncertainty; theory-based reasoning was always employed in support of a yes or no judgment.)

As reflected in Table 13, indeterminacy responses were nonexistent or very rare until ninth grade. Ninth graders and noncollege adults were slightly more likely to recognize the insufficiency of the one-ball evidence than they were the six-ball evidence. College subjects, in contrast, were slightly more likely to recognize the insufficiency of the six-ball than the one-ball evidence, though college subjects were considerably more likely than noncollege adults or ninth graders to recognize the insufficiency of both forms of evidence. Statistical analysis of the data in Table 13 showed an effect of age group, $F(4, 95) = 17.21$, $p \le .001$, no effect of evidence type (one-ball versus six-ball), and a significant interaction, $F(4, 95) = 4.49, p \le .002$. Post hoc comparisons showed significant differences between college subjects and all other groups and between ninth graders and both younger and college subjects. No differences appeared as a function of whether the single ball (in the one-ball problems) or the majority of balls (in the six-ball problems) was in the *Good* (versus *Bad*) basket. The

Table 13

Mean Frequencies of Indeterminacy (Uncertainty) Responses for
Insufficient Evidence Problems

Group	One-ball problem	Six-ball problem
Third graders	0.00	0.00
Sixth graders	0.30	0.05
Ninth graders	1.80	0.70
Noncollege adults	1.05	0.50
College adults	2.35	2.85

justifications subjects of all ages gave for their indeterminacy judgments were primarily of the IIIb1 type (Table 12), in which the lack of variation of the variable is noted. The IIIb3 type (recognition of other potential causes) was rare among other than college subjects.

These results indicate, then, that rarely before ninth grade do subjects recognize that evidence reflecting lack of variation of the critical variable is insufficient to permit an inference regarding the relation between that variable and an outcome. In fact, a substantial number of college students fail to achieve this recognition. Though a single ball or a majority of balls reflecting one variable level "came out good" (or bad), it is not recognized that balls reflecting the other variable level may have come out equally good (or bad). This lack of recognition is comparable to the failure to attend to base rates, described by Tversky and Kahneman and discussed in Chapter 2. We see this phenomenon again in examining subjects' evaluation of asymmetric evidence (Problems 4a–4d). In that case the base rate or alternative-level information is available but not considered. In the case of the present problems, the information is unavailable, but subjects tend not to recognize the significance of its absence.

Interpretation of Mixed Evidence

In Study 4 we never presented evidence reflecting perfect covariation between variable and outcome. Instead, a number of forms of what we term *mixed evidence* were presented. The two basic forms were one that portrayed a very modest covariation between variable and outcome (4/2 evidence) and another that portrayed a stronger covariation (5/1 evidence). In addition we included a form of evidence (3/3 evidence) equivalent to that included in the earlier studies, reflecting absence of covariation, or independence, between variable and outcome. (See "Study 4 Method" section for full descriptions of each form of evidence.) The interpretation of mixed evidence (that showing neither perfect covariation nor perfect noncovariation) proved to be a formidable challenge for many subjects. In the case of 5/1 evidence, the covariation pattern was strong and readily observable, but the subject still had to deal with the one ball of each variable level that deviated from the pattern, and, as we shall see, this deviation was sufficient to lead many subjects to deny the presence of any relationship between variable and outcome. The 4/2 evidence proved particularly interesting because it allowed for two opposing but both reasonable interpretations. One was to interpret the evidence as showing covariation, as in the 5/1 case, though in the 4/2 case two balls of each variable level deviate from the pattern. Alternatively, the evidence could be interpreted as showing independence between variable and outcome, with the 4/2 pattern reflecting simply a random deviation from perfect noncovariation.

Inclusion

Shown in Table 14 are the frequencies of inclusion responses to each evidence type, and in Table 15 the frequencies of exclusion responses, by age group (maximum frequency in each case is 4.00). Also included in Tables 14 and 15 are the numbers of subjects showing any responses of inclusion (Table 14) or exclusion (Table 15).

As reflected in Table 14, at least half of the subjects of all age groups regarded the 4/2 and 5/1 mixed evidence as sufficient evidence to justify an inference of inclusion. The large majority of these inferences were justified by reference to the covariation of antecedent and outcome (e.g., "The rough balls are usually good and the smooth balls are usually bad," Type Ib, Table 12). The frequencies of inclusion inferences and the numbers of subjects making them increased by age group to a near ceiling level among the college group. These same age trends appear for the equal-evidence (Category 2) and unequal-evidence (Category 3) problems considered separately. In the case of the equal-evidence problems, this age trend is notable in that it reflects an increase with age in an *incorrect* response (as the common covariation of two variables with outcome in fact makes it impossible to attribute the variation in outcome to either one). Very few subjects recognized this indeterminacy in either the 4/2 or the 5/1 equal-evidence problems. Only four college subjects did so, referring to the multiple covariates as their reason (e.g., "You can't tell because it could be either the ridges or the size that's making them good," Type IIIb3), and one of these four did so only in response to the "proof" question ("Do the results prove that Mr./Ms. ___ is right?"), that is, she claimed that the evidence did show that the variable makes a difference (inclusion response) but did not prove that it did, because of the common covariation of another variable. One other college subject, two noncollege adults, and one ninth grader also made uncertainty responses to the 4/2 or 5/1 equal-evidence problems (Problems 2a and 2b), but all cited one of the grounds indicated in Table 12, other than additional covariates.

In contrast to 4/2 and 5/1 evidence, 3/3 evidence elicited inclusion responses primarily from third and sixth graders and much less frequently from older subjects. These findings parallel those from Studies 1a and 1b, and as we see in the next chapter, the selective use of noncovariation evidence to support an inference of inclusion was often motivated by theoretical belief. As in Studies 1a and 1b, these inclusion responses were justified by referring either to a single co-occurrence or a limited covariation of antecedent and outcome, ignoring those pieces of evidence that deviated from a covariation pattern.

Statistical analysis of frequencies of inclusion responses showed a significant effect of age group, $F(4, 95) = 2.87$, $p = .027$; a significant effect of problem type (3/3, 4/2, or 5/1), $F(2, 95) = 104.75$, $p \leq .001$; as well as a significant

Table 14

Mean Frequencies and Numbers of Subjects Showing
Inclusion Responses by Evidence Type

Group	5/1 evidence	Number of subjects	4/2 evidence	Number of subjects	3/3 evidence	Number of subjects
Third graders	1.40	14	1.10	11	0.90	9
Sixth graders	2.20	15	1.55	12	1.20	9
Ninth graders	2.20	14	2.05	14	0.20	1
Noncollege adults	2.10	16	1.80	13	0.40	6
College adults	3.70	19	3.20	17	0.00	0

Table 15

Mean Frequencies and Numbers of Subjects Showing
Exclusion Responses by Evidence Type

Group	5/1 evidence	Number of subjects	4/2 evidence	Number of subjects	3/3 evidence	Number of subjects
Third graders	0.45	4	0.55	5	0.90	7
Sixth graders	1.40	12	1.90	12	2.35	15
Ninth graders	1.65	10	1.85	13	3.45	19
Noncollege adults	1.05	11	1.55	13	2.75	18
College adults	0.25	3	0.50	4	3.20	19

interaction, $F(8, 95) = 12.75$, $p \leq .001$. Post hoc analyses showed only third graders and college subjects to differ significantly, while a simple effects analysis of the interaction showed that all groups except third graders responded differently to the different evidence types.

Exclusion

Equally notable are the frequencies of exclusion responses to the three kinds of evidence. Statistical analysis of frequencies of exclusion responses showed a significant effect of age group, $F(4, 95) = 5.26$, $p \leq .001$; a significant effect of problem type, $F(2, 95) = 92.80$, $p \leq .001$; as well as a significant interaction, $F(8, 95) = 8.30$, $p \leq .001$. Post hoc comparisons showed only the third graders to differ significantly from all other groups except the college group, while a simple effects analysis of the interaction showed that all groups except third graders responded differently to the different evidence types. Because a high proportion of third graders' responses were theory-based responses, it is important to note that there was no indication in the theory-based responses of an implicit discrimination among the different types of evidence: The distribution of yes versus no theory-based responses did not vary significantly across the three types of evidence.

Results for the 3/3 problem parallel those reported for Studies 1a and 1b. By ninth grade almost all subjects show some ability to exclude a variable based on evidence of noncovariation with outcome, though the performance of noncollege adults in this study was somewhat below that of ninth graders. The data in Table 15 reflect pronounced development of this ability, however, between third and ninth grades. It should be noted, however, that between third and sixth grades it is largely evidence-based responding, not exclusion itself, that is increasing.

Of even greater interest are exclusion responses to the 4/2 and 5/1 forms of evidence. Exclusion responses to evidence of perfect covariation, recall from Studies 1a and 1b, were infrequent. In contrast, when the evidence is mixed, that is, shows some but less than perfect covariation, exclusion responses become common. In such cases, the subject focuses on the discrepant evidence—on those balls that deviate from a covariation pattern—as the basis for rejecting a causal inference. The subject could make reference to this discrepancy in either of two ways: (a) by noting that the same variable level (e.g., big balls) is associated with two different outcomes (Type IIb1, Table 12) or (b) by noting that the two different variable levels (e.g., both big and small balls) are both associated with the same outcome (Type IIb2). Both types were prevalent. (Type IIb3, comparison of ratios, is applicable only in the case of genuine independence, i.e., 3/3 evidence.)

Exclusion responses to 4/2 and 5/1 evidence were most common among sixth and ninth graders, slightly less common among noncollege adults, and, interestingly, declined to a negligible level among college subjects (Table 15), who typically interpreted the 4/2 as well as the 5/1 evidence as showing a relationship between variable and outcome. Also reflected in Table 15 is the fact that exclusion responses were almost as frequent to the 5/1 problem as they were to the 4/2 problem. The stance of the sixth and ninth graders (and to a lesser extent noncollege adults) who exhibited this broad exclusion pattern of response seemed to be that if the covariation was less than perfect, even if, as in the 5/1 problem, 10 of the 12 outcomes conformed to a covariation pattern, there was no possibility that the variable in question could be related to the outcome. In other words, such subjects were unwilling to acknowledge presence of a pattern in the midst of some unexplained variation. Because the outcome for the exceptions could not be explained, the subject rejected the possibility of the variable in question being one to which the variation in outcome could be attributed. As a ninth grader put it:

> In order for there to be like a comparison, you have to have like all the light in one [basket] and all the dark in the other.

As a result of this approach, such subjects treated all forms of mixed evidence as equivalent, failing to acknowledge any differences among them.

Another strategy for dealing with the mixed 5/1 and 4/2 evidence, less common than exclusion but one that nevertheless was shown by some subjects of all age groups, is reflected in what we will refer to as a qualified inclusion response (Type Ia2). The subject making such a response claimed that the variable in question "sometimes" makes a difference and that the theory is therefore "sometimes" right or "partly" right. Probing of these inclusion responses confirmed that what the subject was claiming was that the theory was right with respect to those instances that conformed to the covariation pattern but was wrong with respect to those instances that did not. These qualified inclusion responses occurred occasionally in response to 3/3 evidence as well, which of course provides no basis for inclusion. A sixth grader, for example, made this response:

> Miss R was a little bit right, because there's three balls in the *Good* basket that have ridges and three balls in the *Bad* basket that have ridges, so she was a little bit right because there's an equal amount in the *Good* and the *Bad*.

These qualified inclusion responses are particularly significant in that they reflect a willingness to regard each individual segment of the available evidence as interpretable by itself, in contrast to an effort to interpret the pattern reflected in the evidence as a whole. This willingness to interpret partial evidence of course leaves the subject particularly susceptible to interpretation biased by theoretical beliefs, a susceptibility we examine in the next chapter. In addition, it reflects a limited and incorrect understanding of what it means for there to exist a relationship between two variables, as the above example illustrates.

Interpretation of Unequal Evidence

Study 4 subjects were asked to evaluate two complex forms of mixed evidence, unequal and asymmetric. The unequal evidence problems (Problems 3a–3d) consisted of all adjacent combinations of the three basic evidence types, 5/1, 4/2, and 3/3. Of interest in the case of unequal evidence is whether the subject is able to regard a body of evidence as providing different degrees of support for two different theories, i.e., as supportive of both theories but more supportive of one than the other. The main question subjects were asked with respect to each set of evidence ("Do these results help more to show that Mr./Ms. ____ is right that (*variable*) makes a difference or do they help more to show that Mr./Ms. ____ is right that (*variable*) makes a difference . . . ?") allowed the subject to make such a relative judgment. The subject who does so we refer to as making a "relative inclusion" response with respect to the theory claimed to be supported by the evidence but supported less strongly than the alternative theory (not to be confused with the "qualified inclusion" responses listed in Table 12 and described above). Of interest, then, are the frequencies with which subjects recognize relative support and make these relative inclusion responses in the case of the four problems in which the degrees of support are in fact unequal (Problems 3a–3d).

Relative inclusion responses occurred occasionally when the evidence was in fact equal, motivated presumably by the difference in theoretical belief regarding the two theories; these cases are examined further in Chapter 9. In the case of unequal evidence (Problems 3a–d), mean frequencies of relative inclusion responses to one or the other of the two theories were (of a possible 4.00): .15 for third graders (2 subjects), .30 for sixth graders (3 subjects), .65 for ninth graders (6 subjects), .35 for noncollege adults (5 subjects), and 1.40 for college subjects (15 subjects). This difference in means across age groups was statistically significant, $F(4, 95) = 5.36$, $p \leq .001$, with post hoc comparisons showing college subjects to differ from all other groups and ninth graders to differ from younger subjects and from college subjects. College subjects, then, were the only ones to appreciate the idea of relative support with any regularity, though a few ninth graders and noncollege adults also did so. It should be noted that though the possible mean frequency was 4.00, as there were four unequal evidence problems, the relative inclusion response is actually correct only on two of those four (the two involving a comparison between the 4/2 and 5/1 evidence types), as the other two involve comparisons in which there is actually no support for one of the theories (i.e., 3/3 evidence). Most relative inclusion responses did occur in response to 4/2-versus-5/1 problems, though a few were made in response to the 3/3-versus-4/2 problems.

Interpretation of Asymmetric Evidence

The asymmetric evidence problems (Problems 4a–4d) are difficult ones that require fairly complex quantitative reasoning for correct solution. To evaluate presence or absence of a relationship for one variable requires the comparison of two ratios, in this case usually the ratio of good to bad balls for one variable level compared to the ratio of good to bad balls for the other variable level. Making this same evaluation for the second variable likewise requires comparison of two ratios. Without resorting to a mathematical formula, the only way to then compare the extent or degree of relationship for the two variables (or theories, in this case) would be to compare the difference between the two ratios for one variable to the difference between the two ratios for the other variable, that is, to examine the difference between differences. We did not anticipate that many subjects would exhibit this strategy and were not surprised to find only two college subjects who attempted it. Yet the request to compare the extent of the relationship for each variable (via the question "Do these results help more to show that one person is right rather than the other?") proved an excellent vehicle for engaging the subject in reasoning about the nature of the relationship for each of the variables, and the asymmetric problems proved to be a rich source of data regarding both the interpretation of evidence and the influence of theoretical belief.

Our results are consonant with those of earlier work on correlational reasoning, discussed in Chapter 2, in showing that the most common interpretation strategy is to base an inference on the frequencies in two of the four cells of a contingency table containing the frequencies for each antecedent/outcome combination. In the present case, the two cells were most commonly the good and bad outcome cells for one of the variable levels. An equivalent but less common strategy was to base an inference on the frequencies of the two variable levels for one outcome (e.g., the number of large versus small balls with good outcomes). Rarely, only the two diagonal cells were considered, as those that confirmed the relationship (e.g., large good-outcome and small bad-outcome balls). One-cell strategies also may have occurred, but these were rare and difficult to diagnose, as in most cases it appeared that the subject was making an implicit comparison to a second cell; for example the statement "There are a lot of big balls that are good" suggests the subject's implicit recognition of a smaller number of big balls that are bad or a smaller number of small balls that are good.

The likelihood of subjects' going beyond a two-cell strategy and basing their interpretation on the evidence contained in all four cells was strongly related to age group. No sixth graders and only 2 ninth graders and 1 noncollege adult did so, in contrast to 14 of the 20 college subjects who did so. These frequencies also showed a relation to sex. Though 1 of the 2 ninth graders and the noncollege adult were female, of the 14 college subjects who showed a four-cell strategy, only 4 were female, while all 10 male college subjects showed some use of the four-cell strategy.

Despite the frequent appearance of a four-cell strategy among college subjects, their performance on the asymmetric problems was far from optimal. No college subject (or subject in any group) used a four-cell strategy consistently. Typically a subject used it in only one or two of the four asymmetric problems and often used it in conjunction with a two-cell strategy. Even the subjects who used it, then, tended not to see the four-cell strategy as providing a definitive and indeed the only correct solution to the problem.

Moreover, the responses of subjects who did show some use of a four-cell strategy provided insight into a variety of further obstacles that must be overcome in order to reason correctly about correlation. A number of subjects, for example, correctly compared the two ratios but failed to draw an appropriate inference. These failures were occasionally the result of miscalculation of the ratios, but more often they reflected more fundamental misconceptions. For example, the following is the response of a ninth grader to the 6/3/2/1 evidence (in which the ratio of good to bad balls for one variable level—6:3—is identical to that for the other variable level—2:1—and variable and outcome are therefore independent):

> (What do these results have to say about Ms. C's view?) That dark-colored is better, because in the *Good* basket there are more dark-colored than light-colored, and in the *Bad* basket there are more dark-colored than light-colored. (So what does that show?) That dark is the most preferred color. (Do the results prove that Ms. C is right that color makes a difference?) Yes.

One of the college subjects made a more precise comparison of ratios in evaluating the 6/3/2/1 evidence but nevertheless failed to understand their implication:

> (What do these results have to say about Ms. S's view?) I'd say there is not enough to prove either way. (Why not?) Because of the fact that it is pretty close. Oh well, there is actually, It is two to one, or so. (What are you looking at when you say two to one?) Well, for . . . there are two good smalls and one bad small, and there are six large good and three large bad, so that is a two to one ratio for each thing, so. . . . (What does that show?) It shows that one out of two cases . . . it shows that size is fifty percent influential, I guess. (So size makes a difference?) Yes.

Another college subject also made a precise ratio comparison in evaluating the 6/3/2/1 evidence but was reluctant to base an inference on this comparison:

> (Do these results help more to show that one person is right . . . ?) I don't think it proves anything. (Why not?) Because you didn't start out with an equal number of dark balls and light

balls or an equal number of smooth balls and textured balls. (What is wrong with that?) It skews the results in favor of whatever texture or color you used more of. . . . You started off with nine dark balls and only three light balls and you didn't give the light balls a chance to prove themselves. I don't think it's fair. (Okay. What *can* you say based on the way it's come out?) Well, if you go and look at the fraction of balls of each color on the good side and the bad side is two thirds. Two thirds of the dark balls you started out with are good and two thirds of the light balls you started out with are good. (What does that show?) Nothing. Well, it shows that color does not matter. (But you are still unhappy with that conclusion?) Yeah, because it's not fair.

This concern about the asymmetry in the marginal frequencies of the two variable levels in fact occurred frequently among the college subjects, though no subjects in other groups mentioned it. Seven college subjects raised the issue, though only the subject quoted above and one other were concerned enough for it to prevent them from making a determinate inference. While the concern of the subject quoted above that the light balls had not been given "a chance to prove themselves" is legitimate, the idea that one must start off with an equal number of instances of the two categories to be compared reflects an inadequate understanding of the concept of ratio. If only absolute values were to be compared, it indeed would be crucial that the initial number of instances be equal, but a ratio calculation in fact amounts to a procedure for equalizing them.

While those subjects who did attend to all four frequencies encountered the additional obstacles we have just illustrated, the majority of subjects never attended to all of the four frequencies, as they would need to in order to make a correct inference. These subjects based their inferences on at most two cell frequencies, in effect ignoring half of the evidence that had been presented. What makes these two-cell strategies so prevalent? Part of the answer, of course, is the complexity of dealing with four quantities at the same time, which may well exceed the information-processing capacities of younger subjects, and part as well is the need to draw the appropriate inference based on these quantities once they have been attended to.

Another factor, however, may be the compellingness of the two-cell strategy. Various combinations of the four frequencies permit a number of different two-cell comparisons to be made. There is likely always to be a two-cell comparison available, then, that will support the particular inference being made, diminishing the likelihood that the subject will look any further. Responses to the 6/3/2/1 evidence provide an excellent example. Responses such as this one were common:

It makes a difference for the rough because six rough came out good and only three rough came out bad. (And what about the smooth?) Well, two smooths came out good and one bad. But roughs are still better because in the good basket you have six rough and only two smooth. (So the texture makes a difference?) Yes.

The existence of a variety of potential two-cell comparisons of course leaves the way open for conflict among them, since some comparisons dictate different conclusions than others. It is particularly noteworthy, then, that many subjects in evaluating a single set of evidence made two and sometimes even three two-cell comparisons that led to different conclusions. College subjects were most likely to make multiple conflicting two-cell comparisons (80% did so), but so did many other subjects. Frequencies were 50% of noncollege adults, 55% of ninth graders, and 35% of sixth graders. These comparisons of course led to a conflict that the subject then needed to resolve, and the prevalence of these self-generated conflicts is an indication of the richness of the reasoning that the asymmetric problems elicited.

The most interesting sets of evidence in this respect, and the ones most likely to generate conflict, were those that contained a zero frequency in one of the cells, in other words, the 4/4/4/0 or 6/4/6/0 evidence. The zero frequency served to focus the subject's attention on the perfect association with outcome for one variable level, for example, "All the large ones came out good," based on which the subject might make the inference that "size makes a difference for the large ones." In the 4/4/4/0 case, the distribution of good and bad outcomes for the other variable, in contrast, was equal, leading the subject to conclude, "For the small ones, the size makes no difference." In the case of the 6/4/6/0 evidence, the distribution was 6:4, rather than equal, but the same conflict nevertheless appeared between the 6/4 and the 6/0 comparisons, as the subject claimed that the 6/4 distribution indicated the variable made no difference because both outcomes occurred. This response of course reflects the same unwillingness to interpret mixed evidence that was observed in the simpler evidence evaluation problems. Its additional significance in the case of the asymmetric problems is that it promotes the qualified, or "sometimes," inclusion response: The variable sometimes (for the instances of one variable level) makes a difference and sometimes does not (for the instances of the other variable level). When the evidence was mixed for both variable levels, as in the simpler problems, subjects were able to use this mixed status as the basis for their response regarding the entire evidence set. When a single evidence set contains both mixed and non-mixed evidence, however, as illustrated above, the problem cannot be solved so readily, and the subject must somehow resolve the conflict between the two opposing conclusions that the two different reasoning strategies dictate.

We observed three modes of resolution of this conflict. One was the qualified inclusion, or "sometimes" response just noted, in which the two opposing reasoning strategies, one leading to an inclusion inference and the other to an exclusion inference, are essentially juxtaposed with no conclusion drawn regarding the relationship "overall" between variable and outcome. A second mode of resolution was an indeterminacy inference. For example:

> For the balls that came out bad, it looks like there's a relationship, because they are all smooth. For the balls that came out good, there doesn't seem to be a relationship because some are smooth and some are rough. So, you really can't tell.

The third and most common mode of resolution was to note the conflicting conclusions that could be drawn, as the subject just quoted did, but then simply to ignore one of them and base a conclusion on the other. Not surprisingly, which line of reasoning was ignored and which was used as the basis for a conclusion typically was influenced by theoretical belief, and it is to the nature of that influence that we now turn.

9

THE COORDINATION
OF EVIDENCE
WITH MULTIPLE THEORIES

In this chapter we consider each of the major types of evidence subjects were asked to evaluate, and, for each, we examine how subjects' beliefs in the truth of one and the falsity of the other affected the way they related the evidence to each of the two theories they were asked to consider. We also examine what light these data shed on the processes in terms of which theories and discrepant evidence are reconciled. As in Part II, we shall first examine examples and then proceed to group-level quantitative analysis. The same two major forms of bias that we examined in Part II can be predicted: (a) subjects will be more likely to acknowledge evidence consistent with their own theories and less likely to acknowledge evidence inconsistent with their theories, and (b) subjects will more readily draw inferences from evidence that are consistent with their own theories and less readily draw inferences that are inconsistent.

STUDY 4 RESULTS:
ACKNOWLEDGMENT OF THE EVIDENCE

As indicated in Chapter 8, Study 4 subjects, except for the third graders, made evidence-based responses most of the time. Yet, when they did not, they were much more likely to ignore the evidence that conflicted with their theory. There were, however, a few younger subjects—mostly third graders but occasionally sixth graders—who ignored the evidence virtually entirely. These subjects were unable to set aside their own beliefs regarding the theories to the extent necessary

133

to carry out the assigned task of evaluating how a set of evidence related to those theories. Their attitude in effect was that Mr. S (for example) was right because size indeed does make a difference and Mr. C was wrong because color does not. In the process, the evidence itself, to which the subject was being asked to relate these theories, was lost. Sarah, a sixth grader, provides a good example of a subject who did not see the presented evidence as relevant to the matter at hand. The following is her response to the initial problem:

(Do these results help more to show that one person is right . . . ?) I think it shows S is right. (Why?) Well . . . see, the way I say is because really, it's my opinion, size really matters and I never believed that color makes a difference. (Do you think *these results* show that S is right?) Right. (Because?) Because size is what makes a difference. (Do these results prove that Ms. S is right?) Yes it does. (What do these results have to say about Ms. C's view?) I think she's wrong. (Why?) Because she's forgetting that color goes everywhere, color goes on balls, so I think that she has no right arguing about it. And she [Ms. S] does. She has a right arguing because the way, I would believe the way God makes you, he makes you in a certain size and keeps the size — the way the company wants the size. I mean, no one will want a tiny ball.

In the next problem, the large size that Sarah favors in fact came out bad, but this result did not deter her from her position:

(What do these results have to say about Ms. S's view?) The big ball came out bad. (Does that show that Ms. S is right or wrong?) I think it shows that she's right. (Why?) Well, first of all the ball came out bad and now she has won the decision that size does make a difference. (Why has she won it?) Because, see, the way that she wanted, she doesn't really believe that colors make a difference. The size she really wants it to be.

In some of the subsequent problems, Sarah noted some of the features of the evidence, but she clung to the view that Ms. S was right because she cares about the size and Ms. C was wrong because

she don't really care about their size. All she cares about is color. (And do the results show she's right or wrong about the color making a difference?) She's wrong because the idea of the game, I mean, not the idea of the game, but I mean the idea is that, in my opinion, the balls should be about the size of the face of the paddle [i.e., large].

Ultimately, Sarah proposed what some might regard as a feminine resolution:

I could say both of them are wrong because they really shouldn't be arguing about it. What they can do is have an agreement — she (Ms. S) chooses the size and she (Ms. C) chooses the color.

Few subjects were as unable to separate their own beliefs from the evidence as was Sarah, but many subjects showed resistance to acknowledging the implications of evidence that was not consistent with their own beliefs and gave theory-based responses instead. In the sections below, data regarding the frequency of theory-based versus evidence-based responses as a function of theoretical belief are examined individually for each evidence type. In addition we examine how each evidence type is interpreted in relation to the two theories when the subject does attend to the evidence.

STUDY 4 RESULTS:
COORDINATING EVIDENCE AND THEORIES

Insufficient Evidence

Not surprisingly, perhaps, the insufficient-evidence problems, in which the most minimal and ambiguous evidence was presented, were the ones that elicited the most bias in interpretation. Problem 1a, in which a single ball was portrayed as having a good outcome, consistent with both subject's and other's theory, very frequently elicited a response like the one given by a third grader, Allen. Allen had theorized size to be causal (with large favored) and color noncausal. When presented with a single ball, a large, light-colored, rough-textured ball without ridges in the *Good* basket, he responded as follows:

> (Do these results help more to show that one person is right . . . ?) Mr. Size would win. (Why?) Because this ball is big. And it came out good. (Do these results prove that Mr. S is right?) Yes. (What do these results have to say about Mr. C's view?) He loses. (Why?) Because the color doesn't really matter. (And this ball coming out good, what does that say about Mr. C's view?) That says that the color doesn't matter.

Denny, a ninth grader with the same theories and shown the same evidence, gave a more sophisticated but equally biased response:

> It shows that Mr. S is right, because the size is big. They are more easy to hit. (Do these results prove that Mr. S is right?) Yes. (What do these results have to say about Mr. C's view?) It doesn't say too much. If there was another ball . . . (pause). . . . (What ball would you need?) A dark one. (Why would you need another ball?) Because this doesn't prove that you need the ball to be dark-colored or light-colored.

This same recognition of the insufficiency of the evidence Denny failed to apply to the preferred theory, size. He showed no hesitation in regarding the very same evidence as proving the preferred theory but insufficient in relation to the opposing theory.

With the introduction of the six-ball problems (Problems 1c and 1d), the balls become distributed across the two outcomes, but the evidence is still insufficient because only one variable level is represented. The approach illustrated above by Allen, in which the theory-consonant evidence for a theory the subject does not believe is ignored, was also common in the six-ball problems. Subjects also, however, often interpreted the evidence with respect to both theories but used different standards or strategies of evaluation. Lorraine, a ninth grader who had theorized texture to be causal (with smooth texture favored) and color noncausal, made this evaluation of the six smooth balls, four in the *Good* basket and two in the *Bad:*

> T is right. But in this test all of them are smooth, so you can't really be sure unless. . . . You'd have to use more balls that are rough *and* smooth. You can't really tell. (What do these results have to say about Ms. C's view?) She's wrong, because all of them so far are dark colored. (So what does that show?) That color doesn't make a difference. (But for texture you can't be sure?) No. (Why not, exactly?) Because if they were testing four kinds of balls with and without ridges and with and without texture, you have to test all four of them.

Thus, in comparison to Denny, who treated the evidence as a basis for inclusion with respect to his theory but as uncertainty with respect to the other's theory, Lorraine saw the evidence as indicating uncertainty with respect to her theory but exclusion with respect to the other's theory. Yet both subjects show comparable bias in evaluating the same evidence in variable ways in a manner that enhances consistency of the evidence with their theoretical beliefs.

Quantitative Analysis

Several different kinds of analyses were done to assess the extent of bias of various types. The first approach was based on a simple index of whether bias was or was not exhibited by a subject in response to a particular problem, irrespective of the specific nature of the bias, and, if so, whether the bias was in the direction favoring subject's theory or other's theory. For example, if the subject evaluated the evidence as indicating inclusion with respect to the theory favored by the subject and exclusion with respect to the opposing theory, response to that problem would be counted as an instance of bias favoring the subject's theory (the evidence in fact being identical with respect to the two theories). Other combinations counted as instances of bias would be (a) inclusion inference for one theory and uncertainty inference for the other, (b) inclusion for one theory and relative inclusion (evidence supports the theory but less strongly than it supports the alternative theory) for the other, and (c) uncertainty for one theory and exclusion for the other. (In cases in which one or both evaluations were theory based, the theory-based judgment was taken as the basis for comparison, with a no judgment comparable to exclusion and a yes judgment comparable to inclusion; theory-based maybe or can't tell responses did not occur.)

One-Ball Problem. For Problem 1a, 44 of 100 subjects showed bias favoring subject's theory, 2 showed bias favoring other's theory, and the remainder showed no bias, that is, evaluated the identical evidence for the two theories in a comparable way. For Problem 1c (six-ball), 26 subjects showed bias favoring subject's theory, 4 showed bias favoring other's theory, and the remainder showed no bias. Problems 1b (one-ball) and 1d (six-ball) were equivalent except outcomes were reversed (so that the variable level the subject believed favorable more often had a bad outcome). This reversal had the effect of reducing bias, but bias was still more frequent favoring subject's theory in both cases, 19 versus 11 for Problem 1b and 18 versus 5 for Problem 1d. Sign tests performed on these differences were statistically significant for each problem, with $p \le .001$ for Problems 1a and 1c and $p = .015$ for Problem 1b and .046 for Problem 1d.

While these comparisons establish that significant bias did occur in the direction favoring the theory the subject believed was correct, they do not establish exactly what forms this bias took. Comparisons were therefore made of subject's versus other's theory with respect to (a) frequencies of evidence-based responses, (b) frequencies of inclusion responses, and (c) frequencies of exclusion responses. In the case of one-ball evidence (Problem 1a), 82% of responses were evidence based when subjects were evaluating the bearing of the evidence on the theory they believed true, compared to 61% when evaluating the bearing of the evidence on the theory they did not believe to be true, $F(1, 95) = 31.15$, $p \le .001$. Thus, subjects frequently avoided acknowledging the implications of evidence not consistent with their beliefs. Examination by age group showed this difference to be greater for younger subjects, with ninth graders and college subjects showing no difference. (Statistical analysis of theory by age group effects is presented below.) A slight difference also occurred with respect to the frequencies with which subjects recognized that the evidence was insufficient to allow an inference. Subjects made inferences of indeterminacy (uncertainty) with respect to the theory they believed false slightly more often than with respect to the theory they believed true—30% versus 25%, though this difference did not reach statistical significance.

If subjects did make determinate inferences based on the evidence and did not recognize its insufficiency, did they show bias in the types of inferences they made? Analyses of inclusion response frequencies indicated that they did. Subjects regarded the single-ball evidence as sufficient to justify an inference of inclusion 55% of the time with respect to the theory they believed true, compared to 29% with respect to the theory they did not believe true, $F(1, 95) = 36.28$, $p \le .001$. Included in this 29% are cases in which subjects interpreted the evidence as showing only relative inclusion with respect to the theory they did not believe in (evidence supports it but less strongly than it supports the favored theory). Younger groups showed the largest differences in frequencies of inclusion for subject's versus other's theories, with the college group showing no difference. As scarcely any were made in the insufficient evidence problems, no analysis of exclusion inferences was undertaken.

Six-Ball Problem. Results for Problem 1c were similar. In evaluating evidence consonant with both a theory they believed true and a theory they believed false, 89% of responses were evidence based when subjects were evaluating the bearing of the evidence on the theory they believed true, in contrast to 74% when evaluating the bearing of the evidence on the theory they believed false, $F(1, 95) = 15.77$, $p \leq .001$. Examination by age group showed this difference to be greater for younger subjects, with ninth graders and college subjects showing no difference.

A difference also occurred with respect to frequency of inclusion responses. The six-ball evidence was regarded as sufficient to justify an inference of inclusion 34% of the time with respect to the theory the subject believed true, compared to 18% with respect to the theory the subject believed false, $F(1, 95) = 14.80$, $p \leq .001$. Examination by age group indicated that younger groups showed the largest differences, with the noncollege adults and college groups showing no difference. No differences appeared with respect to uncertainty and exclusion response frequencies; they occurred to an equal extent in the case of subject's and other's theories. For the six-ball problem, then, bias was shown with respect to willingness to evaluate the evidence and to infer inclusion but not in willingness to infer uncertainty or exclusion.

Analyses for Problems 1b and 1d were comparable.

Age-by-Theory Effects.   If all four insufficient-evidence problems are considered together in a single statistical analysis, it becomes possible to examine frequencies of evidence-based, inclusion, and exclusion responses as a function of the multiple factors of theory (subject's versus other's) and age group, with a significant interaction between the two factors indicating that extent of bias varies by age group. These analyses indicated the presence of such interaction effects. For frequencies of evidence-based responses, effect of theory was significant, $F(1, 95) = 50.11$, $p \leq .001$, as was the interaction of theory and age group, $F(4, 95) = 11.27$, $p \leq .001$. For frequencies of inclusion responses, effect of theory was likewise significant, $F(1, 95) = 33.08$, $p \leq .001$, as was the interaction of theory and age group, $F(4, 95) = 5.35$, $p \leq .001$. For frequencies of exclusion responses, neither theory nor interaction effect reached significance. (Simple effects of age group are not reported for these analyses as they are comparable to those reported in Chapter 8.) Means are shown in Table 16. Maximum score in each case is 4.00.

Equal Evidence

Problems 2a–2c presented subjects with evidence identical with respect to the two theories and sufficient to allow some determinate inferences, though in the case of Problems 2a and 2b (5/1 and 4/2 evidence), the evidence was indeterminate with respect to which of the two critical variables were causal. As discussed in Chapter 8, very few subjects recognized this indeterminacy, and

Table 16

Mean Frequencies of Evidence-Based, Inclusion,
and Exclusion Responses for Subject's Theory (S)
and Other's Theory (O) for Insufficient Evidence Problems

Group	Evidence-based responses		Inclusion responses		Exclusion responses	
	S	O	S	O	S	O
Third graders	2.90	1.25	1.90	0.70	1.00	0.55
Sixth graders	3.50	2.30	1.85	0.85	1.55	1.20
Ninth graders	3.85	3.90	1.25	0.85	1.45	1.70
Noncollege adults	3.15	2.45	1.10	0.70	1.25	1.00
College adults	4.00	4.00	0.65	0.75	0.70	0.70
Total sample	3.48	2.78	1.35	0.77	1.19	1.03

most made determinate (inclusion or exclusion) responses. In doing so, they exhibited a variety of biases.

Michael, a ninth grader, provides an example in the case of 5/1 evidence. He theorized texture as causal (with smooth favored) and color noncausal. He was presented the set of balls shown in Figure 6. As indicated in the figure, light color is always paired with smooth texture and dark color with rough texture, making it impossible to ascertain whether one, the other, or both have a causal effect on outcome. Michael responded as follows:

> (Do these results help more to show that one person is right. . . ?) In this case it would probably show that smooth is better than rough. (Why?) The smooth ones came out good. (Do the results prove that Mr. T is right?) Yes. (Why?) The smooth came out good. (What do these results have to say about Mr. C's view?) There is no difference. (Why not?) Because five dark and one light came out bad and five light and one dark came out good. (So what does that show?) They are pretty much neutral. (So does color makes a difference?) It doesn't matter.

Michael's response is notable in that he accurately characterized the evidence but drew opposite implications with respect to the two theories despite the equivalence of the evidence. Other subjects, in contrast, characterized the evidence inaccurately. Cynthia, a third grader, theorized size as causal (with large favored) and presence or absence of ridges as noncausal. In response to the 3/3 evidence (in which the distributions across good and bad outcomes are equal for all variables), Cynthia responded as follows:

> (Do these results help more to show that one person is right. . . ?) Size. (Why?) Because most of the big ones came out good and one little one came out good too. (Do the results prove that Ms. S is right?) Yes. (Why?) Because size does make a difference. (What do these results have to say about Ms. R's view?) It makes no difference. (Why not?) Because some balls have ridges and some don't.

While Cynthia's response reflects a gross distortion of 3/3 evidence (which

Figure 6.   Example of equal 5/1 evidence.

clearly reflects independence), the most interesting responses in many ways are those made to the 4/2 evidence, for this evidence could reasonably be interpreted either as reflecting covariation of antecedent and outcome or as reflecting independence between the two. Matt, a noncollege adult, provides an example of response to the 4/2 evidence. Matt theorized that texture was causal (with rough favored) and ridges noncausal. The 4/2 evidence Matt was asked to evaluate is shown in Figure 7. He responded as follows:

Figure 7. Example of equal 4/2 evidence.

(Do these results help more to show that one person is right. . . ?) Texture. Because you have more balls that have smooth texture that came out with bad serves than you do balls that have rough texture and bad serves. (Do these results prove that Mr. T is right?) Yes. Because the balls with smooth texture, larges and small, have bad serves. (What do these results have to say about Mr. R's view?) It's not showing nothing about ridges. (Why not?) Because you have balls that have ridges that have bad serves and balls that have ridges that have good serves.

We thus see the two different inference strategies described in the last chapter, one focused on the covariation and used as justification for inclusion and the other focused on the mixture of outcomes for a single variable level and used as justification for exclusion. In this case, the subject applies them to the same set of evidence, one with respect to one theory and one with respect to the other, in a way that serves his theoretical beliefs.

Quantitative Analysis

The same set of analyses used in the case of the insufficient evidence problems was employed. For 5/1 evidence, 30 subjects showed bias in the direction of subject's theory, 3 in the direction of other's theory, and the remainder no bias. For 4/2 evidence, 21 subjects showed bias in the direction of subject's theory, 4 in the direction of other's theory, and the remainder no bias. For 3/3 evidence 10 subjects showed bias in the direction of subject's theory, 1 in the direction of other's theory, and the remainder no bias. Overall, then, the greater adequacy of the evidence reduced bias, compared to its frequency in response to the insufficient-evidence problems, but did not eliminate it. Sign tests were statistically significant for each of these comparisons, with $p \leq .001$ in the case of the 5/1 and 4/2 evidence and $p = .006$ in the case of the 3/3 evidence.

5/1 Evidence. In the case of 5/1 evidence, more detailed comparisons indicated a difference first of all for frequencies of evidence-based responses. In evaluating evidence consonant with both a theory they believed true and a theory they believed false, 90% of responses were evidence based when subjects were evaluating the bearing of the evidence on the theory they believed true, in contrast to 77% when evaluating the bearing of the evidence on the theory they believed false, $F(1, 95) = 11.27$, $p \leq .001$. Examination by age group showed this difference to be greater for younger subjects, with ninth graders and college subjects showing no difference.

Comparison of inclusion response frequencies indicated that subjects regarded the 5/1 evidence as sufficient to justify an inference of inclusion 67% of the time with respect to the theory they believed true, compared to 48% with respect to the theory they believed false, $F(1, 95) = 17.72$, $p \leq .001$. Younger groups showed the larger differences, with only the college group showing no difference. A difference also appeared in the case of exclusion responses. Subjects regarded the 5/1 evidence as justifying an inference of exclusion 27% of the time with respect to the theory they believed false, compared to 20% with respect to the theory they believed true, though this difference did not reach statistical significance. (Frequencies of uncertainty responses were too small to analyze in any of the equal, unequal, or asymmetric evidence problems.)

4/2 Evidence. In the case of 4/2 evidence, a difference also occurred in frequencies of evidence-based responses. When subjects were evaluating the bearing of the evidence on the theory they believed true, 85% of responses were evidence-based, compared to 78% when evaluating the bearing of the evidence on the theory they did not believe to be true. This difference did not reach statistical significance. Comparison of inclusion response frequencies indicated that subjects regarded the 4/2 evidence as sufficient to justify an inference of inclusion 51% of the time with respect to the theory they believed true, compared to 41% with respect to the theory they believed false, $F(1, 95) = 7.79, p \leq .01$. These differences were greater for younger subjects, with ninth graders and college subjects showing no difference. In the case of exclusion response frequencies, no differences occurred.

3/3 Evidence.   In the case of 3/3 evidence, differences were slight for evidence-based responses, as well as for inclusion and exclusion responses, and none reached statistical significance.

Summary

The results for equal evidence problems suggest overall, then, that bias is present chiefly with respect to inclusion and less so with respect to exclusion. In other words, subjects are quite likely to regard covariation evidence as supporting a causal theory they believe true (inclusion) while ignoring the same implications of this evidence with respect to a causal theory they believe false. But they are less likely to see noncovariation evidence as disconfirming a causal theory they believe false (exclusion) while ignoring the same implications of this evidence with respect to a theory they believe true. Let us go on now to consider the extent to which these conclusions hold true in the case of unequal evidence.

Unequal Evidence

Matt, the noncollege adult quoted above, had two strategies for dealing with mixed evidence, as the previous quotation illustrated, and he applied them selectively in evaluating the same evidence in a way that served his theoretical beliefs. It is interesting, then, to observe how he draws on these strategies when the evidence is not in fact equal with respect to the two theories. In Matt's case of texture and ridges, one set of unequal evidence appeared as shown in Figure 8 (Problem 3c, combining 4/2 and 3/3 evidence). Matt had no problem detecting the slight difference favoring his theory.

> (Do these results help more to show that one person is right. . . ?) This result says that T's theory on texture [is more right]. (Why?) We have four balls that gave good serves that have rough texture and we have two balls with rough texture that gave bad serves. (Do these results prove that Mr. T is right?) Yes. Because we have more balls with rough texture that gave a good serve and more balls without rough texture that gave a bad serve. (What do these results have to say about Mr. R's view?) It proves nothing about R and his theory on ridges. (Why not?) Because we have three balls with ridges that gave a good serve and three balls with ridges that gave a bad serve.

Figure 8.   Example of unequal (4/2 and 3/3) evidence.

What happened when we simply reversed the evidence regarding texture and ridges, as shown in Figure 9? Matt acknowledged the modest difference in favor of ridged balls:

> This result shows that a ball with ridges could give you a better serve. (Why?) Because we have more balls with ridges that gave you a good serve and more balls without ridges that gave you a bad serve.

In the case of his preferred theory, texture, however, Matt was unwilling to apply the inference he did when this same noncovariation evidence had been presented regarding ridges (Figure 8).

Figure 9.   The reverse of the unequal evidence in Figure 8.

(What do these results have to say about Mr. T's view?) Well, it still says to me that a ball with rough texture will give you a better serve. (Why?) Because we still have balls with rough texture that have a better serve than a ball with smooth texture. (So is there a difference in how much the results help to show that Mr. R is right and how much they help to show that Mr. T is rignt?) I'd say they're equally right.

Thus, Matt, in addition to applying very different standards to the same comparison of unequal evidence depending on the relation of that evidence to his theoretical beliefs, is willing to consider only part of the evidence available, in a way that serves his theoretical beliefs. Because there is *some* evidence that can be found to support it, his theory is right.

Also of interest is the response of a sixth-grade boy, Steven, to this same combination of 4/2 and 3/3 evidence, this time in the case of ridges (which he believed causal) and color (which he believed noncausal). The 4/2 evidence was present for color and the 3/3 evidence for ridges.

> (Do these results help more to show that one person is right. . . ?) Well, I'd say Mr. R, because with the ridges they're saying that it's an equal amount with the ridges that have a good serve and a bad serve, and with color it could be light would make a good serve. (So which one is right?) R. (Why?) Because with the ridges you're saying. . . . No, in some ways supporting C because you're saying that with the ridges it could make a bad serve. (R says the ridges make a difference and C says color). Well, with the ridges it's pretty equal because you're saying that with ridges . . . wait. . . . I say supporting. . . . R is wrong, C with the color, it's C, I mean R (C is for color, R is for ridges) . . . I don't think C is right with the color. . . . Wait a minute. . . . I'm, saying that C is right with the colors because that one dark ball made a bad serve and two yellow balls did, and in the good . . . two dark balls made a good serve and one light ball made a good serve [the 4/2 ratio present in the evidence is thus reduced to a 2/1 ratio]. (Do the results prove Mr. C is right?) Yeah. (Why?) No . . . yeah, with the color because it's saying that. . . . Wait, I'm getting confused. . . . I'd say. . . . Now I've looked it over again it's saying R, because he's saying that it could be dark or light and make a bad serve and dark or light and make a good serve. (So it supports R?) Why? Because it's saying that dark and light could make good serves and dark and light could make bad serves. (And what does it say about the ridges that it supports R?) That the ridges they could make the possibility of a bad serve and they could make the possibility of a good serve. (So it supports R?) Yeah, but I can't explain it.

Steven was thus in the end unable to offer a justification for his belief that the evidence favors the effectiveness of ridges over color. His response to this evidence set reflects a strong bias in his reading of the evidence, as he claims the evidence to show no support for C and some support for R while it in fact shows the reverse. Unlike Matt, Steven recognized both the covariation and the "mixture" interpretations of 4/2 evidence as applicable with respect to the same theory (color). But in the service of drawing a conclusion compatible with his theoretical beliefs, he focused on one as the basis for his inference and ignored the other. In the case of his preferred theory, ridges, no interpretation of the evidence was compatible with his belief in the causal role of ridges. Instead of distorting the evidence by focusing on only part of it, as did Matt, Steven acknowledged the same "mixture" interpretation with respect to ridges but then drew a conclusion at variance with it, in effect offering no justification at all for his interpretation of the evidence. Thus, even the absence of an available interpretation strategy sometimes does not deter the subject from a theory-motivated inference.

In addition to what it illustrates with respect to the reasoning itself, Steven's response is notable as an illustration of the extent to which the task of coordinating the evidence with two theories often engages subjects in concerted thought, requiring them to exercise and coordinate a variety of cognitive strategies. It is this exercise that we believe is likely to promote development of the skills that are the subject of this work. We have more to say about this issue in Chapter 11 and again in Chapter 13.

Quantitative Analysis

The same analyses used for the previous evidence types were employed, but in this case the subject-other comparison was made across rather than within problems, so as to keep the evidence that was being evaluated equal. In other words, as illustrated above in the case of Matt, the subject was asked to compare 4/2 evidence for one theory and 3/3 evidence for another theory. In another problem the subject was again asked to compare 4/2 and 3/3 evidence, but the matching of theory and evidence type were reversed. The question of interest, then, is whether when 3/3 evidence is compared to 4/2 evidence, the 3/3 evidence is evaluated any differently when the subject believes a relationship exists for that variable (subject's theory) than when the subject believes one does not (other's theory). The same question can then be asked with respect to the 4/2 evidence. In two other problems, the subject was asked to compare 4/2 evidence for one theory and 5/1 evidence for the other. The sames questions can be asked, then, with respect to 4/2 evidence (this time when it is evaluated in comparison to 5/1 evidence) and with respect to 5/1 evidence (evaluated in comparison to 4/2 evidence).

For 5/1 evidence (always evaluated in comparison to 4/2 evidence in the unequal evidence problems), 20 subjects showed bias in the direction of subject's theory, 8 in the direction of other's theory, and the remainder no bias. For 4/2 evidence evaluated in comparison to 5/1 evidence, 28 subjects showed bias in the direction of subject's theory, 8 in the direction of other's theory, and the remainder no bias. Sign tests were statistically significant for each of these comparisons, with $p = .015$ for the 5/1 evidence and $p = .001$ for the 4/2 evidence. For 4/2 evidence evaluated in comparison to 3/3 evidence, 25 subjects showed bias in the direction of subject's theory, 5 in the direction of other's theory, and the remainder no bias. For 3/3 evidence, 23 subjects showed bias in the direction of subject's theory, 3 in the direction of other's theory, and the remainder no bias. Sign tests were significant for each of these comparisons, with $p \leq .001$ in each case.

5/1 Evidence. More detailed comparisons indicated a difference for subject's theory versus other's theory in the frequencies of evidence-based responses and the frequencies of inclusion responses. When subjects were evaluating the bearing of 5/1 evidence on a theory they believed true, 88% of responses were evidence based, compared to 79% when evaluating the bearing of 5/1 evidence on a theory they believed false, $F(1, 95) = 8.06, p \leq .005$. The same percentage difference was present in the case of frequencies of inclusion responses, 63% versus 54%, but in this case the difference was just below statistical significance. Examination by age group showed that in both cases the younger groups contributed most heavily to the differences, with differences absent in the ninth grade and college groups. No differences occurred in frequencies of exclusion responses.

4/2 Evidence.   No differences appeared in frequencies of evidence-based responses when 4/2 evidence was evaluated in comparison to 5/1 evidence or when it was evaluated in comparison to 3/3 evidence. Differences did occur, however, in frequencies of inclusion responses for both cases. In the case of comparison to 5/1 evidence, 59% of responses to 4/2 evidence were inclusion responses when the subject believed the theory true, compared to 47% when the subject did not believe the theory true, $F(1, 95) = 8.88, p \leq .005$. In the case of comparison to 3/3 evidence, the percentages were 56% and 46%, with the difference just below statistical significance. In both cases these differences were contributed to by the third graders, sixth graders, and noncollege adults, but not ninth graders or college subjects. Likewise in both cases, a difference appeared in frequency of exclusion responses, with exclusion responses more frequent when the subject did not believe the theory true. This difference was slight, however, in the case of comparison of 4/2 and 3/3 evidence (29% versus 33%) and reached statistical significance only in the case of comparison of 4/2 and 5/1 evidence (27% versus 36%, $F[1, 95] = 6.84, p \leq .01$), with the difference again contributed to most heavily by younger subjects.

3/3 Evidence.   In the case of 3/3 evidence, there were slight differences in expected directions, but none reached statistical significance.

Age-by-Theory Effects.   By considering all 5/1 evidence sets together (pooled across the equal and unequal problem types) in a single statistical analysis, it becomes possible to examine frequencies of evidence-based, inclusion, and exclusion responses as a function of the multiple factors of theory (subject's versus other's) and age group, with a significant interaction between the two factors indicating that extent of bias varies by age group. Similar analyses are possible for the 4/2 and the 3/3 evidence sets. These analyses, similar to those carried out in the case of the insufficient evidence sets (Table 16), indicated the presence of such interaction effects. In the case of 5/1 evidence, for frequency of evidence-based responses, effect of theory was significant, $F(1, 95) = 17.55, p \leq .001$, as was the interaction of theory and age group, $F(4, 95) = 2.65, p \leq .04$. For frequency of inclusion responses, effect of theory was significant, $F(1, 95) = 17.57, p \leq .001$, as was the interaction of theory and age group, $F(4, 95) = 3.23$, $p \leq .02$. Neither effect was significant for frequency of exclusion responses. (Simple effects of age group are not reported for these analyses, as they are equivalent to those reported in Chapter 8.) Means are shown in Table 17 (maximum frequency is 2).

In the case of 4/2 evidence, for frequency of evidence-based responses, neither theory nor interaction effect reached significance. Effects were significant, however, for frequencies of inclusion responses: $F(1, 95) = 14.93$, $p \leq .001$ for theory and $F(4, 95) = 2.98$, $p \leq .03$ for the interaction. Neither effect was significant for frequencies of exclusion responses. Means are shown in Table 18 (maximum frequency is 3). In the case of 3/3 evidence, no effects reached significance. Means are shown in Table 19 (maximum frequency is 2).

Summary

Two general conclusions hold true across subjects' performance on both the equal and unequal evidence evaluation problems. First, biased evaluation of evidence is more likely to occur in the evaluation of covariation evidence than in the evaluation of noncovariation evidence. Correspondingly, bias in making inclusion inferences is more likely than bias in making exclusion inferences. Subjects are quite likely to regard covariation evidence as supporting a causal theory they believe true (inclusion) while ignoring the same implications of this evidence with respect to a causal theory they believe false. It is much less likely, however, that subjects will regard noncovariation evidence as disconfirming a causal theory they believe false (exclusion) while ignoring the same implications of this evidence with respect to a theory they believe true. The second general conclusion is that the likelihood of bias is age related, with younger subjects the more likely to exhibit it and college subjects, and sometimes ninth graders, showing little or none.

Table 17

Mean Frequencies of Evidence-Based, Inclusion, and Exclusion Responses to 5/1 Evidence for Subject's Theory (S) and Other's Theory (O)

Group	Evidence-based responses		Inclusion responses		Exclusion responses	
	S	O	S	O	S	O
Third graders	1.15	0.70	0.95	0.45	0.20	0.25
Sixth graders	1.95	1.70	1.35	0.85	0.60	0.80
Ninth graders	2.00	1.95	1.15	1.05	0.80	0.85
Noncollege adults	1.80	1.45	1.25	0.85	0.50	0.55
College adults	2.00	2.00	1.80	1.90	0.15	0.10
Total sample	1.78	1.56	1.30	1.02	0.45	0.51

Table 18

Mean Frequencies of Evidence-Based, Inclusion, and Exclusion Responses to 4/2 Evidence for Subject's Theory (S) and Other's Theory (O)

Group	Evidence-based responses		Inclusion responses		Exclusion responses	
	S	O	S	O	S	O
Third graders	1.45	1.10	1.15	0.60	0.30	0.50
Sixth graders	2.85	2.55	1.15	0.95	1.65	1.55
Ninth graders	2.90	2.95	1.05	1.00	1.85	1.95
Noncollege adults	2.60	2.45	1.35	0.75	1.25	1.65
College adults	3.00	3.00	1.65	1.65	1.15	1.10
Total sample	2.56	2.41	1.27	0.99	1.24	1.35

Asymmetric Evidence

As discussed in Chapter 8, the asymmetric problems were very difficult but also particularly interesting ones in that they presented the opportunity for a variety of different two-cell comparisons that led to different conclusions. Subjects often made two or even three of these comparisons in evaluating a single evidence set and then had to resolve the conflict created by the different conclusions these comparisons led to. This of course left the way open for theoretical belief to influence the choice between conflicting lines of reasoning.

Most interesting is the fact that college subjects, who showed negligible bias in the simpler evidence evaluation problems, began to be biased by their theoretical beliefs when they reached the more difficult asymmetric problems. Jennifer, a college subject who theorized size as causal (with small favored) and color noncausal, provides an example. When presented the 6/4/6/0 evidence in the case of color, she responded as follows:

Table 19

Mean Frequencies of Evidence-Based, Inclusion, and Exclusion Responses to 3/3 Evidence for Subject's Theory (S) and Other's Theory (O)

Group	Evidence-based responses		Inclusion responses		Exclusion responses	
	S	O	S	O	S	O
Third graders	0.90	0.90	0.55	0.35	0.35	0.55
Sixth graders	1.90	1.75	0.65	0.55	1.20	1.15
Ninth graders	1.90	1.95	0.10	0.10	1.70	1.75
Noncollege adults	1.75	1.50	0.30	0.10	1.40	1.35
College adults	2.00	2.00	0.00	0.00	1.60	1.60
Total sample	1.69	1.62	0.32	0.22	1.25	1.28

(What do these results have to say about Ms. C's view?) Color is the same, because both dark-colored and light-colored gave good serves [six dark and six light in *Good*], and only the dark gave bad serves [four dark and no light in *Bad*]. (So what does that show?) Color does not make a difference. (Why not?) Because there is mixed color in the *Good* basket.

Thus, though she noted the exclusive presence of one variable level (dark) for one of the outcomes, which could be interpreted as evidence in support of a relationship, she did not pursue this implication and focused only on the mixture of balls in the *Good* basket, which served to support an inference of exclusion. When presented (in the next problem) this same 6/4/6/0 evidence with respect to her preferred theory, size, she initially focused on this same mixture as evidence for exclusion but then shifted course and ended with a quite different conclusion:

(What do these results have to say about Ms. S's view?) I think she is wrong. (Why?) It doesn't make a difference. Because you have both small and large balls that gave you the good serve, and no small balls that gave you bad serves. So she still has not proven it that either the large one or the small ones give you a better serve. (So what do you conclude about size?) She is maybe a little right, but . . . she is not wrong and she is not right. (Why is that?) Because the mixture of sizes gave you the good serve, but then there are large ones that gave you the bad serve. (So?) So you could say that the little ones gave you a better serve, but not necessarily. I guess you would say that the little ones give you a better serve. (Do the results prove that Ms. S is right?) Not one hundred percent, but close to it.

Thus, both inference strategies are exhibited with respect to each of the theories, but one dominates in one case and the other in the other case, in a way that serves the subject's theoretical beliefs.

Jennifer showed a similar bias in her interpretation of the 4/4/4/0 evidence. With respect to her preferred theory, size, she reasoned as follows:

(What do these results have to say about Ms. S's view?) It shows it partially but it doesn't prove it. (Why is that?) Oh, yes, in this one it does. No, it does not, because you have large ones that gave a bad serve and also gave a good serve. (So what does that show?) So it doesn't *prove* that size makes a difference. But it shows that it makes some difference, because all the small ones came out good.

In evaluating this same 4/4/4/0 evidence with respect to color, however, she reasoned as follows:

(What do these results have to say about Ms. C's view?) Well it may show . . . see there are more . . . it could show that light is a little better than the dark because the dark gave some bad serves [and the light didn't]. But there are more dark balls to give bad serves with than there were light balls. (Yes, so what can you conclude?) That color still does not make a conclusive difference. (Why?) Because all the light ones gave good serves, but there are twice as many dark ones.

This issue of the asymmetry in the overall frequencies of the two variable levels, recall, we observed in Chapter 8 as a concern for some college subjects. In Jennifer's case, it did not occur to her as a problem in evaluating the evidence with respect to her preferred theory, size, and arose only when considering a theory at odds with her theoretical beliefs.

Quantitative Analysis

As noted in Chapter 8, and as the preceding examples illustrate, it was the evidence sets containing a zero-cell frequency (4/4/4/0 and 6/4/6/0) that were highly likely to elicit conflicting two-cell comparisons and therefore provided the greatest opportunity for theoretical bias to enter into the resolution of the conflict. As Jennifer's reasoning illustrates, the comparison including the zero suggested that variable and outcome were related, while the comparison not including the zero indicated a mixture of outcomes for a single variable level and thus suggested variable and outcome were not related; this conflict afforded the subject the opportunity to choose the line of reasoning compatible with theoretical belief.

Statistical analyses confirmed that bias was most likely to occur in the cases of the zero-cell evidence sets. As in the case of the unequal evidence problems, the subject-other comparison was made across rather than within problems, so as to keep the evidence that was being evaluated identical. For the 4/4/4/0 evidence set, 23 subjects showed bias in the direction of subject's theory, five in the direction of other's theory, and the remainder no bias. A sign test was statistically significant, $p = .001$. More detailed comparisons indicated that subjects regarded the 4/4/4/0 evidence as sufficient to justify an inference of inclusion 67% of the time with respect to the theory they believed true, compared to 46% of the time with respect to the theory they did not believe true, $F(1, 72) = 11.63$, $p = .001$. A difference also appeared in the case of exclusion responses. Subjects regarded the 4/4/4/0 evidence as sufficient to justify an inference of exclusion 22% of the time with respect to the theory they believed true, compared to 41% of the time with respect to the theory they did not believe true, $F(1, 72) = 11.29$, $p = .001$. In contrast to the analyses presented for the earlier, simple evidence evaluation problems, these differences were contributed to to an equal extent by all age groups. In other words, college subjects were as likely as younger subjects to exhibit bias. (Analyses of evidence-based responses or uncertainty responses were not undertaken as frequencies of both uncertainty and non-evidence-based responses were very low, the latter due in large part to the absence of third graders from the sample.)

For the 6/4/6/0 evidence set, 16 subjects showed bias in the direction of subject's theory, 6 in the direction of other's theory, and the remainder no bias. A sign test was statistically significant, $p = .026$. More detailed comparisons indicated that subjects regarded the 6/4/6/0 evidence as sufficient to justify an inference of inclusion 58% of the time with respect to the theory they believed true, compared to 44% of the time with respect to the theory they did not believe true, $F(1, 73) = 6.29$, $p = .01$. A slight difference appeared in the case of exclusion responses. Subjects regarded the 6/4/6/0 evidence as sufficient to justify an inference of exclusion 38% of the time with respect to the theory they believed true, compared to 43% of the time with respect to the theory they did not believe true. This difference did not reach statistical significance.

Indices of bias for the other two evidence sets, 6/3/2/1 and 8/2/4/2, were in the predicted directions but did not reach statistical significance. Bias in the asymmetric evidence problems, then, was focused on the zero-cell evidence sets, but in contrast to the simpler evidence evaluation problems, it was not limited to younger subjects and was exhibited by all age groups to a comparable extent.

Overall Prevalence of Bias

A total of 15 evidence evaluation problems of four types—insufficient, equal, unequal, and asymmetric —were presented to subjects, except for third graders, who were not presented the asymmetric problems and for whom the total was therefore 11 problems. To provide an indication of the overall prevalence of bias among the various age groups, the number of problems of the 15 on which each subject exhibited bias favoring the subject's theory was counted (with bias defined in the same way described earlier as the basis for the reported sign tests). Means and ranges of these frequencies by age group are shown in Table 20. (The maximum for third graders is 11, rather than 15.) Also included in Table 20 are the numbers of subjects who *ever* showed bias favoring their own theory, without regard to how frequently they showed it. One-way analysis of variance showed a signifcant age group effect, $F(4, 95) = 13.85$, $p \leq .001$.

Examination of these frequencies by sex revealed no differences. Thus, one sex showed no greater propensity toward bias than the other. In contrast, as Table 20 reflects, prevalence of bias was strongly associated with age group. While most subjects showed some bias, the prevalence was high among third and sixth graders, dropped substantially among ninth graders, but then diverged sharply for the two adults groups. The substantial difference in the performance of the college and noncollege adults groups in all of the analyses presented in this and the preceding chapter is an important result that we discuss further at the end of

Table 20

Mean Frequencies, Ranges, and Numbers of Subjects
Exhibiting Bias toward Own Theory

Group	Mean	Range	Number exhibiting
Third graders	5.30	1–11	17
Sixth graders	4.35	1–15	20
Ninth graders	1.45	1–4	14
Noncollege adults	4.85	1–14	20
College adults	1.20	1–3	16

this chapter and again in the concluding chapter. Also notable is the individual variation reflected in the ranges shown in Table 20. While ranges were restricted among ninth grade and college groups, among the other three groups some subjects showed bias favoring their own theory on every problem or every problem but one, while other subjects in these groups showed bias on only a single problem.

STUDY 4 RESULTS:
THE RECONCILIATION OF THEORY
AND DISCREPANT EVIDENCE

In contrast to the studies described in Part II, in Study 4 subjects were not asked to evaluate the same evidence set repeatedly after each additional instance was presented. Instead, the complete evidence set was presented at one time and the subject evaluated it. As a result, Study 4 did not afford us the same opportunity that the earlier studies did to observe how the subject reconciled his or her theory with increasingly discrepant evidence over the course of the evidence presentation. Nevertheless, the same two mechanisms for maintaining theory and evidence in alignment that were observed in the studies in Part II were also evident in subjects' responses to the complete sets of evidence presented in Study 4. The major mechanism, biased evaluation of evidence, has been described and illustrated in the preceding sections of this chapter.

The other mechanism observed in Part II, the adjustment of theory to fit the evidence, was also observed, but much less frequently, most likely because, as in Study 3 (Chapter 7), theories were held with greater certainty than they were in the studies reported in Part II. A few subjects from all age groups except the college group, however, did exhibit theory adjustment to fit the evidence. As in the earlier studies, this was done instead of or before referring to the evidence. Such changes occurred in both directions: modification of a noncausal theory to a causal theory to fit covariation evidence and modification of a causal theory to a noncausal theory to fit noncovariation evidence. As in the earlier studies, however, the latter change was less prevalent, with 8 subjects (1 third grader, 3 sixth graders, 2 ninth graders and 2 noncollege adults) exhibiting it on a total of 16 responses. In contrast, modification of a noncausal theory to a causal theory was exhibited by 11 subjects (2 third graders, 3 sixth graders, 2 ninth graders, and 4 noncollege adults) on a total of 30 responses.

The fact that Study 4 evidence was almost always mixed evidence (i.e., it never reflected perfect covariation between variable and outcome and in only a few problems did it reflect perfect noncovariation, or independence) afforded an additional opportunity to examine how subjects reconciled discrepant evidence with their theories. If the subject's belief was that variable and outcome were not related, the encounter with discrepant evidence could be avoided. The subject needed only to note a "mixture" of outcomes for a single variable level (e.g., a small ball with a good outcome and a small ball with a bad one) or a "mixture" of variable levels occurring with a single outcome (e.g., a large and a small ball with good outcomes), and this evidence was readily regarded as sufficient justification for an inference of exclusion, as we have observed. If the subject's theoretical belief was that variable and outcome were related, however, the situation was different. Even if the covariation evidence was strong, for example, the 5/1 case, there remained 2 balls of the 12 that deviated from the covariation pattern. Assuming the subject noted the predominant pattern of covariation as the basis for an inference of inclusion, how did the subject regard these deviant cases?

Unsurprisingly, perhaps, the most common approach was simply not to acknowledge the discrepant instances as posing any problem for the theory. The existence of these discrepant instances might be ignored ("The big ones came out good and the small ones came out bad"), or they might be acknowledged ("The big ones mostly came out good and the small ones mostly bad"), but any possible significance these discrepant instances might have is not acknowledged. When this approach became particularly noteworthy was when there in fact existed a preponderance of discrepant evidence. Consider for example, the response to the 6/3/2/1 evidence by a sixth grader, Maria, who theorized size causal with large favored:

> (What do these results have to say about Ms. S's view?) S is still right. (Why?) Because five, no six big balls came out [good], and only three percent [three balls] came out bad. And that two of these [small balls] came out good. But still at least one [small ball] came out bad.

In the case of the small balls, the distribution is actually counter to the subject's theory: More small balls have good outcomes than have bad outcomes. Nevertheless, she focused on that minority outcome as the significant one and dismissed the fact that the outcome is the opposite for the majority of cases. Her treatment of the 8/2/4/2 evidence is very similar:

> (Do these results help more to show that one person is right. . . ?) Yes. She has eight balls [in the *Good* basket] and only two percent [two balls] messed up. (So what does that show?) It shows that she's still right and size does make a difference. And that she only has three [small ones] that went [had good outcomes]. [Four small balls are in fact present in the *Good* basket.] And only two [small ones] messed up. (So what does that show?) She's right about size. Because little ones just came out a little bit good, and these two [small balls in *Bad* basket] messed up because it's a small ball.

Again, the minority outcome she attributed to the theorized causal effect, while the majority outcome she both misrepresented quantitatively and dismissed as not significant.

While most subjects on most occasions simply failed to acknowledge the possible significance of the discrepant instances, a significant minority of instances in which inclusion inferences were made in response to mixed evidence, roughly 20%, were accompanied by some attempt on the subject's part to address the discrepant evidence (i.e., that deviating from the covariation pattern). We observed four approaches:

1. *Discrepant evidence rejected as wrong* (4% of cases). Subjects showing this approach regard the discrepant evidence as a mistake and refuse to accept that the outcomes could be as portrayed, as in "This large ball doesn't belong in the *Bad* basket; it's supposed to be over here [in the *Good* basket] with the other large balls."

2. *Discrepant evidence regarded as an exception or anomaly* (2% of cases). Subjects showing this approach accept the evidence as displayed but note the discrepant cases as deviating from the pattern and express puzzlement over the deviation, as in "I don't understand what happened to this one big ball—why it didn't come out good like the others."

3. *Theory constructed to account for the discrepant evidence* (7% of cases). Slightly more prevalent were approaches that attempt to explain the discrepant outcomes once noted. Most common is the invoking of another variable as responsible for the deviant outcome(s), even though the influence of this other variable is otherwise ignored, as in "This one big ball came out bad because it has ridges and they were messing it up."

4. *Theory qualified to accommodate discrepant evidence* (7% of cases). Subjects displaying this approach adjust their theory as a way of accommodating the discrepant evidence. They do so by making the "qualified" inclusion inference noted previously (Table 12), as in "Size sometimes matters, because sometimes the big balls come out good but sometimes they don't."

These attempts to deal with discrepant evidence were exhibited by subjects of all age groups, with no particular approach favored by one age group significantly more than by another, except for the approach listed first above (rejection of evidence as wrong), which did not occur among college subjects.

GENERAL DISCUSSION

The studies in Part II provided an indication of weaknesses in inference skills that leave people susceptible to bias arising from their theoretical beliefs. Subjects fail to infer exclusion from evidence of noncovariation. In addition, they readily infer inclusion from a single co-occurrence or limited covariation (ignoring the conflicting portion of the evidence), or from covariation in the presence of multiple covariates. The failure to interpret noncovariation correctly, we noted in Chapter 4, coupled with lax criteria for inferring causality, is a particularly lethal combination, leaving one extremely prone to fallacious inference.

The results of Study 4 both corroborate these findings and further illuminate the inference skills necessary for correct interpretation of covariation and noncovariation evidence. While third and sixth graders showed limited ability to interpret the meaning of noncovariation, by ninth grade (or even sixth grade in some cases), a phenomenon that can be regarded as "overinterpretation" of noncovariation became prevalent. If covariation was less than perfect, even if, as in the 5/1 problem, 10 of the 12 outcomes conformed to a covariation pattern, the subject rejected the possibility that the variable in question "made a difference" to the outcome. Thus, all mixed evidence was interpreted as indicating exclusion. Since all of the evidence presented in Study 4 was mixed evidence, such subjects made nothing but exclusion responses, thus not acknowledging the presence of any patterns in the evidence they were asked to evaluate, even when there was substantial (i.e., 5/1) covariation evidence relative to a theory they believed true. The one or two instances of nonconformity to a covariation pattern may have violated the subject's theory of the causal mechanism connecting variable and outcome. Yet the subject was not willing to consider these exceptions as due to random or other unexplained sources of variability. As a result, such subjects made no distinction between sets of evidence showing independence between variable and outcome and sets showing substantial covariation. Though this pattern of response declined among older subjects and was absent among college subjects, its prevalence among sixth and ninth graders is noteworthy. Much of the covariation that people might detect in the physical or social environment is in fact less than perfect covariation. Subjects' responses in the case of the simple stimuli used in this study suggest that such patterns of covariation frequently may be ignored, with the information that they provide thus remaining unutilized.

Another, very fundamental limitation in the interpretation of covariation was revealed by Study 4 subjects' frequent use of the qualified, or "sometimes," inclusion response to mixed evidence: The variable sometimes makes a difference (for those instances that conform to the covariation pattern) and sometimes does not (for those instances that depart from the pattern), and the theory is therefore "sometimes" right or "partly" right. This conception, of course, reflects a limited and incorrect understanding of what it means for there to exist a relationship between two variables, as the example of the reasoning of a sixth grader given in Chapter 8 illustrated. The theory that ridges were causally related to outcome was "a little bit right," the subject claimed, because three balls with ridges had good outcomes and three balls with ridges had bad outcomes.

The reasoning of the subject just referred to reflects the belief that the "good outcome" instances can be interpreted in their own right, apart from the "bad outcome" instances. A comparable misconception that occurred more commonly is the idea that the presence of a relationship can be examined separately for the two variable levels. Subjects frequently expressed the idea that the small balls, for example, have one sort of relationship to outcome, while the large balls have another. This conception, of course, reflects a misunderstanding of the very concept of covariation. Covariation of any two variables indicates that they vary together—variation in one is accompanied by variation in the other. If no variation occurs in one of the variables, for example, if only small balls are considered, the concept of covariation becomes meaningless. Taken to its extreme, the "sometimes" strategy means that each individual co-occurrence or non-co-occurrence of variable level and outcome can be interpreted in isolation. The occurrence of an antecedent in the presence of an outcome is thus sufficient to implicate that antecedent as having played a causal role in the outcome. Such an inferential rule is of course false inclusion in its most blatant form.

Closely related to the "sometimes" strategy is the willingness subjects displayed to base an interpretation on only partial evidence, as reflected both in the use of two-cell strategies in the asymmetric problems and in the frequency of determinate inferences in response to the insufficient evidence problems. In the case of the asymmetric problems, it is not surprising that subjects showed very limited command of the correct four-cell strategy entailing comparison of the two ratios. What is noteworthy is the inferences that they *were* willing to make based on very limited evidence. What these subjects are lacking, then, is not only knowledge of the correct strategies and how to apply them but the metacognitive knowledge that these are the necessary strategies to apply to the problem and that no others will suffice.

The limitations in inference skill that have just been summarized have profound implications with respect to the coordination of evidence with theories. The biases observed in Study 4 were primarily in differential acknowledgment of the evidence (frequencies of evidence-based responses) and differential inclusion and only infrequently in differential exclusion; that is, subjects only occasionally drew on noncovariation evidence to disconfirm the opposing theory while ignoring the same implications of this evidence with respect to the favored theory. In contrast, they frequently drew on covariation evidence to support the favored theory while ignoring the same implications of this evidence with respect to the opposing theory.

It is notable that the effects of theoretical belief on interpretation of evidence were greatest when the evidence available was the most minimal and ambiguous (the insufficient evidence problems). In other words, subjects were willing to take a little bit of evidence and use it for their own purposes, that is, as support for their theoretical beliefs. When more adequate evidence was available, subjects' willingness to interpret partial evidence, as well as their "sometimes" conception of relations between variables, fostered the selective use of evidence. This aspect or segment of the evidence suggests this; another aspect suggests something else, with no need perceived to evaluate the available evidence as a whole. The result is that some evidence can be found to support just about any theory. As many of the excerpts from subjects' responses have illustrated, the person says in effect, " My theory is right, and just as right as the other person's, because here is *some* evidence that supports my theory."

Another factor that the Study 4 results show to be strongly implicated in susceptibility to bias is the availability of multiple interpretation strategies that the subject can apply to the same set of evidence. While the simple covariation and noncovariation evidence presented in the earlier studies allowed for less variability in strategies, the mixed evidence, and particularly the asymmetric evidence, presented in Study 4 gave rise to a wider potential set of strategies. This variety of strategies was very prevalent within a single subject's reasoning, even within a single problem, as well as across problems and across subjects. The availability of multiple interpretation strategies clearly affected the ways in which subjects coordinated evidence and theories. Having to coordinate the same identical evidence set with two opposing theories we thought would enhance subjects' performance by making it difficult not to acknowledge a discrepancy between the evidence and at least one of the theories. To an extent it did have this effect, but subjects were able to circumvent this simply by applying different strategies, in other words, different standards of evaluation, when evaluating the evidence with respect to each of the theories. If the subject has two strategies available in his or her repertoire that apply satisfactorily to the problem at hand, it is quite likely that the subject will select the strategy to apply in a way that will minimize discrepancy between theoretical belief and interpretation of the evidence. The fact that the evidence with respect to the two different theories was embodied in the same physical objects made these variable standards difficult to maintain, but a large number of subjects nevertheless exhibited them.

In Part II, we suggested that the bias subjects exhibit in evidence evaluation reflects limitations in the differentiation and coordination of theory and evidence. Identical evidence means one thing in relation to a theory that is favored and something else in relation to a theory not favored, which suggests that in both cases the evidence is not sufficiently differentiated from the theory itself. It does not retain its own identity, its constancy of meaning, across a range of theories to which it might be related. It could be, then, that exercise in relating evidence of different forms to a number of different theories would serve to foster this coordination skill and thereby to reduce bias. It is this idea that we pursue in Chapter 11.

We also suggested in Part II that bias was one manifestation of subjects' effort to maintain theory and evidence in alignment with one another. The other strategy, change of theory to fit the evidence, was also observed in Study 4, though it was less prevalent. The presence of mixed evidence afforded us the opportunity to observe how subjects dealt with those instances of evidence that were counter to their theory, and these results reflected similar efforts to maintain theory and evidence in alignment. The qualified inclusion ("sometimes") response reflected one approach, one resembling but more moderate than the theory change strategy. The other notable approach was to appeal to the influence of other variables to account for the discrepant evidence, thereby "saving" the theory. The most common approach, however, was simply not to acknowledge evidence that posed a problem for the theory.

The results of Study 4 give a clearer indication of the age-group relatedness of bias than did the studies in Part II. Bias was most prevalent among third and sixth graders and declined substantially by ninth grade. College subjects showed virtually no bias on the initial problems, but once the problems became more complex, their performance indicated that they were likewise susceptible. The fact that the noncollege young adults performed very differently than the college subjects is particularly significant. Their performance was in the range intermediate between that of sixth and ninth graders. This tells us, of course, that the decline in bias is not a simple age-related phenomenon but has a great deal to do with the experiential backgrounds of the subjects. At the end of Chapter 5, we discussed the ability to bracket belief in a theory as a means of evaluating the bearing of the evidence on it and the possible association of this skill with school experience. The superiority of college students and even ninth grade high school students over young adults not in school certainly supports such an association. Also significant, however, is the wide individual variation in susceptibility to bias that we observed within each of the age groups. In the concluding chapter, we say more about the implications of each of these findings.

10

THE GENERATION
OF EVIDENCE
TO EVALUATE THEORIES

In all of the results described thus far, we have focused on subjects' abilities to evaluate and to coordinate with theories the various forms of evidence presented to them. We purposely focused the investigation on subjects' skills in interpretation of evidence, for these skills seemed to us to be the most significant ones with regard to reasoning in general, particularly everyday reasoning, if not to scientific reasoning as well. It is true of course that professional scientists in many fields frequently design and conduct experiments to generate evidence that they then interpret. Yet, other than some professional scientists, few people in their work or everyday lives ever have the opportunity, or the inclination, to conduct experiments to generate evidence. We nevertheless included in Study 4 an assessment of subjects' abilities to generate their own evidence, in other words, to design experiments the results of which they believed would provide tests of the theories in question.

We had two reasons for doing so. First, we thought it likely that an examination of the evidence that subjects generated—the evidence that they regarded as critical to their own and the opposing theories— would yield insight into their understanding of the relations between evidence and theories and therefore into the meaning they attributed to various forms of evidence. Second, as discussed in Chapter 2, there already exists a sizable research literature on the development of the ability to conduct controlled experiments, stemming from the original work on the topic by Inhelder and Piaget (1958). These studies indicate marked changes in strategy during the same preadolescent and adolescent age range covered in the present work. These changes almost certainly are related to the ones investigated in the present work. Our investigation of evidence generation skills as part of Study 4, then, as well as contributing to our understanding of their development and their relation to skills in evidence evaluation, should facilitate the relating of our results to existing literature on the development of controlled experimentation skills.

The evidence generation segment of Study 4 differs in several respects from most of the studies of control, or isolation, of variables, that is, studies of strategies of experimentation, in the Piagetian research literature. In most of these studies, the subject is instructed simply to experiment with the materials to find out which of several potential variables have a causal influence on outcome. Such studies are focused on the experimentation strategies themselves rather than on the products of the experimentation which must then be interpreted. In Study 4, in contrast, subjects were asked to construct a finished set of evidence which would then serve as a demonstration, or proof, that a particular theory were either correct or incorrect. The focus, then, was on the product, on the evidence generated, rather than on the process of generation (experimentation), and the subject was asked to link the evidence to specific theories, with a focus on demonstrating what is not causal (exclusion) as well as what is (inclusion). In addition, unlike previous studies of experimentation strategies, the study was designed in a way that enabled us to examine skills as a function of subjects' theoretical beliefs.

STUDY 4 METHOD: GENERATION OF EVIDENCE

Though secondary in focus to the evidence evaluation segments of Study 4, the evidence generation segment was administered first, so that subjects would not be influenced in their generation of evidence by having previously viewed displays of evidence generated by the interviewer. The subject was asked to generate evidence for and against two theories, one stating that Variable X makes a difference and the other that Variable Y makes a difference. Variable X was always the one the subject had claimed to be the one that made the most difference. Variable Y was always the one the subject had claimed to be the one least important of the four and one that made no difference. The first theory we refer to as "subject's theory" and the second as "other's theory." Assuming for purposes of illustration that "size makes a difference" is subject's theory and "color makes a difference" is other's theory, the following instructions were given:

> You said that *size* makes a difference in how a serve comes out. Suppose now that the company did a test using these balls, and the results of the test proved that you're right. In other words, the results showed that *size* makes a difference in how a serve comes out. Can you show how the results would have to come out to prove that you're right? In other words, what balls would result in a good serve and what balls would result in a bad serve in order to prove that you're

right that size makes a difference in how a serve comes out? Can you put them in the baskets to show me? You can use as many or as few balls in your test as you want. (Subject completes the placement of balls in baskets.) Can you explain how this proves that size makes a difference in how a serve comes out?

The following additional questions were then asked:

1. *Other balls:* Is there any other combination of balls in the two baskets that could prove that you're right? (If yes) Can you show me? (Subject places balls.) Which way shows better that you're right? Why?

2. *Fewest balls:* Suppose that you wanted to prove that *size* makes a difference using the fewest balls possible. Could you do it using fewer balls than you have here? (If yes) Can you show me? Can you explain how this proves that *size* makes a difference?

3. *Two balls:* (If more than two balls were used in preceding proof) Could you prove it using just two balls? (If yes) Can you show me? (Subject places balls.) Can you explain how this proves that *size* makes a difference?

The subject was then asked to generate evidence to prove that the subject's theory (size in this illustration) was wrong:

> Suppose now that someone else thinks that you're wrong when you say that *size* makes a difference, and they believe that *size* does not makes a difference. Can you show me how the results would have to come out to prove that you're wrong and this other person is right? In other words, what balls would result in a good serve and what balls would result in a bad serve in order to prove that you're wrong when you say that size makes a difference in how a serve comes out? Can you put them in the baskets to show me? You can use as many or as few balls in your test as you want. (Subject completes the placement of balls in baskets.) Can you explain how this proves that you're wrong in saying that *size* makes a difference in how a serve comes out?

The three additional questions indicated above (other balls, fewest balls, and two balls) were then asked with respect to proving the subject's theory wrong.

The identical format was used with respect to other's theory. In the case of color, the instructions were as follows:

> Suppose a Mr./Ms. C who works at the company thinks that *color* makes a difference in how a person's serve comes out. Suppose now that she did a test using these balls, and the results of the test proved that he/she is right. In other words, the results of the test showed that *color* makes a difference in how a serve comes out. Can you show how the results would have to come out to prove that he/she's right? In other words, what balls would result in a good serve and what balls would result in a bad serve in order to prove that he/she's right when he/she says that *color* makes a difference in how a serve comes out? Can you put them in the baskets to show me? You can use as many or as few balls in your test as you want. (Subject completes the placement of balls in baskets.) Can you explain how this proves that he/she's right in saying that *color* makes a difference in how a serve comes out?

The three additional questions indicated above (other balls, fewest balls, two balls) were then asked. As in the case of subject's theory, the subject was then asked to generate evidence that would prove this other person wrong, followed again by the three additional questions.

After generation of each set of evidence, the subject was asked to indicate on a 10-point scale (use of which was explained and illustrated): "How sure are you that this evidence proves that (*variable*) makes (doesn't make) a difference?"

The subject was thus asked to generate, explain the basis for, and indicate certainty regarding four major sets of evidence: (1) for subject's theory, (2) against subject's theory, (3) for other's theory, and (4) against other's theory. In each case the subject was subsequently asked to generate the requested evidence using other balls, fewest balls, and two balls. The "for" evidence generation task always preceded the "against" task. The "subject's theory" and "other's theory" tasks, however, were counterbalanced, with half the subjects in each subject group receiving one first and half the other first.

The evidence generation phase, for the reasons already noted, was administered before the evidence evaluation phase. A final phase of the procedure, occurring immediately after the main evidence evaluation phase, was the presentation of several multiple-evidence evaluation problems. The procedure for these final problems (which relate directly to the evidence generation problems and were therefore included in this chapter) is described below. The initial instruction was as follows:

> Now I'm going to ask you some questions about different ways of doing a test. I am going to show you two different tests that were done, and I'm going to ask you which you think shows best what makes a difference in how a serve comes out. To show you the two sets of test results, I will use these two sets of baskets. The *Good* and *Bad* baskets over here (interviewer indicates left side of table) show how one test came out, and the *Good* and *Bad* baskets over here (interviewer indicates right side of table) show how the other test came out.

After placement of balls in the four baskets by the interviewer, the subject was asked (again using size and color as illustrative variables):

> Which result best shows that Mr./Ms. S is right that *size* makes a difference in how a serve comes out? Can you say why?

The placement of balls was changed, and the same question was repeated with respect to the other variable (color in this illustration). Following placement of a different set of balls in the four baskets, the interviewer asked:

> Which result best shows that Mr. S is wrong in saying that *size* makes a difference? In other words, which result best shows that *size* does not make a difference? Can you say why?

The placement of balls was changed, and the same question was repeated with respect to the other variable (color in this illustration).

For the first two (inclusion) questions, the comparison is between evidence that reflects controlled versus uncontrolled tests. In the case of size, for example, one evidence set consisted of a large, dark-colored, rough ball with ridges in the

Good basket and a small, dark-colored, rough ball with ridges in the *Bad* basket. The other evidence set consisted of the same ball in the *Good* basket and a ball with all opposite characteristics in the *Bad* basket: a small, light-colored, smooth ball without ridges. For the second two (exclusion) questions, the comparison is between conclusive and inconclusive evidence for exclusion. Though both reflect noncovariation between variable and outcome, they differ in form. Conclusive evidence is defined as that in which two different levels of the variable produce the same outcome, with all other variables held constant. Inconclusive evidence is defined as that in which two balls reflecting the same level of the variable have different outcomes. This evidence is inconclusive as the variable level has not been varied, and the different outcomes conceivably could have resulted from the operation of some different variable.

STUDY 4 RESULTS:
GENERATION OF EVIDENCE

Generation of Covariation Evidence

Each subject was asked to generate a total of eight sets of evidence to support a causal theory, one for a theory the subject believed correct (subject's theory) and one for a theory the subject believed incorrect (other's theory), each under the four task conditions described: initial, other balls, fewest balls, and two balls. In this section we consider the generation of covariation evidence. We first examine the physical evidence that subjects produced, that is, the arrangement of balls in the two baskets, and then go on to consider subjects' understanding of this evidence as reflected in their explanations.

Not all subjects produced such evidence. Some were unable or unwilling to do so, especially in the second through fourth conditions. Numbers of subjects who attempted generation of supporting evidence are shown in Table 21, for subject's theory and other's theory for each task condition. In the initial condition, as Table 21 reflects, refusals always occurred for other's theory and can therefore be attributed to the discrepancy between the theory the subject was being asked to generate evidence to support and the subject's own theoretical belief (an interpretation that our later examination of explanations supports). In the second task condition, in contrast, more than half the subjects claimed for both belief conditions that there was no other set of balls that could prove the theory correct, implying that the initial set that had been generated was the only possible one. In the next (fewest-balls) condition, the number of subjects willing to generate evidence increased to more than 80, and remained at this level in the last (two-balls) condition, though in this condition again subjects appeared slightly more willing to generate evidence for a theory they believed. Increase in

Table 21

Numbers of Subjects Attempting to Generate Covariation Evidence
for Subject's Theory (S) and Other's Theory (O) in Each Task Condition

Group	Initial		Other balls		Fewest balls		Two balls	
	S	O	S	O	S	O	S	O
Third graders	20	17	7	9	17	15	19	16
Sixth graders	20	19	8	8	18	18	17	15
Ninth graders	20	19	6	9	17	17	20	15
Noncollege adults	20	17	8	8	14	14	16	15
College adults	20	19	13	15	18	16	19	16
Total	100	91	42	49	84	80	91	77

willingness from second to third task condition is most likely attributable to the
fact that subjects often met the "fewest-balls" task requirement simply by
removing one or two balls from their previously generated evidence set.
Statistical analysis of the data in Table 21 showed a significant effect of task only,
$F(3, 285) = 81.94$, $p \leq .001$. Mean number of balls used was 11.7 (of 16) in the
initial condition, 8.7 in the other-balls condition, 5.3 in the fewest-balls
condition, and of course 2.0 in the two-balls condition. These means did not
differ significantly by age group or belief condition. (Statistical analysis across
task conditions was not undertaken due to the large variation in sample size
across task conditions, because of refusals.) No sex differences emerged in this
or any of the analyses reported in this chapter.

Once evidence generation was attempted, a number of challenges to a
successful demonstration remained. First, did the subject succeed in showing
covariation between the variable in question and the outcome? Not all subjects
were successful in showing *any* covariation between variable and outcome
(whether or not the covariation was perfect). Failures were of two types. Either
the evidence the subject generated showed noncovariation (e.g., equal numbers
of large and small balls appeared in each basket), or the variable was not varied
(e.g., the subject included only large balls in the evidence that was produced).
Presented in Table 22 are the numbers of subjects who were successful in
demonstrating covariation (whether perfect or not) between variable and outcome
(relative to the numbers who attempted evidence generation, shown in parentheses), for the initial and the two-balls conditions. Performance in the two
middle task conditions was omitted from this analysis as it deviated very little
from that in the initial condition. As reflected in Table 22, ninth graders and
college subjects who attempted evidence generation were almost always successful in demonstrating covariation; subjects of the other three age groups often
were not. As the percentages at the bottom of Table 22 reflect, differences in
successful demonstration of covariation by belief condition (subject's theory vs.

Table 22

Number and Percentage of Subjects Correctly Generating Covariation Evidence
for Subject's Theory (S) and Other's Theory (O) in Two Task Conditions

Group	Initial		Two balls	
	S	O	S	O
Third graders	19 (95%)	13 (76%)	10 (53%)	9 (56%)
Sixth graders	20 (100%)	17 (89%)	12 (71%)	11 (73%)
Ninth graders	19 (95%)	19 (100%)	20 (100%)	15 (100%)
Noncollege adults	15 (75%)	16 (94%)	9 (56%)	11 (73%)
College adults	20 (100%)	19 (100%)	18 (95%)	15 (94%)
Total	93 (93%)	84 (92%)	69 (76%)	61 (79%)

Note. Percentages are of those attempting evidence generation.

other's theory) were negligible; differences in subject frequencies by belief condition in Table 22 therefore are attributable to differences in numbers of subjects who attempted evidence generation. Percentages at the bottom of the table also reflect the greater difficulty subjects experienced in showing covariation for the appropriate variable in the two-balls condition. Statistical analysis of frequencies of subjects successfully demonstrating covariation between variable and outcome for initial and two-balls task conditions showed a significant effect of age group, $F(4, 95) = 5.91$, $p \leq .001$; a significant effect of task condition, $F(1, 95) = 38.62$, $p \leq .001$; a nonsignificant effect of belief condition; and no significant interactions. Of all demonstrations of covariation between variable and outcome, about 20% reflected less than perfect covariation. This percentage varied only slightly across age groups and conditions, from a low of 3% for college subjects in the fewest-balls condition to a high of 24% for third graders in the initial condition. In examining their explanations, we gain some insight into the factors that led to imperfect covariation in the evidence subjects generated.

The next issue to consider in assessing the quality of the evidence that subjects generated is the extent to which the three variables not involved in the demonstration were controlled. In Table 23 appear the numbers of subjects who generated completely controlled evidence, that is, evidence in which no other variable covaried with outcome other than the variable that was the focus of the demonstration. As reflected in Table 23, achievement of control varies sharply as a function of task condition and age group. (The other-balls condition is omitted due to its reduced sample size and the similarity of performance to that in the initial condition.) In the initial condition, third graders appear almost as skilled at controlling variables as college subjects. Once they were asked to constrain their evidence sets, however, all subjects except college students showed a decline in control, with the decline most pronounced among third graders.

Table 23

Number and Percentage of Subjects Controlling Other Variables
for Subject's Theory (S) and Other's Theory (O) in Three Task Conditions

Group	Initial		Fewest balls		Two balls	
	S	O	S	O	S	O
Third graders	13 (68%)	9 (69%)	2 (14%)	2 (18%)	0 (00%)	1 (11%)
Sixth graders	11 (55%)	13 (76%)	7 (41%)	6 (35%)	7 (58%)	5 (45%)
Ninth graders	11 (58%)	15 (79%)	7 (41%)	13 (76%)	10 (50%)	13 (87%)
Noncollege adults	9 (60%)	13 (81%)	4 (36%)	7 (70%)	3 (33%)	8 (73%)
College adults	15 (75%)	17 (89%)	13 (72%)	11 (73%)	16 (89%)	15 (100%)
Total	59 (63%)	67 (80%)	33 (43%)	39 (56%)	36 (52%)	42 (69%)

Note. Percentages are of those generating covariation evidence.

Statistical analysis of the data in Table 23 showed no effect of belief condition; an effect of task condition, $F(2, 190) = 28.26, p \leq .001$; an effect of age group, $F(4, 95) = 4.50, p \leq .001$; and a significant interaction between age and task, $F(8, 190) = 2.68, p = .008$. (Subjects achieving complete control were compared to all remaining subjects in this analysis.) Though ninth graders and noncollege adults tended to do better in the other's-theory belief condition, overall effect of belief condition did not reach significance.

Related to these data on achievement of control are the results of the multiple-evidence problems administered at the end of the evidence evaluation segment of the interview. In one of the two problems, the subject was asked to choose which of two evidence sets presented by the interviewer provided a better demonstration of the correctness of the theory, one a completely controlled demonstration and the other a completely uncontrolled demonstration (all four variables covaried with outcome). Choices revealed little recognition of the superiority of the controlled evidence, except among college subjects. Of 20 college subjects, 16 chose the controlled demonstration for subject's theory, and 17 of 20 did so for other's theory. Among other subject groups, choice of the controlled demonstration was at no greater than chance level. Interestingly, though, there was some suggestion that the inferiority of the uncontrolled demonstration is recognized with respect to a theory that is believed false before it is recognized with respect to a theory that is believed true: A total of 15 subjects preferred the controlled demonstration only for other's theory, compared to 6 subjects who preferred it only for subject's theory. The results for the multiple-evidence covariation problem suggest that the apparently substantial degree of control that noncollege subjects appear to have attained in the initial evidence generation condition (Table 23) is not the result of intentional efforts to achieve control, for few of these subjects recognized the superiority of a controlled demonstration. Instead, the apparently high degree of control in this condition is most likely attributable to the fact that all or nearly all of the balls were often used in the initial condition, especially among younger subjects. (More than half of third and sixth graders and almost half of the noncollege adults used between 14 and 16 balls.) In such cases, when the balls are sorted as to outcome based on one variable, even distribution is automatically obtained with respect to all other variables (as each unique combination of variables is represented by a single ball in the set of 16). Thus, performance under the subsequent, constrained conditions provides a more accurate picture of ability to control variables.

Explanations

Subjects were asked to justify each set of evidence they generated, in response to the question, "Can you explain how this proves that (*variable*) makes (doesn't make) a difference?" The most immediately apparent and striking feature of these explanations was the frequency with which they were theory based rather than evidence based. This feature is made especially noteworthy by the fact that, except for third graders, subjects' responses in the evidence evaluation task were almost always evidence based, as we reported in Chapter 8. Frequencies of theory-based, mixed (both theory-based and evidence-based explanations given), and evidence-based responses are reported in Table 24 for subjects who successfully generated covariation evidence in the initial task condition. Data for the remaining task conditions are comparable and are not reported. As reflected in Table 24, only college subjects differed from the others in showing a minimum of theory-based responding. Among other groups, over half of the subjects made no reference to the evidence in their explanations, and well over half failed to make exclusive reference to the evidence. Statistical analysis of the data in Table 24, based on exhibition of any evidence-based responding (either exclusive or

Table 24

Number and Percentage of Subjects Showing Evidence-Based, Theory-Based, and Mixed Explanations in Initial Task Condition

Group	Subject's theory (S)			Other's theory (O)		
	Theory based	Mixed	Evidence based	Theory based	Mixed	Evidence based
Third graders	12 (63%)	3 (16%)	4 (21%)	7 (54%)	4 (31%)	2 (15%)
Sixth graders	11 (55%)	4 (20%)	5 (25%)	10 (59%)	3 (18%)	4 (24%)
Ninth graders	11 (58%)	3 (16%)	5 (26%)	12 (63%)	3 (16%)	4 (21%)
Noncollege adults	10 (67%)	1 (07%)	4 (26%)	9 (56%)	4 (25%)	3 (19%)
College adults	1 (05%)	4 (20%)	15 (75%)	2 (11%)	0 (00%)	17 (89%)
Total	45 (48%)	15 (16%)	33 (35%)	40 (48%)	14 (17%)	30 (36%)

Note. Percentages are of those generating covariation evidence.

mixed), showed only an effect of age group, $F(4, 95) = 14.66$, $p \leq .001$, with post hoc analysis showing only the college group differing from all other groups.

Particularly notable about the high proportion of theory-based responding reflected in Table 24 is the fact that it occurred as often when subjects were generating evidence for a theory they believed false (other's theory) as it did when subjects were generating evidence for a theory they believed true (subject's theory). The latter instances were fairly straightforward. Lorraine, for example, the ninth grader quoted in Chapter 9, placed eight smooth balls in the *Good* basket and eight rough balls in the *Bad* basket as evidence for her theory that texture makes a difference. When asked to explain how this shows that texture makes a difference, she responded:

> The rough texture will make the ball heavier so it won't go so far when hit.

In other words, she justified not why she had chosen this particular arrangement of balls but why the relationship reflected in this arrangement was a theoretically sensible one. We can assume that it is her lack of a firm differentiation between theory and evidence that prevented her from acknowledging explicitly the meaning of covariation evidence, though she obviously had some appreciation of its meaning.

The instances in which the subject is generating evidence to demonstrate the correctness of a theory he or she does not believe true are quite different. In these cases the subject's theoretical belief conflicts with the evidence that has been generated (if the subject has correctly demonstrated covariation between variable and outcome), which might lead us to predict that theoretical considerations would be set aside in explaining how this covariation evidence demonstrated the relationship between variable and outcome, as the subject does not believe such a relationship exists and thus presumably has no theory that would account for such a relationship. Instead, and quite strikingly, we find that subjects of all age groups except college often construct such a theory and use it as the basis for explaining why the covariation evidence that has been generated is plausible, in the same way as does the subject quoted above. It is worthwhile to present several examples.

Melissa, a ninth grader, initially declined to generate evidence demonstrating correctness of other's theory, in this case the theory that color was causally related to outcome:

> I would say that either of them would come out good.

The interviewer repeated the task instructions, in response to which Melissa correctly placed eight light-colored balls in the *Bad* basket and eight dark-colored balls in the *Good* basket. She was then asked to justify this arrangement.

> (Can you explain how this proves that color makes a difference?) These [dark in *Good* basket] are more visible in the air. You could see them better.

Melissa, strikingly, turned to this theory to explain the covariation evidence she had generated even though she had just previously voiced the theory that color makes no difference. Though this immediate juxtaposition of the two opposing theories was unusual, subjects often exhibited this need to explain why the evidence they had just generated was plausible or sensible, even though they had produced the evidence in response to an explicit instruction to generate evidence supporting an opposing theory and not as evidence that they believed to be true. In other words, they were unwilling to generate evidence without having a compatible theory in place.

The next example is somewhat different and also instructive, as the subject managed to keep both his own theory and the newly constructed opposing theory intact, by stipulating the range of conditions under which each applies. John, a noncollege adult, was asked to demonstrate the correctness of other's theory color. Before placing any balls in the baskets, he said:

> All right. If you're playing at nighttime and you have lights, the dark ones ain't gonna work. The light ones will work. (Can you show me which balls you would use?) Again, for the daytime it doesn't make any difference. For the nighttime it does make a difference, even if you have spotlights. [Subject then placed one light-colored ball in the *Bad* basket and one dark-colored ball in the *Good* basket.] (Can you explain how this proves that color makes a difference?) Again in the night a light ball you got a good chance of seeing it and a nice chance of returning the serve. With the dark ball, even with the spotlight, it ain't gonna work.

Interestingly, to anticipate results from the next section on noncovariation evidence, when John was then asked to generate evidence showing the color theory wrong, he did so without difficulty and resorted to his original theory to explain his arrangement of balls, without including the special circumstances of nighttime play:

> (Can you explain how this proves that color does not make a difference?) Like I said, in the daytime it doesn't matter. Use both balls in the day. It doesn't make a difference.

Unlike the cases categorized as theory based in Table 24, those categorized as mixed typically did not involve construction of a new theory to fit the evidence that had been generated. Instead, the subject's original theory coexisted in an uneasy relationship with the subject's evidence-based explanation of the generated evidence. Lorraine, the ninth grader quoted above, again provides an example. In response to the request to demonstrate the correctness of other's theory color, she began with the comment:

> One pile has to be light, the other dark. [She then placed two light balls and two dark balls in the *Good* basket and two light balls and two dark balls in the *Bad* basket, thus demonstrating noncovariation rather than covariation.] (Can you explain how this proves that color makes a difference?) It doesn't show it, because I varied it! I put lights and darks together. (Can you arrange the balls to prove that color does make a difference?) [She then placed two light balls in the *Bad* basket and two dark balls in the *Good* basket.] (Can you explain how this proves that

color makes a difference?) It still proves nothing, because color doesn't make a difference. Unless each color varies with the material made [i.e., covaries with the texture variable, which the subject believed effective]. The dark would be good and the light would be bad. Dark came out good and light came out bad, so dark are better.

Thus, though she eventually produced a correct demonstration and evidence-based explanation, it is clear that the implausibility of the theory from her perspective constituted a serious obstacle to achieving this goal.

Examination of subjects' explanations revealed another major respect in which theoretical beliefs influenced ability to generate evidence. Many of the subjects' explanations indicated that their aim was not just to demonstrate that the variable in question had an effect on outcome but to demonstrate that all of the variables the subject believed effective had an effect on outcome. In other words, subjects arranged the balls in the way they thought they ought to appear if their theories with respect to all four variables were correct. As a result, the subject typically placed in the *Good* basket only those balls that had the desirable characteristics with respect to all variables the subject believed effective. Sometimes, as well, the subject restricted placement in the *Bad* basket to those balls that had only undesirable characteristics. For example, Warren, a ninth grader, in the initial task condition used only two balls to demonstrate the correctness of his preferred theory, size. His justification was as follows.

Because this one is big and has ridges and is a bright color. This one [in the *Bad* basket] is small and very unseeable to the person.

Another subject, Randall, also a ninth grader, used all 16 balls, but his intent was similar.

The light colored would be better. [Subject placed two light-colored balls in *Good* basket and all others in *Bad* basket.] (Can you explain how this proves that color makes a difference?) These [in *Bad* basket] are not smooth and have no ridges.

The example of Warren suggests why, in their evidence generation, subjects often failed to achieve control of other variables. Similarly, the example of Randall suggests why they may have failed to produce perfect covariation between the focal variable and outcome. Among subjects whose demonstrations reflected lack of control and/or imperfect covariation, roughly half manifested in their explanations some intent to demonstrate the effects of variables other than the focal one, but this intent of course may have been operating in the case of other subjects who did not reveal it in their explanations. Evidence of this intent also suggests why many subjects achieved more control in generating evidence for other's theory than for subject's theory (Table 23): In generating evidence to support a theory that is the subject's own, the subject is more likely to expand that theory into a global theory that incorporates all the variables the subject believes effective. When asked to generate evidence to demonstrate the effectiveness of a variable the subject does not believe effective (other's theory), in contrast, subjects are more likely to confine their focus to that single variable.

Certainty

One final set of results suggests the influence of theory on evidence generation. After each arrangement and explanation, the subject was asked to indicate on a 10-point scale how sure he or she was that the evidence generated proved that the variable in question makes (or does not make) a difference. Subjects overall reported high certainty. While there were no age group effects, certainty ratings were higher for subject's theory than they were for other's theory. Means were 8.8 and 7.0 (for subject's and other's theory respectively) in the initial condition, 8.2 and 7.4 in the fewest-balls condition, and 8.0 and 7.4 in the two-balls condition. (The other-balls condition was omitted due to reduced sample size.) This difference was significant in the initial condition, $F(1, 87) = 18.32$, $p \leq .001$, and in the fewest balls condition, $F(1, 63) = 4.75$, $p \leq .05$, and approached significance in the two-balls condition. Examination of subject's explanations of their certainty ratings suggested that these differences were a result of subjects' confusion of certainty regarding the theory and certainty regarding the evidence. This response of Maria, a noncollege adult, illustrates:

> I'm not too sure [that this evidence proves it], because I don't know if it's true that texture makes a difference.

Failures and Refusals

Before concluding this section, some mention should be made of subjects' explanations of their refusals or failed attempts to generate covariation evidence, for these provide some insight into the factors responsible for subjects' weaknesses overall. As reflected in Table 21, failed attempts to generate covariation evidence occurred mostly in the two-balls condition, where the constraint of using only two balls often led subjects to overlook the need to demonstrate covariation of variable and outcome that they had successfully demonstrated in the earlier conditions. Most often, this error took the form of placement of two balls with the positive level of the focal variable in the *Good* basket, to demonstrate that they both produced a good outcome, without recognition that failure to include any balls with the negative level of the variable fails to establish a relation between variable and outcome. Other subjects failed to vary the focal variable due to their preoccupation with demonstrating other aspects of their global theories, as described earlier, or due to their resistance to demonstrating covariation for a variable they did not believe causal. For example, Freda, a noncollege adult, had no trouble demonstrating covariation to show the correctness of the theory she believed true. In the case of the opposing theory, color in her case, she placed both light- and dark-colored balls in the *Good* basket and offered this explanation:

> It would make a difference because one is light and one is dark. (How does this show that color makes a difference?) Because one is lighter and one is darker and both came out good.

The nine subjects who in the initial condition refused to generate evidence refused only in the other's theory condition. They had no difficulties in generating covariation evidence to demonstrate the correctness of a theory they believed true. In subsequent task conditions, in contrast, the constraints imposed by the task condition became a factor, as described earlier. In the case of the initial condition, the explanations for these refusals were like the following response of a noncollege adult, Lisa.

> What about if you don't choose nothing? I don't think color matters. (Interviewer repeated instruction.) My God, I don't want to choose anything, cause color doesn't matter to me. (You couldn't show it?) No, it's just a color.

Or the subject sometimes invoked the opposing theory that he or she believed true, as illustrated by a third grader, Carrie:

> [Subject rapidly placed all 16 balls in the *Bad* basket]. (Can you explain how this shows that ridges make a difference?) Ridges don't make a difference. (Interviewer repeated instruction.) It doesn't make a difference. It really doesn't. It has to go by the size. (Could you show how the balls should look if ridges *did* make a difference?) No.

Or, finally, worth quoting is the striking response of a college subject, Marion, who clearly had not resolved her efforts to incorporate the realm of subjectivity (a topic we return to in Chapter 12):

> [Following extended deliberation] No. (You can't show how the balls should look to prove that ridges make a difference?) Not really. (Why not?) Because I think it's psychological. (What do you mean?) If you say to yourself ridges will make a difference then it will, but if you say it won't then it won't. (And what are you telling yourself?) I'm saying that it won't make a difference. That's why. (So why can't you do it exactly?) Because I have this set thought. If I say ridges will make a difference and if I did it that way, I would unconsciously do it that way, but right now I feel it doesn't make a difference because when you asked me I felt it didn't. (Could you show it for another person?) No, but, I'll keep trying even though I know I would be trying really hard without really feeling it. That's how I really feel.

Generation of Noncovariation Evidence

As in the generation of covariation evidence to demonstrate the correctness of a causal theory, not all subjects were willing to attempt the generation of evidence to demonstrate the incorrectness of a causal theory. Presented in Table 25 are the numbers of subjects who attempted generation of evidence to demonstrate a theory wrong, by age group, belief condition, and task condition

Table 25

Numbers of Subjects Attempting to Generate Noncovariation Evidence
for Subject's Theory (S) and Other's Theory (O) in Each Task Condition

Group	Initial		Other balls		Fewest balls		Two balls	
	S	O	S	O	S	O	S	O
Third graders	17	19	7	7	15	18	15	18
Sixth graders	19	20	8	6	17	19	16	19
Ninth graders	20	20	13	14	14	14	15	16
Noncollege adults	18	20	12	9	15	14	15	19
College adults	20	20	17	18	14	18	12	11
Total	94	99	57	54	75	83	73	83

(parallel to the presentation in Table 21 for generation of evidence to demonstrate a theory correct). Comparison of the two tables indicates their similarity. Refusals were overall more frequent when the evidence to be generated conflicted with the subject's theoretical belief (subject's theory condition in this case, since the theory was to be demonstrated wrong). Attempts dropped to only slightly over half in the other-balls task condition but then returned to roughly the 80% level in the two remaining conditions, except for college students, almost half of whom were unwilling to generate two-ball evidence. Statistical analysis showed an effect only of task condition, $F(3, 285) = 36.92$, $p \le .001$. Mean number of balls used was 11.5 in the initial condition, 9.4 in the other-balls condition, 5.3 in the fewest-balls condition, and of course 2.0 in the two-balls condition. These means did not differ significantly across age group or belief condition, except for an age-group effect in the initial condition, $F(4, 88) = 3.72$, $p = .01$, with ninth graders using fewer balls than other subjects.

Of subjects who attempted evidence generation, not all were successful in showing noncovariation between variable and outcome. Presented in Table 26 are the numbers and percentages (of those subjects attempting evidence generation) of subjects who successfully demonstrated noncovariation, by age group, belief condition, and task condition. The other-balls task condition is omitted due to the reduced sample size and comparability of the results to those in the initial condition. Omitted from the frequencies reported in Table 26 are subjects whose arrangements of balls actually reflected less than perfect covariation for the focal variable but whose explanations made it clear that the intent underlying the arrangement was otherwise and that the noncovariation pattern was an unintentional byproduct of the intended strategy. These other strategies are considered shortly.

Noncovariation evidence could be of three types: (1) a selection of balls of a single variable level distributed across two outcomes, (2) a selection of balls of both levels of the variable yielding the same outcome, and (3) a combination of

Table 26

Number and Percentage of Subjects Correctly Generating Noncovariation Evidence
for Subject's Theory (S) and Other's Theory (O) in Three Task Conditions

Group	Initial		Fewest balls		Two balls	
	S	O	S	O	S	O
Third graders	10 (58%)	13 (69%)	7 (47%)	11 (61%)	5 (33%)	8 (44%)
Sixth graders	11 (58%)	18 (90%)	11 (65%)	16 (84%)	7 (44%)	14 (74%)
Ninth graders	15 (75%)	17 (85%)	12 (86%)	11 (79%)	12 (80%)	10 (63%)
Noncollege adults	11 (61%)	13 (65%)	8 (53%)	8 (57%)	7 (47%)	10 (52%)
College adults	19 (95%)	18 (90%)	12 (86%)	17 (94%)	10 (83%)	10 (91%)
Total	66 (70%)	79 (80%)	50 (67%)	63 (76%)	41 (56%)	52 (63%)

Note. Percentages are of those attempting evidence generation.

the two preceding types, that is, a selection of balls of both levels of the variable
distributed across both outcomes. Only the second and third types of evidence,
of course, constitute conclusive evidence of the absence of relation between
variable and outcome, since the first type does not include a manipulation of the
variable to assess its effect. Among the subjects shown in Table 26 who
demonstrated noncovariation, a majority (92% over all subjects and conditions)
produced demonstrations of the second or third type. This percentage did not
differ significantly across subject groups or conditions. Interestingly, however,
when subjects were asked in the multiple-evidence noncovariation problem (see
method above) to choose between an inconclusive and conclusive demonstration,
only college subjects consistently regarded the conclusive demonstration as
preferable (17 of 20 subjects in the subject's theory condition and 18 of 20 in the
other's theory condition). Other groups showed no consistent preference.

Statistical analysis of the data in Table 26 showed significant effects of task
condition and belief condition and an effect of age group just below significance:
For age group, $F(4, 95) = 2.29$, $p = .065$; for task, $F(2, 190) = 27.91$,
$p \leq .001$; for belief, $F(1, 95) = 8.44$, $p = .004$. Older subjects were more likely
to demonstrate noncovariation, and subjects were more likely to demonstrate
noncovariation when it was consistent with their theoretical beliefs (other's
theory condition), an effect that did not appear in the generation of covariation
evidence. Comparable to what was found in the case of control in the
demonstration of covariation evidence (Table 23), performance declined as task
constraints increased: Subjects were less likely to demonstrate noncovariation
using only two balls than they were when the number of balls was unconstrained,
and performance in the fewest-balls condition was intermediate between the two.

Explanations

Not all subjects who generated noncovariation evidence were able to produce
appropriate explanations of how the arrangement showed that the variable in

question did not make a difference. Of those subjects who made any reference to the evidence, virtually all made at least some minimal reference to noncovariation, either the occurrence of multiple outcomes with a single variable level or more often the occurrence of both variable levels with a single outcome, depending on the form of noncovariation evidence the subject had produced (see above). A typical evidence-based explanation, for example, was this one given by a sixth grader:

> I guess I'd put all [16] of them in there [*Good* basket] if it makes no difference. That means all of them are the correct size. It doesn't matter.

The percentages of subjects (of those who generated noncovariation evidence) whose explanations made at least some reference to the evidence in the initial task condition were 88% in the subject's theory condition and 89% in the other's theory condition. These percentages remained roughly comparable in the remaining task conditions and are substantially higher than those reported in the preceding section for generation of covariation evidence. The remaining subjects gave exclusively theory-based explanations. As in the case of generation of covariation evidence reported in the previous section, theory-based responding (whether used exclusively or in conjunction with an evidence-based response) was most frequent among younger subjects and rare among college subjects.

Also as for covariation evidence, theory-based responding occurred almost as frequently when the evidence to be generated was contradictory to the subject's beliefs (subject's theory condition in this case, since the evidence was disconfirming the theory) as it did when the evidence was compatible with the subject's beliefs (other's theory condition). In the latter case, the subject already held the theoretical belief that the variable in question was not causal. In justifying an arrangement of balls that reflected noncovariation, the subject substituted an explanation of why this noncovariation was correct theoretically for an explanation of how this arrangement of balls demonstrated a lack of relationship between variable and outcome, exemplifying the same confusion between theory and evidence that was illustrated in the preceding section on generation of covariation evidence. For example, Fred, a noncollege adult, after placing balls in the two baskets, gave this explanation:

> (Can you explain how this proves that color does not make a difference?) Because if a person's eyesight is very good, and they would be able to see the ball, then color doesn't matter.

Theory-based responses also occurred, however, in the condition in which the subject was asked to generate evidence to show that the theory the subject believed true was incorrect (subject's theory condition). In this case the subject constructed a new noncausal theory, compatible with the evidence that he or she had generated. For example, a third grader, Allen, quoted in Chapter 9, had just previously expressed the theory that size makes a difference. When asked to generate evidence to show that size does not make a difference, he placed two large, smooth balls without ridges, one dark- and one light-colored, in the *Good* basket and two large rough balls, one with ridges and one without and one dark- and one light-colored, in the *Bad* basket.

> (Can you explain how this proves that size does not make a difference?) The results show that size doesn't matter because it would still bounce and you would still hit it.

Another subject, Carl, a noncollege adult, gave a mixed theory-based and evidence-based explanation. Though he was perfectly capable of providing an explanation based on the evidence, and did so, he added a theory-based qualification that enabled him to retain his original theory. To show that texture makes no difference, he placed two rough, large balls and one smooth, small ball (all dark-colored without ridges) in the *Good* basket and two smooth balls, both light-colored without ridges, one large and one small, in the *Bad* basket.

> (Can you explain how this shows that texture does not make a difference?) It wouldn't have to come out any particular way. (Can you explain what you mean?) Because here [*Good* basket] you have rough and smooth. It wouldn't make a difference. All depending on the game you were playing. In some cases it would make a difference, in others it wouldn't.

Failed Attempts to Generate Noncovariation Evidence

Shown in Table 26 are the numbers of subjects who correctly generated noncovariation evidence to demonstrate the incorrectness of a causal theory. What of the remaining subjects who attempted the task but did not generate noncovariation evidence? These subjects all produced covariation evidence of one sort or another. Three types of strategies were identified. They occurred in roughly the same proportions across task conditions and across age groups, except for college subjects, who showed little use of any incorrect strategies.

Inverse Covariation. The first type, which occurred in 40% of failed attempts, was to disconfirm a causal theory by showing that variable and outcome were related but in a direction opposite to that predicted by the causal theory. For example, Stuart, a sixth grader, theorized ridges to be causal with their presence associated with a *Good* outcome. When asked to generate evidence to demonstrate that ridges do not make a difference, he placed six balls with ridges and three balls without ridges in the *Bad* basket and two balls with ridges and five balls without ridges in the *Good* basket.

> (Can you explain how this shows that ridges do not make a difference?) Because there's more ridges in the bad serve than in the good serve. (What does that show?) That ridges don't make a difference.

In the case of the other's theory condition, in which the subject's own belief was noncausal, this strategy occurred equally often. In this case the subject simply produced covariation evidence in the direction opposite to the direction in which it had been produced in the preceding problem, in which the subject had been asked to generate evidence to show the variable did make a difference. These cases are interesting in that the subject's own professed theory is that the variable makes no difference and yet the subject fails to generate any evidence that supports this theory.

Covariation for Another Variable. Subjects exhibiting this strategy (25% of all failed attempts cases) likewise showed no awareness of the existence or significance of a noncovariation pattern of evidence. Instead, they undertook to demonstrate that the variable in question did not make a difference by demonstrating that another variable did, typically one of the variables held to be causal in their own global theory. For example, Calvin, a third grader, when asked to generate evidence to prove that size makes no difference, placed all eight balls with rough texture in the *Good* basket and all eight balls with smooth texture in the *Bad* basket.

(Can you explain how this shows that size does not make a difference?) They're better to catch, these [rough-textured balls in *Good* basket]. I still think these are better. You said size didn't matter. (Can you explain how this shows that size does not make a difference?) Because these [in *Good* basket] are easier to catch.

Covariation for a Focal Variable. In the remaining cases (35% of all failed attempts), the subject produced for the variable in question covariation rather than noncovariation evidence—typically no different from the covariation evidence generated earlier to show that the variable did make a difference. In some cases, the subject's reluctance to generate evidence counter to his or her own beliefs was clearly an obstacle. For example, Jean, a noncollege adult, to demonstrate that texture does not make a difference, placed one smooth ball in the *Good* basket and one rough ball in the *Bad* basket.

(Can you explain how this shows that texture does not make a difference?) I think it [texture] really does make a difference. (Interviewer repeated instruction.) The texture makes no difference because of the balance. I could weigh these two and the rough ball is gonna be a little bit heavier because of the ridges.

The generation of covariation evidence to demonstrate the correctness of a noncausal theory, however, was equally frequent when the subject did not believe the variable to be causal, suggesting that a major difficulty for subjects in both cases may have been the generation of noncovariation evidence per se.

Certainty

Results of subjects' certainty ratings follow the same pattern as those reported for generation of covariation evidence. Subjects reported greater certainty that the evidence that had been generated proved that the variable in question does not make a difference when what was being demonstrated accorded with their theoretical beliefs (other's theory condition in this case), and the same confusions of certainty regarding the theory and certainty regarding the evidence were evident in subjects' explanations for their certainty ratings. Means (based on the 10-point certainty scale) were 7.6 and 9.0 (for subject's and other's theory respectively) in the initial condition, 7.8 and 8.4 in the fewest-balls condition, and 8.0 and 8.0 in the two-balls condition. (The other-balls condition was omitted due to reduced sample size.) Effect of belief condition reached statistical significance only in the initial condition, $F(1, 88) = 10.96$, $p \leq .001$. In the two-balls condition, there was an age-group effect, $F(4, 60) = 5.01$, $p \leq .001$, with college subjects less certain (mean of 6.0 in both belief conditions) than other groups that the theory could be proved correct using just two balls.

Refusals

Those subjects who refused to generate evidence to demonstrate a theory wrong (see Table 25) exhibited in their explanations the same difficulties described previously: If the subject believed the theory correct, the subject had difficulty in generating evidence counter to this theory, as illustrated by Lisa's and Carrie's explanations of their refusals in the section on covariation evidence. The explanations of other subjects, in both belief conditions, suggested that their difficulties lay in the generation of noncovariation evidence per se, similar to the difficulties described above that were experienced by those subjects who attempted but failed to produce noncovariation evidence. In addition, consonant with the decline in certainty reported above, college subjects showed a sharp increase in refusals in the two-balls condition. In explaining their refusals, these subjects tended either to claim that a minimum of four balls was necessary, to demonstrate the occurrence of both outcomes with each variable level, or to claim that the result for two balls could have been due to chance and required replication.

GENERAL DISCUSSION

In the discussion at the end of Chapter 9, we described a variety of respects in which subjects' performance in the evidence evaluation problems reflected limitations in their understanding of covariation and noncovariation evidence. Their performance in problems that required them to generate the two kinds of evidence reflects similar limitations. Subjects had less difficulty generating covariation evidence to demonstrate the correctness of a causal theory than they did generating noncovariation evidence to demonstrate the incorrectness of a causal theory. Yet, in the attempt to generate covariation evidence, younger subjects and noncollege adults sometimes generated evidence that included only a single variable level. This lack of recognition of the fact that variation in both variables is required to demonstrate their relationship is the same lack of recognition observed in responses to the evidence evaluation problems and discussed in Chapter 8. The major source of error in the generation of covariation evidence, however, was the failure to recognize the potential effects of other variables and the need to control them in order to produce a valid demonstration.

The difficulties subjects exhibited in generating noncovariation evidence were more pronounced and more varied. While over 90% of subjects succeeded in generating covariation evidence, in the case of noncovariation evidence, only the college group reached that level of performance, and the percentage for other groups averaged only about two thirds. Subjects who failed to produce a noncovariation pattern of evidence produced patterns such as an inverse covariation or the covariation of a different variable with outcome—patterns reflecting fundamental misconceptions regarding the evidence that indicates absence of a causal relationship. This difference in skill in dealing with the two kinds of evidence is consistent with that observed in the case of evidence evaluation, as described in earlier chapters. The results taken together indicate that both the generation and the interpretation of noncovariation evidence pose challenges, particularly for younger subjects, that the generation and interpretation of covariation evidence do not.

The performance of ninth graders in the evidence generation problems was inferior to that of college subjects in most critical respects. Ninth graders successfully generated noncovariation evidence less frequently than did college subjects and in generating covariation evidence, controlled variables less often than did college subjects. In the evidence evaluation problems, in contrast, performance of ninth graders equaled that of college subjects, suggesting that, at this age level at least, generation of noncovariation evidence poses difficulties that evaluation of this same evidence does not. In both evidence generation and evidence evaluation, however, performance of noncollege adults was consistently below that of both college subjects and ninth graders, suggesting the important role in performance played by experience, in particular academic experience.

The other major respect in which the results reported in the present chapter are consonant with those reported in Part II and in the preceding chapters of Part III is in their demonstration of the influence of theoretical belief. Subjects had greater success in generating evidence compatible with their own theoretical beliefs than they did in generating evidence incompatible with those beliefs. They also exhibited in their explanations of the evidence they had generated a tendency to justify not why this particular arrangement of balls had been selected but why the relationship (or lack of relationship) reflected in this arrangement was theoretically sensible. This tendency was very prevalent when the theory that would justify the generated evidence was a causal one and less so when the theory was noncausal (a difference that did not appear in the evaluation, as opposed to generation, of evidence, either in Study 4 or in the studies reported earlier), presumably because causal theories were more salient. These theory-based responses to questions about evidence reflect the same confusion between the two that was common in response to evidence evaluation questions in the studies reported in Part II but less common in evidence evaluation problems in Study 4, reported in the two preceding chapters. Evidently, as we noted in Chapter 8, the Study 4 evidence evaluation procedure (in which the subject was asked explicitly to compare two theories with respect to the bearing the evidence had on each) was successful in focusing the subject's attention on the evidence (except for third graders, who continued to show a high level of theory-based responding). In the evidence generation problems, in contrast, the subject is dealing only with a single theory and the relation of evidence to it. Though performance improved when evidence was generated to disconfirm a theory, this procedure evidently does not promote differentiation of theory and evidence and the focusing of attention on the evidence in the effective way that the Study 4 evidence evaluation procedure does, and only college subjects consistently referred to the evidence. The lesser degree of focus on the evidence in the evidence generation problems is paradoxical, since in the evidence generation case subjects have actually produced the evidence, which one might predict would serve to focus their attention on it. Evidently, however, it is not the surface involvement provided by construction of the evidence itself that is effective but rather the challenge (and potential contradictions) inherent in the subject's examining that evidence as an element in two different relationships (to the two opposing theories involved in the evidence evaluation problems).

In their explanations of the evidence they had generated, many subjects confirmed their inability to confine their focus to the single variable that was the subject of the demonstration. Instead, they undertook to demonstrate the correctness of their own theoretical beliefs with respect to all of the variables present, especially when the evidence to be generated for the focal variable was compatible with their own theoretical beliefs. This failure to set aside or temporarily bracket one's own theories regarding other variables in order to demonstrate a relationship (or lack of relationship) between a focal variable and outcome, thereby compromising the demonstration, parallels the difficulties we observed in the chapters on evidence evaluation, in which subjects were unable to set aside their own theoretical beliefs to evaluate what the evidence would mean for the theory were it the only basis for making a judgment.

The other phenomenon we encountered that links directly to what was observed in evidence evaluation performance was the willingness to construct a new compatible theory in conjunction with the generation of evidence contradictory to the subject's original theory. The phenomenon is not precisely the same in the evaluation and generation situations since in the latter it could be argued that the subject does not explicitly claim as his or her own the theory being espoused to justify the evidence. Yet, what such a subject is unable to say is, "This is the way the evidence should look if this theory is correct, though you have given me no reason to think that the theory is correct." In both the evidence evaluation and evidence generation cases, subjects exhibited the need to maintain theory and evidence in alignment with one another. Both this and the phenomena described in the two preceding paragraphs, we would claim, reflect weaknesses in ability to differentiate and coordinate theory and evidence.

Finally, we should establish a connection between the present results and the literature on formal operations, in particular isolation of variables. At the end of Chapter 4, we suggested that poor performance in isolation-of-variables tasks, which has been assumed to be due to lack of appropriate experimentation strategies, may be at least partly due as well to problems in the interpretation of evidence once it has been generated, particularly noncovariation evidence. In a similar vein, we suggest that failure to employ an experimentation strategy in which all variables are controlled may not be due to inattention to the effects of these other variables, as typically has been assumed. To the contrary, it may be *overattention* to these other variables, that is, the failure to focus attention on the single variable whose effect is to be assessed, that leads to lack of control. In other words, the subject is not able to set aside the agenda created by his or her own theoretical beliefs in order to perform the test that is required. If this interpretation is correct, it constitutes but one example of a broad range of ways in which theoretical belief compromises both generation and evaluation of evidence.

11

THE DEVELOPMENT OF
SKILLS IN COORDINATING
THEORY AND EVIDENCE

In this chapter we examine change that occurs in subjects' thinking skills as they engage over a period of several months in repeated encounters with problems that require the coordination of theories and evidence. The question of the nature of the change process is one we have not addressed until now and, indeed, is one that until recently has received a relatively small share of research attention given its importance. During the 1960s and 1970s, those empirical studies in developmental psychology that did concern themselves with the change process virtually all adhered to the training study paradigm. A training experience hypothesized to induce the cognitive competency under consideration is administered to half of a group of subjects whose pretest performance indicated absence of this competency. All subjects are then reassessed, and the posttest performance of those subjects exposed to the training is compared to the posttest performance of those not exposed.

The fact that use of the training study method declined sharply after only a decade or two of popularity is suggestive of its limitations. The most telling evidence against the training study method is probably the fact that training study research has not served to constrain theories of the change process. After hundreds of training studies devoted to concepts of conservation, theories of how conservation develops remain as numerous and varied as they were before conservation training studies were undertaken. The major problem with the training study method is that, even when training is successful, no assurance exists that the process by which the competency was achieved in the experimental setting is anything like the process in terms of which that competency develops naturally. Indicative of this limitation is the fact that the data from training studies are confined to subjects' performance on pretest and posttest assessments, with attention rarely being paid to the nature of the subject's experience during the training period itself.

The object of a series of studies by Kuhn and Phelps (1982) was to examine the change process itself. Fourth and fifth grade subjects engaged in repeated encounters with problems that required scientific thinking skills resembling those investigated in the present volume. The object was to increase subjects' exercise of existing cognitive strategies beyond the level at which it would occur normally. Underlying the approach is the premise that such exercise is sufficient to lead at least some subjects to modify their strategies, providing the researcher the opportunity to observe the process of change. Content of the problems subjects encountered was chemical reactions (either color change or formation of a precipitate). Subjects were asked to plan, carry out, and interpret their own experiments, in order to determine which elements of a mixture played a causal role in producing the chemical reaction. Subjects encountered a new problem of this form once each week over a period of 3 months. No instruction or guidance was provided as to what form the subject's experiments should take or how results of the experiments should be interpreted. Nor was any feedback given with respect to the strategies the subject chose to use. The only feedback the subject received was thus the feedback from his or her own actions on the materials. The interviewer did, however, ask a variety of questions, the purpose of which was to promote exercise of the subject's existing cognitive strategies, for example, ''What are you going to find out by trying it these ways?'' ''How do you think it will come out?'' ''Why do you think it will come out that way (following experimentation) ?'' ''What do you think about how it came out?'' ''What did you find out from doing this experiment?''

Cognitive exercise of this sort proved sufficient to lead to change for a majority of subjects. One of Kuhn and Phelps's major observations regarding this change was that a subject's performance over time was variable, with the skill or insight manifested at one session not necessarily being maintained at a later session or even later in the same session. Overall progressive change nevertheless occurred. The dominant pattern of change observed was one marked by the period of variable performance just mentioned followed by eventual stabilization at the more advanced level. A few subjects, however, did not adhere to this dominant change pattern and, instead, exhibited a more abrupt transition from a less advanced to a more advanced skill level. For all subjects, the greatest challenge appeared to lie not in mastering the more advanced skill but in abandoning the less advanced skill that was being replaced, a reversal of the way in which development is typically conceived.

Almost all of the subjects in these studies early in the series of sessions showed at least occasional use of the more advanced strategies they would eventually apply consistently. If these superior strategies were within their competence, why did it take subjects so long to achieve consistent use of them? The answer Kuhn and Phelps proposed is that during the period of exercise subjects not only were perfecting use of the more advanced strategies (which they did not always apply correctly), but also were gaining in metacognitive knowledge about both more and less advanced strategies. If subjects were doing no more than gaining practice in the application of a set of strategies to a problem, Kuhn and Phelps (1982) argued, strategy use would remain relatively constant, rather than change. As we noted in in Chapter 2, "metastrategic" knowledge about what strategies are effective for a given problem is at least as important as strategic knowledge of how to execute effective or ineffective strategies. It entails an understanding of why the advanced strategy provides a more efficient or more correct approach to the problem, what its range of application is, why all other strategies are less efficient or incorrect, and what errors they lead to. In comparison to knowledge of the first type, knowledge of how to execute a strategies, which is largely ascertainable from the surface features of the performance—knowledge of this second type is subtle and complex (Kuhn, 1983). In order to know that a strategy is the best one for solving a particular problem, one must understand the strategy, understand the problem, and understand how the strategy and the problem intersect or map onto one another. As we discuss further in Chapter 13, it is the absence of such knowledge that is responsible for the common failures of generalization following training interventions: The subject learns the strategy in the particular context in which it is taught but fails to apply it subsequently in other contexts in which it is equally appropriate. Until such knowledge was secure, Kuhn and Phelps (1982) claimed, their subjects were unlikely to discard the less advanced, incorrect strategies.

In recent years, attention has turned increasingly to the question of the mechanisms in terms of which development occurs, and a number of researchers have begun to use what might be given the general label of *microgenetic* methods for studying the process of change. These studies may entail a period of observation ranging from a single session to a year, and they differ in a number of other ways as well. But they have in common the researcher's objective of learning about the nature of the change process by careful observation of it as it takes place. The focus of the present volume is on the identification and description of scientific thinking skills, and not on the mechanisms in terms of which they develop. We nevertheless have included the small-scale study of change processes reported in this chapter because of the insight we believe that an examination of patterns of change is likely to provide into the nature of the skills themselves.

The research reported in this chapter is similar in intent and design to the Kuhn and Phelps (1982) studies. Fifth- and sixth-grade subjects participated in weekly individual sessions during which they encountered the same evidence generation and evidence evaluation tasks involved in Study 4. Also included in each session was a more open-ended task similar in structure to the chemicals problems designed by Kuhn and Phelps. In this task, designed by Leona Schauble, the subject was asked to explore a microworld of race cars, presented on a microcomputer, and to determine how the various features of the cars affect the distance they travel in test runs along a racetrack. The cars varied on five dimensions, four dichotomous, two of which had no effect on outcome and two of which had an interactive effect, and one trichotomous, which had a curvilinear effect. These relations did not vary, and subjects' knowledge of the microworld thus accumulated over the series of sessions. A second, matched group of subjects worked on the race cars problem each week but were presented the evidence generation and evaluation (balls) problems only at the initial and final sessions. The intent underlying the design was to examine how subjects learned about the race car microworld and how specific skills in evidence generation and evaluation (particularly those that may have shown development during the research period) influenced this process. Because this study as a whole goes beyond the scope of the present volume, only the data pertaining to the evidence generation and evaluation (balls) problems is presented in this chapter.

STUDY 5 METHOD

Subjects

Subjects were 20 students from a mixed fifth- and sixth-grade classroom in an urban parochial school in a working-class neighborhood. Median age was 10 years, 11 months, with a range from 8 years, 10 months to 12 years, 1 month. There were 7 girls and 13 boys.

Procedure

Each of the 10 subjects in what we term the experimental group was presented the balls problems once per week over a series of 9 weeks. The remaining 10 subjects, who made up the control group, were presented the balls problems only at the initial and final (ninth) sessions. The same interviewer administered the balls problems at the initial and final sessions. Two other interviewers conducted the intervening balls problem sessions for experimental subjects, with the same interviewer working with a given subject throughout.

Evidence evaluation problems presented at each session were identical to those presented in Study 4, except that the latter two insufficient evidence problems (Problems 1c and 1d, described in Chapter 8) were omitted and in their place were substituted two problems in which variable and outcome covaried perfectly. (Study 4, recall, did not include any perfect covariation problems, as these had been examined in the studies presented in Part II.) The second of the two perfect covariation problems was of a new form, not previously examined, in which the covariation of variable and outcome was in the direction opposite of that predicted by the subject's theory. This problem was added as a result of our observation based on Study 4 evidence generation data that subjects had difficulty distinguishing inverse covariation and noncovariation. This led to the prediction that subjects might have difficulty in recognizing covariation if it was not in the direction predicted by their theoretical beliefs and would confuse this inverse covariation with noncovariation.

The asymmetric evidence evaluation problems (Problems 4a–4d) were omitted for all subjects, and the unequal evidence problems (Problems 3a–3d) were included only at the initial and final sessions. Multiple-evidence problems were not included. Only the first (unconstrained) and last (two-balls) task conditions for the evidence generation problems were included. The entire set of problems, then, consisted of: generation of evidence to show theory correct, generation of evidence to show theory incorrect, evaluation of insufficient evidence (Problems 1a and 1b), evaluation of theory-consistent and theory-inconsistent covariation evidence (Problems 2a and 2b), evaluation of mixed (5/1, 4/2, and 3/3) evidence (Problems 2c–e), and evaluation of unequal (4/2 versus 3/3 and 5/1 versus 4/2) evidence (Problems 3a–d). Order of presentation within the mixed- and unequal-evidence problems was varied across sessions, but presentation order was otherwise held constant. Each session lasted from 30 to a maximum of 45 min.

Interview Format

The format and interviewer's questions at the first and final sessions were exactly as described for Study 4. In the intervening (second through eighth) sessions, the interviewer posed a variety of additional questions. The purpose of these questions was to encourage the subject to think further about the problem, to extend the application of existing strategies, and to consider new possibilities that resulted. A general set of questions used throughout the session, for example, drew the subject's attention to those aspects of the evidence that the subject had ignored. If the subject's response addressed only balls in the *Good* basket, the interviewer asked, "What about these balls over here in the *Bad* basket? What do they have to do with it?" If the subject's response dealt only with balls of a single variable level, the interviewer asked, "What about the other kind of balls, the small ones? How did [would] they come out?" (The particular variables and variable levels referred to in this and subsequent quotations are arbitrary and chosen merely for illustration.) If the subject's response dealt only with balls that were consistent with the subject's interpretation of the evidence, the interviewer asked, "What about these other large balls that didn't come out good? What do they have to do with it?"

Another general technique was to extend to the other variable (or theory) the same strategy the subject had exhibited but used only in a theory-consistent way. This extension was presented in the context of a hypothetical "other person" whose suggestion reflected extension of the strategy. For example, in both the insufficient-evidence and equal-evidence covariation problems, subjects frequently made inclusion inferences for their theoretically preferred variable but failed to make the same inference for the other variable, though the evidence for the two was identical. In these cases, the interviewer said, "Another person thought that Ms. S was right, because the ball[s] that came out good is [are] large. What do you think of that person's idea?" Once a subject began to apply the inclusion inference uniformly for both variables, the interviewer included questions aimed at getting the subject to recognize the indeterminacy, in other words, that inclusion in fact can be inferred for neither variable. A question the interviewer typically asked was, "Does the evidence coming out this way settle the argument [between Ms. S and Ms. C]?" Often, at either the same or the next session the interviewer went on to ask, "What *caused* these balls in the *Good* basket to come out good [or, alternatively, balls in the *Bad* basket to come out bad]?" If necessary, the interviewer added, "Another person thought that it was the color that caused them to come out good. What do you think of that person's idea?" After each of the preceding questions, the interviewer typically asked, "Is there another ball or balls that could be tested that would settle the argument [or that would show what caused the balls in the *Good* basket to come out good]?" If the subject indicated a ball that would correctly unconfound the two variables, the interviewer asked, "How would Ms. S expect this ball to come out? How would Ms. C expect it to come out?"

A similar set of questions was asked in the evidence generation problems when the subject generated confounded covariation evidence. The interviewer said, "Another person thought that the size is what's making them come out different. What do you think of that person's idea?" To promote the subject's recognition of the insufficiency in the insufficient evidence problems, the interviewer asked (in the case, for example, in which only large balls had been tested), "How would a small one come out?" If this did not lead the subject to recognize the insufficiency, the interviewer then added, "Another person thought that it might come out just as good. What do you think of that person's idea?" These same questions were asked when the subject generated insufficient evidence intended to show covariation—evidence that included only a single variable level. If insufficient evidence was generated to show noncovariation (e.g., two small balls, one with good and one with bad outcome), the second question took the form "Another person thought that the large balls might always come out good."

To promote recognition of the possibility of covariation in dual directions (both theory consistent and theory inconsistent), when the subject misinterpreted covariation in one of the directions as noncovariation, the interviewer referred to another person who "thought this evidence shows that size *does* make a difference but that small, not large, balls work better." To promote the interpretation of mixed evidence when the subject interpreted any mixed evidence as indicating noncovariation, the interviewer asked, "Does this evidence suggest that large balls usually work better or small ones?"

More problematic were cases in which the subject failed to see any evidence as indicating noncovariation and hence exclusion. Such subjects most often interpret noncovariation evidence as indicating that the theory is "both right and wrong, because three [of the type in question] came out good and three came out bad." To recognize exclusion, the subject must resist interpreting each instance of evidence individually and look for a broader pattern across instances, and it was not obvious what sort of questions would encourage the subject to do this. One that was tried was to ask the subject whose inferences were always of the "both right and wrong" or "half right" sort, "How would the balls look if the theory was *totally wrong?*" Rather than leading to a recognition of exclusion, this question often produced the generation of covariation evidence in the opposite direction, in which case the interviewer proceeded to the line of questioning indicated in the preceding paragraph.

The wording of all of the interviewer's probes described in the preceding paragraphs is approximate and meant to convey only the general nature of the interviewer's questionning. Exact wording varied from session to session. The interviewer made intuitive judgments as to whether or not to probe a particular incorrect response. Typically, no more than two or three responses were followed by probes at any one session. No probes occurred before the third session, and none were used at the final session. Because the time available for each session was limited to 45 min, it was occasionally necessary to omit some of the evidence evaluation problems when the questioning with regard to some of the problems proved fruitful and as a result consumed more time than average. The particular evidence evaluation problems omitted alternated across sessions, so that no problem was omitted over two sessions in a row. The typically less time consuming evidence generation problems were never omitted.

The standard procedure of selecting one variable the subject believed causal and one the subject believed noncausal as variables for the evidence generation and evidence evaluation problems was not always followed in the intervening (second through eighth) sessions. Instead, for several of these sessions, pairs of variables were selected both of which the subject believed causal or both of which the subject believed noncausal. The purpose was to remove discrepant theoretical belief as an additional challenge, permitting the subject a greater opportunity to focus on correct evidence generation and evaluation skills themselves. Only later in the series of sessions was belief variation reintroduced.

STUDY 5 RESULTS

Subjects' progress across the sessions was assessed in terms of 25 specific skills entailed in the problems subjects engaged in, 15 pertaining to evidence evaluation and 10 to evidence generation. They appear by name in the left-hand side of Table 27. With the exception of Skill 7, all of these have been examined in detail in the preceding chapters and are organized here in list form only to facilitate presentation of the present data. In parentheses next to each of the evidence evaluation skills (1–15) are the numbers of the particular evidence evaluation problems on which assessment of the skill is based. In the right-hand side of Table 27, the progress of one subject, Randy, is charted. After providing some necessary explanations regarding the skills themselves and the notation used, we examine Randy's performance across the sessions.

The columns in Table 27 each represent one of the nine sessions. A circle in the cell representing a particular skill and session indicates that the subject displayed the skill at that session. Only subjects' responses before introduction of any of the interviewer's probes (described above) were considered in making this assessment. For all skills except those dealing with use of evidence-based reasoning and avoidance of theory bias (Skills 3, 4, 8, 9, 11–14, 19–20, and 24–25), a skill was counted as displayed if it ever appeared in the subject's responses to the problems indicated. Use of evidence-based reasoning and avoidance of theory bias, in contrast, were counted as displayed only if the subject displayed them consistently, that is, made some reference to the evidence in response to each of the problems indicated (though theory-based reasoning could appear in addition) and never exhibited theory bias. A pair of parentheses in the cell indicates that there was no opportunity to assess the skill at that session. Parentheses appear for all theory bias skills (4, 9, 12, 14, 20, and 25) for Sessions 3–6 in Table 27, as theoretical belief for the two variables did not differ at those sessions, as explained above. Parentheses appear for all unequal evidence skills (13–15) for Sessions 2–7, as the unequal evidence problems were omitted from all except first and last sessions for all subjects, as noted earlier. Other parentheses occur because the relevant problem was omitted from that session due to time constraints. Parentheses around a circle indicate that the skill was assumed to be present. This designation arose for two sequences of skills that were substitutive rather than additive in nature, one for the generation of covariation evidence and the other for the generation of noncovariation evidence. These skills are marked with asterisks in Table 27. In each case the skill appearing later in the list replaces the one immediately preceding it, so that the earlier one does not actually appear if the later one is exhibited. Finally, it should be noted that Skills 11–15 overlap, as Problems 3a and 3b are unequal evidence problems but also involve noncovariation evidence.

Table 27

Randy's Progress across Sessions

Skill	S1	S2	S3	S4	S5	S6	S7	S8	S9
Evaluation									
1. Recognizes insufficiency of single-ball ev. (problem 1a)	0						0	0	0
2. Recognizes insufficiency of single-var. ev. (problem 1b)	0						0	0	0
3. Evidence-based evals. of insufficient ev. (problems 1a and 1b)	0		0	0	( )	0	0	0	0
4. Avoids theory bias in eval. of insufficient ev. (problems 1a and 1b)			( )	( )	0	( )	0	0	0
5. Recognizes indeterminacy w/ mult. covariates (problems 2a-2d)			0	0	0		0	0	0
6. Recognizes inverse covariation (problem 2b)				( )	( )				
7. Recognizes less than perfect covariation (problems 2c and 2d)	0	0	0	( )	0	0	0	0	0
8. Evidence-based evals. of covariation (problems 2a-2d)		0	0	0	0	0	0	0	0
9. Avoids theory bias in eval. of covariation ev. (problems 2a-2d)			( )	( )	( )	( )	0	0	0
10. Exclusion inf. based on noncovariation ev. (problems 2e, 3a, and 3b)									
11. Evidence-based evals. of noncovariation ev. (problems 2e, 3a, and 3b)			0	0	0	0	0	0	0
12. Avoids theory-bias in eval. of noncov. ev. (problems 2e, 3a, and 3b)		( )	( )	( )	( )	( )	( )	( )	0
13. Evidence-based evals. of unequal ev. (problems 3a-3d)		( )	( )	( )	( )	( )	( )	( )	0
14. Avoids theory bias in eval. of unequal ev. (problems 3a-3d)		( )	( )	( )	( )	( )	( )	( )	0
15. Recognizes relative degrees of covariation (problems 3c and 3d)		( )	( )	( )	( )	( )	( )	( )	
Generation									
16. *Imperfect covariation ev.	(0)	(0)	0	(0)	(0)	(0)	(0)	(0)	(0)
17. Perfect covariation ev.	0	0	0	0	0	0	0	0	0
18. Controlled covariation ev.			0	0	0	0	0	0	
19. Evidence-based expls. of covariation ev.			0	0	0	0	0	0	0
20. Avoids theory bias in gener. of cov. ev.		0	( )	( )	0	0	0	0	0
21. *Single-variable-level noncov. ev.	(0)	(0)	(0)	(0)	(0)	(0)	(0)	(0)	(0)
22. *Imperfect dual-variable-level noncov. ev.	0	(0)	(0)	(0)	0	(0)	(0)	(0)	(0)
23. Perfect dual-variable-level noncov. ev.		0	0	0	0	0	0	0	0
24. Evidence-based expls. of noncov. ev.		0	0	0	0	0	0	0	0
25. Avoids theory bias in gener. of noncov. ev.			( )	( )	( )	( )	0	0	0

Note. See text for explanation of symbols.

Randy, the subject whose progress is charted in Table 27, was a subject in the experimental group. He was 11 years, 8 months old at the beginning of the sessions and in the sixth grade. Like most subjects, he showed a fair degree of consistency in his theoretical beliefs across the series of sessions. At the first session, he cited texture as causal and the most important variable, with smooth balls yielding the good outcome. Rough-textured balls, Randy explained, would be likely "to get tangled up in the racket." The texture variable remained causal and most important over all the sessions. The ridges variable Randy always cited as noncausal and least important. "Ridges is just to get a grip on the ball," he explained. "It doesn't make a difference to the serve." His beliefs regarding the two middle-ranked variables showed some vacillation but were predominantly noncausal. Color he claimed to be causal at Sessions 1, 5, and 9, and "maybe" at Session 8. At these sessions, he explained that the light color was inferior as it would be hard to see on a sunny day "because it matches the color of the [day]light." At the remaining sessions, Randy indicated that color made no difference. Size he claimed to be causal only at Sessions 6 and 9, claiming that the big balls "would be easier to see and easier to hit." At the remaining sessions, he asserted that size made no difference.

Texture and ridges were the two variables Randy was asked to consider at Sessions 1 and 2. At Sessions 3, 4, and 5, two noncausal variables were examined (color and size at Sessions 3 and 4, and size and ridges at Session 5). At Session 6, two causal variables were examined (texture and size), and at Session 7, the combination returned to one causal and one noncausal variable (texture and color at Session 7 and texture and ridges at Sessions 8 and 9).

Inspection of the first column on the right side of Table 27 indicates that, like most of the Study 5 subjects, Randy displayed only a minority of the skills at the initial session. By the final session, however, he exhibited almost all of them. What form did this change take? Consider first Randy's evaluation of insufficient evidence (Skills 1–4). It is not a typical case, as at the initial session he clearly exhibited Skill 1, rejecting the single-ball evidence as insufficient with respect to either theory:

> (Do these results help more to show that one person is right. . . ?) No, because they only tested one ball. You can't really tell. Because sometimes you have to test the others.

When the six-ball insufficient evidence was presented (four smooth, ridged balls in the *Good* basket and two smooth, ridged balls in the *Bad* basket), however, his responses with respect to the two theories diverged:

> (Do these results help more to show that one person is right. . . ?) It shows that texture makes the difference, because more of these [smooth] balls came out right. Only two came out bad. (Do these results prove that Mr. T is right?) Just sort of shows it. (What do these results have to say about Mr. R's view?) Well, I don't know, because the test needs other balls.

Though the interviewer did not confirm explicitly that it was nonridged balls that

Randy believed needed to be tested, Randy was assessed as having shown some recognition of the insufficiency of both the one-ball and six-ball evidence (Table 27) and also as having made consistent evidence-based responses (Skill 3). He did not, however, avoid theory bias (Skill 4), as the preceding response indicates.

At the beginning of Session 2, Randy's focus became much more theory based, and any recognition of the insufficiency of the evidence disappeared. He evaluated both the one-ball and six-ball evidence as indicating that the texture theory was correct and the ridge theory incorrect, citing his theories in both cases as the basis for his judgments. At Session 3, the theories Randy was questioned about shifted to color and size, and his responses both became evidence based and, since he believed both variables noncausal, did not exhibit any bias. Yet, no recognition of the insufficiency of the evidence reappeared. He regarded both the one-ball and the six-ball evidence as proving both the color and the size theories correct. At Session 4, his responses were comparable.

At Session 5 (in which both theories, size and ridges, were again believed noncausal), after a similar inclusion responses to the one-ball evidence (a large, ridged ball) for both theories, the interviewer first introduced a probe raising the possibility of insufficiency:

> (So the fact that this large, ridged ball came out good proves that both Mr. S and Mr. R are right?) Yes. (Suppose another person said, "You know, I don't think either of you are right, because how do you know that this small ball without ridges might not come out just as good?") Well, they'd say we'd have to test both balls now. (Why?) Because they didn't really test both of them. So they can't really say it came out good. They'd have to test it. (And if they'd only tested this one ball and couldn't test any more, what would we know then?) I'm not sure. (Would we know whether Mr. S's or Mr. R's theories were right?) Not really.

The six-ball evidence was omitted at Session 5. At Session 6 (in which both theories, texture and size, were now causal), Randy showed no recognition of the insufficiency of the evidence and again made inclusion responses for both theories for both the one-ball and six-ball problems. The interviewer again introduced a probe:

> [One-ball evidence:] (Suppose Mr. S said to Mr. T, "You're wrong, because I think this rough ball would come out just as good.") If they were selling this as a tennis ball, the rough one would get tangled up in the tennis racket, unless they're using it for one of those ping pong tables. (But Mr. S and Mr. T are looking at what these results here show. And Mr. S is suggesting that Mr. T might not be right if the rough ball came out just as good as the smooth one. What's your opinion of this argument that he's making? Do you think it's a good argument?) No.

Though Randy was first diverted by theory-based reasoning, even when the interviewer directed his attention back to the evidence, he was unwilling to accept the argument.

Though Randy was at least superficially more receptive to the same suggestion after the six-ball evidence, he misconstrued the insufficiency concept in attempting to apply it to the texture theory and ended with a confusion between inverse covariation and noncovariation, seeing inverse covariation as the only evidence against the theory:

> (Suppose somebody came along and said, "You know, Mr. S, I don't think this shows that you're so right because we've got all these small balls over here [interviewer pointed to box containing remaining balls], and maybe if we tried those they would come out just as good." Would this be a good argument?) Yes. (Okay. Let's talk about Mr. T again. Can you tell me again, then, what these results say about Mr. T's view?) That he's right. Because he wouldn't want small to come out good. (Is there any argument you could make against Mr. T that would show he isn't right or that we don't know if he's right?) Maybe that somebody would come along and say the rough are just as good and would test them out and all the rough would come out good and only a couple smooth would come out good, and that would show Mr. T wrong. But in this case, it shows that he's right.

At Session 7 (in which the theories now varied, as they had at the initial sessions, with texture causal and color noncausal), Randy for the first time indicated the insufficiency of the one-ball evidence without any probe on the part of the interviewer:

> (Do these results help more to show that one person is right. . . ?) They should have tested more balls to tell if it makes a difference. (Why?) Cause they just tested one. One could've come out good or bad. They should have tested more balls to show how they came out.

But Randy did not extend this insight to the six-ball evidence. The evidence proved both theories correct, he claimed, because four of the six smooth, light-colored balls were in the *Good* basket. Though the theories now differed with respect to Randy's beliefs, bias in his evaluations did not reappear. The interviewer again introduced a probe, which Randy accepted:

> (What about dark-colored ones? How might they come out?) [No response.] (Suppose someone said just as good. Would they have a point?) Yes. Then Mr. C. . . . They should have tested the darks too. (And if they didn't?) They don't really know anything because he could test all dark and they all came out good and all light and they all came out good, and then there would be no way that Mr. C would be right or wrong. (And if they just tested the light ones?) It would show C right. But he hasn't tested any dark balls. (So is he right then?) Not actually, no. (Why not?) Because he needs to test the dark balls. Cause if he doesn't then if he was to put these balls in the court the people might want a different color ball. (Let's talk about Mr. T again. Do these results show he is right?) Not for sure because he hasn't tested any rough.

At Sessions 8 and 9 (in which the theories varied, with texture causal and ridges noncausal), Randy recognized the insufficiency without prompts by the interviewer for both one-ball and six-ball evidence, though in the Session 8 one-ball problem, he showed his reluctance to let go of the inclusion inference:

> Mr. T wanted smooth and Mr. R said having ridges was good, so they're both right. But I would have tested more balls. (Do we know for sure with just one?) No. Because you could test more balls and they might come out wrong. (If you tested just one, would you know they were right?) Yes, in a way, but you still have to test more balls.

His responses to the remaining problems were similar, and he noted in response to the Session 8 six-ball problem, "You can't tell. It's the same thing [as the one-ball case]; it's just that there's more balls."

Though Randy showed some recognition of the insufficiency of the one-ball and six-ball evidence at the very first session, his grasp of the concept was unstable across the sessions, and it is impossible to say with certainty that it was firmly in place at the final sessions. The situation is similar with respect to Randy's recognition of the indeterminacy of the covariation evidence, to which we now turn, though in this case he did not display any recognition initially. Randy had no problem in interpreting imperfect as well as perfect covariation as indicating inclusion (Skill 7), though at Session 1 he did not always give evidence-based responses and at Sessions 1 and 2 he exhibited theory bias, proclaiming the other theory either wrong or less right than his preferred theory despite the identical evidence. He continued to make inclusion inferences for both variables (without bias) at Sessions 3–5, after which, at Session 5, the interviewer first introduced a probe bearing on the indeterminacy, after the subject had evaluated the perfect covariation evidence (Problem 2a).

> (So you are saying then that both Mr. S and Mr. R are right?) Yes. (Do these results prove that they are both right?) Yes. (Can you explain why?) Because the [*Good*] balls both have ridges and are bigger. So it's the same. (So what can we tell, then?) We can't really say, but they *are* both right. (Suppose Mr. S said, "The reason these balls in the *Good* basket came out good is that they're big," and Mr. R said, "No, the reason these balls came out good is that they have ridges." Is there any way to settle the argument between them?) They could say the combination of ridges and size might help it to be more better. (Would they know for sure whether it was the combination of ridges and size, or just size, or just ridges that made them come out good?) No. The only way to know is to test the combination of the large size and the ridges.

After the 5/1 mixed covariation evidence problem (Problem 2c), the interviewer further probed the issue:

> They are both right but not so much because Mr. S has a small ball in the *Good* basket, and Mr. R has a nonridged ball in the *Good* basket. (So are they both equally right?) Yes. (Do these results prove that they are both right?) Yes. (Do you think the good balls came out good because they were big or because they were ridged? Mr. S might say it was because they were big, and Mr. R might say it was because they were ridged. What do you think?) If I was Mr. Size, I could like join up, because the bigger balls and the ridges are a nice combination, because they come out right like that. So they could like join companies. (Do we know for sure what's making the balls come out good?) No. (Is it because of the combination or . . .) (Randy interrupted) I think so because . . . (pause) . . . I can't really tell because they . . . (pause) . . . just have everything, and on the other side it comes out different, so you can't really tell. Mr. S thinks it's size and Mr. R thinks it's ridges, but if they put their balls together they'd probably be better. (Could we test another ball that would help us to decide who was right?) [Randy selected another large, ridged ball.] (If we tested this ball, would it settle the argument?) I'm not sure.

The same line of questioning was continued at Session 6 (Problem 2a):

(Did the ones in the *Good* basket come out good because they are big or because they are smooth?) I'd say if you have bad eyesight, then good because they're big. But if I didn't, then probably good because they're smooth. It all depends on how you test it. I could give it to somebody with bad eyesight and they tested it and forgot their glasses and it would be big.

Despite this intrusion of theoretical concerns and confusion between the tester's own preferences and his evaluation of evidence, in the remainder of his response to this same problem, Randy went on to achieve the unconfounding that had eluded him at the previous session:

(Do we know for sure if the ones in the *Good* basket are good because of their size or their texture?) No, we don't know for sure. (Why not?) Because we haven't tested the balls. And Mr. T, they tested the balls, so they say smooth came out good and Mr. S says big came out good, so they would be right. (Could we test another ball that would help us to decide who was right?) A big rough ball, to see if it is size or texture. (How would we find out?) Mr. T would expect it to be bad. Mr. S would expect it to be good. Actually, what they should do is get a big rough ball and test it with a big smooth ball and a small smooth ball . . . to see if it was size . . . or a little rough ball . . . to see if it was size or texture. And then it depends on how the test comes out to see who is right.

At Session 7, Randy indicated that both theories were proven right in response to the perfect covariation evidence (Problem 2a). But then in response to the 4/2 mixed covariation evidence, he for the first time acknowledged the indeterminacy before any interviewer probe:

(Do these results help more to show that Mr. T is right or Mr. C is right, or is there no difference?) You can't say. . . . Oh, yes I can. . . . No, you can't say. (Why not?) Both have equal in the baskets. There are four light-colored, rough ones in the good and two smooth, dark ones in the bad, so you can't tell who is right.

At Session 8 in response to the same problem, he gave a more elaborated explanation of the indeterminacy:

You don't know for sure because you haven't tested the right ball to show. This wouldn't tell because it could be about the ridges or the texture.

At Session 9 he gave a similar response. At Sessions 7–9, however, Randy's recognition of the indeterminacy occurred only in response to some of the covariation problems. For others at each session, he responded that the evidence showed both theories to be right. And, thus, in the cases of both the insufficiency and indeterminacy concepts, Randy's appreciation clearly increased, but we cannot regard either as firmly in place at the final session.

Other respects in which Randy clearly progressed from initial to final session were in his focus on the evidence (Skills 3, 8, 11, and 13) and his avoidance of theory bias. When the potential for theory bias was reintroduced at Session 7 (by including theories for which the subject's beliefs differed), biased evaluation did not reappear. An area in which there was no indication of progress, however, was in recognizing inverse covariation and distinguishing it from noncovariation

(Skill 6). When in Problem 2b, the interviewer simply moved all of the balls that had been in the *Good* basket (in Problem 2a) to the *Bad* basket and likewise moved the *Bad*-basket balls to the *Good* basket, Randy's responses were typical of many subjects. Instead of declaring both theories equally right, as he had in response to the initial (Problem 2a) covariation evidence, Randy (at Session 1) declared his preferred theory, texture, now to be wrong:

> You put them in the *Bad* basket! (Yes, suppose it came out that way.) Then Mr. R would be more right than Mr. T. (Why?) Because all these came out bad. They look okay. They tested them and they didn't come out right. It's not the ridges that make the difference. It's that . . . it's like. . . . I can't really explain. (You think Mr. R is more right?) Yeah. (Does it prove he's right?) Just sort of shows. (And Mr. T?) He is a little right, because I don't see what makes the difference between the ones like this [rough textured balls in *Good* basket]. . . . The strings might come off. My brother cuts the hair off his tennis ball.

It is clear that Randy regarded Mr. R as right only in relation to Mr. T, whom he saw as clearly wrong, and he was preoccupied with making sense theoretically of how the rough-textured balls could have come out good. In later sessions, he shifted to declaring both theories wrong when the contents of the baskets were switched.

Beginning at Session 3, the interviewer introduced probes describing, for example, a Mr. S who thought that size made a difference and that large were better and a Ms. S who thought that size made a difference but that small were better. Randy usually agreed that both could be right but then returned abruptly to the idea that

> in this case, he thinks large are better and they came out bad, so he's wrong. (So do the results show that size makes a difference?) No, it doesn't make a difference.

Randy's difficulty with inverse covariation is most likely linked to the difficulty he exhibited in understanding noncovariation, to which we now turn. If there is no concept of noncovariation in place, then the only pattern that "being wrong" can be associated with is inverse covariation. In fact, the closest Randy came to appreciating inverse covariation was in his efforts to interpret noncovariation evidence. He exhibited the characteristic "half right" or "partly right" interpretation of noncovariation. At Session 4, he evaluated the noncovariation evidence (Problem 2e) as follows:

> If he prefers big, then he's sorta right. Three wrong and three right. (And what if he prefers small?) He's still sorta right. Three of each ball are good.

At this point, the interviewer first introduced a probe:

> (So you think he's sort of right whether he thinks that large balls are better or he thinks that small balls are better. How would the balls look if he weren't right at all—if he were wrong?) If he wants small to be right, then all these [small balls would go] in there [*Bad* basket]. If he wants big to be right, then all these [large] in there [*Bad* basket].

At Session 5, Randy's response to the noncovariation evidence was similar. At session 6, in response to the interviewer's question "How would the balls look if the size theory were wrong?" Randy placed five small balls and one large ball in the *Good* basket.

> (Couldn't someone say that he was right if it looked like this, because most of the balls in the *Good* basket are small?) He could be right; he could be wrong. We don't know which he likes. (Can you show me how the balls would look if we knew for sure that he was wrong?)

After a fair bit of rearranging, taking balls in and out of the baskets, Randy ended with four large and four small balls in the *Good* basket. As an afterthought, he then placed two large and two small balls in the *Bad* basket.

> (What does this show?) It show that in both [baskets] they don't make a difference.

The interviewer then rearranged the balls into the original 3/3 pattern.

> (Remember this is how it was at first. What does this show?) It shows they are right and wrong. Equally right and equally wrong.

The preceding description well illustrates the resistance that many subjects showed to the concept of exclusion. At Session 7, Randy at first reiterated his original "half right" interpretation but then went on in response to the probe to give his first clear explanation of exclusion:

> Mr. C is half right because if he wanted light, three light came out good and if he wanted dark, three dark came out good. (Can you show me how the balls would look if we knew for sure that he was wrong?) [Randy placed five light and five dark balls in the *Good* basket.] (Why does this show he's wrong?) Because it shows that dark balls are as good as light balls. [The interviewer then rearranged the balls into the original 3/3 pattern.] (What does this show?) That he's wrong.

At the next session, however, in evaluating the noncovariation evidence Randy began to confuse exclusion and indeterminacy:

> It's the same [as the previous, 4/2 mixed-evidence problem]. You can't tell. You need a certain kind of ball, with ridges and rough. This shows you don't know who's right or wrong. (What do we know about ridges?) It doesn't make a difference. (What about texture?) It doesn't either. (Why not?) Because six rough and six smooth wouldn't show T or R wrong. You have to test a ball that has both qualities, both alike with ridges and rough texture. (What do these results show about ridges?) They don't make a difference. You need to test others to know. (Are you saying that you know that they don't make a difference or that you can't tell?) You can tell that ridges does not make a difference. (Can you explain how you can tell?) Because three of the ridged ones are good and three are bad. (And what about texture?) Same thing. Texture makes no difference, because there are three smooth in good and three in bad.

Though the exclusion at the end of this response is clear, at the final session Randy's confusion increased and the exclusion concept surfaced only fleetingly:

Well, I can't tell. Cause everything's equal in each basket. (What do these results say about Mr. T's theory?) Unless he thinks it's a coincidence that these came out right. . . . (Would you say he is right, or wrong, or can't you tell?) I would say I can't tell. (What about Mr. R?) Well, I would say Mr. R is . . . (long pause) . . . I would say that he's wrong. Well, I think he is, because these balls don't have ridges and they came out good. And these balls in the *Bad* basket have ridges and they came out bad. So I would say that the smooth texture helped them to come out good in the *Good* basket.

In other words, Randy sees Mr. R's wrongness as due to an inverse covariation between presence of ridges and good outcome. The three ridged balls in the *Good* basket that are exceptions to this inverse covariation, Randy explains away as attributable to the effects of another variable. The interviewer continued:

(So who is more right?) Mr T. Because this shows that the smooth texture helps the ball to come out good. (Do these results prove that for sure?) No. (Why not?) Because he could be wrong. He could be right. Cause I was just guessing, because it looks sort of like he's wrong. (Well, what do you think?) I'll go with my answer. (What about Mr. R?) I'm not certain. He could be more right than Mr. T. (How so?) Well, these balls came out good without the ridges, and this could show that the smooth balls and the ridges did not make a difference. (So what do you think?) I'll say they don't make a difference. (How does it show that neither one makes a difference?) Because there are three rough balls in the *Good* basket and three smooth with ridges in the *Good* basket. Same thing in the *Bad* basket. (So would you say that they are both equally right or equally wrong?) I'd say they're both equally right. (Why did you choose right instead of wrong?) Because you can't really tell if they are. (Before, you said that you thought texture did not make a difference. So is Mr. T right or wrong?) I don't know. (And Mr. R?) I don't know.

We have described Randy's performance in the evidence evaluation problems in some detail, in order to provide a sense of the unevenness that was characteristic of most subjects' performance. The summary provided in Table 27 does not adequately capture this unevenness, as it does not discriminate between cases in which the concept is exhibited barely at all during a session and cases in which it is exhibited much more consistently or clearly. We do not describe Randy's performance in the evidence generation problems in the same detail, because the picture is similar. After the first few sessions, he began to focus consistently on the evidence, and theory bias evident at the first session did not reappear. Like many subjects, Randy progressed from generating imperfect (mixed) evidence to generating perfect covariation or perfect noncovariation evidence as the best demonstrations that a theory was right or wrong. His control of other variables in demonstrations of covariation (Skill 18) was only intermittent, however. Especially notable is his consistent demonstration of perfect noncovariation, beginning at the second session, in light of the great difficulty we have just seen him to have in evaluating noncovariation evidence. Such apparent inconsistencies and anomalies across different areas of a subjects' performance were common, however, rather than exceptions. In Randy's case, it is relevant that the noncovariation evidence he produced always consisted of just 2 balls, one of each of the two levels of the variable, both of which yielded good outcomes. "Both of them came out good," he explained. The noncovariation evidence he was asked to evaluate, in contrast, consisted of 3 balls of each variable level in each basket, a total of 12 balls. This was a more complex array, certainly, based on which a noncovariation pattern had to be detected. But also, and perhaps more significant, there existed the temptation—one that Randy frequently succumbed to—of interpreting segments of this evidence in isolation rather than as part of an overall pattern.

In Tables 28 and 29 appear summaries of the performance of all 10 experimental and 10 control subjects. Each column in these two tables represents one subject, and the subjects appear from left to right in the order of their initial skill level. Although these summaries are based only on initial and final session performance and hence do not capture the variability characteristic of subjects' intervening performance, they provide an overall indication of the progress made with respect to various kinds of skills. A circle in the cell representing a particular subject and skill indicates that the subject displayed that skill at both the initial and final sessions. A triangle in the cell indicates that the subject displayed that skill at the final, but not the initial, session. A dash indicates that the skill was displayed at the initial but not the final session. Other conventions in depicting subjects' performance in these two tables remain as described for Table 27.

As Tables 28 and 29 reflect, the majority of both experimental and control subjects made overall progress, but progress was greater for experimental subjects. At the level of individual skills, however, there were exceptions to this generalization. One is Skill 5, recognition of indeterminacy, which only one experimental subject (Randy, the subject described above) and one control subject ever displayed spontaneously (i.e., not in response to the interviewer's probe). A second is Skill 15, relative inclusion, for which no practice problems were provided in intervening sessions and only two experimental subjects displayed at the final session. Another is Skill 6, recognition of inverse covariation, as initial level was by chance higher for experimental subjects.

Skill 7, recognition of less than perfect covariation, is an interesting case as there were only five instances in which experimental subjects displayed a skill initially but not at the final session (Table 28), and three of these five cases involved Skill 7. It can also be observed from Table 28 that the same three subjects who lost the ability to recognize imperfect covariation gained exclusion ability during this same period. This pattern of change supports the "overgeneralization" interpretation of the refusal to acknowledge covariation in mixed evidence that was suggested in Chapter 8. Once exclusion is achieved, subjects may overgeneralize it to all cases in which covariation between variable and outcome is less than perfect.

In ability to generate perfect covariation and perfect noncovariation evidence, control subjects showed as much progress overall as experimental subjects,

Table 28

Progress of Experimental Subjects

Skill	S3	S6	S10	S1	S2	S5	S7	S9	S8	S4
Evaluation										
1. Recognizes insufficiency of single-ball ev. (problem 1a)	△	△	△	0	△	△	△	△		0
2. Recognizes insufficiency of single-var. ev. (problem 1b)	△	△	△	0	△		0	△		0
3. Evidence-based evals. of insufficient ev. (problems 1a and 1b)		△	△	0	0	△	△	△	0	0
4. Avoids theory-bias in eval. of insufficient ev. (problems 1a and 1b)	△	△	△	△	0	△	△	△	0	0
5. Recognizes indeterminacy w/ mult. covariates (problems 2a-2d)				△						
6. Recognizes inverse covariation (problem 2b)	△	0	0	0	0	0	0	△	0	0
7. Recognizes less than perfect covariation (problems 2c and 2d)		0	–	△	0	–	–	△	0	0
8. Evidence-based evals. of covariation ev. (problems 2a-2d)		△	△	△		△	△	△	0	0
9. Avoids theory-bias in eval. of covariation ev. (problems 2a-2d)		△	△	△		△	△	△	0	0
10. Exclusion inf. based on noncovariation ev. (problems 2e, 3a, and 3b)	△	△	△	△	0	△	△	0		0
11. Evidence-based evals. of noncovariation ev. (problems 2e, 3a, and 3b)	△	△	0	△	△	△	△	0	0	0
12. Avoids theory-bias in eval. of noncov. ev. (problems 2e, 3a, and 3b)	△	△	△	△	△	△	△	0	0	0
13. Evidence-based evals. of unequal ev. (problems 3a-3d)	△	△	△	△	△	△	△	0	△	0
14. Avoids theory-bias in eval. of unequal ev. (problems 3a-3d)	△	△		△	△	△	△	0	△	0
15. Recognizes relative degrees of covariation (problems 3c and 3d)	△	△	△							
Generation										
16. *Imperfect covariation ev.	0	(0)	0	(0)	(0)	0	(0)	(0)	(0)	(0)
17. Perfect covariation ev.	△	△	△	0	0	△	0	0	0	0
18. Controlled covariation ev.	△	△	△	△		△	0	0	0	0
19. Evidence-based expls. of covariation ev.	△	△	△	△	△	△	△	△	0	0
20. Avoids theory bias in gener. of cov. ev.	0	△	△	0	△	0		0	0	0
21. *Single-variable-level noncov. ev.	(0)	(0)	(0)	(0)		(0)	(0)		(0)	(0)
22. *Imperfect dual-variable-level noncov. ev.	0	0	0	0		(0)	0		(0)	(0)
23. Perfect dual-variable-level noncov. ev.	△	△	△	△	△	0	0		–	–
24. Evidence-based expls. of noncov. ev.	△	△	△	△	△	0	△	△	0	0
25. Avoids theory bias in gener. of noncov. ev.	△	0	0	△	0	0	△	0	0	0

Note. See text for explanation of symbols.

Table 29

Progress of Control Subjects

Skill	S16	S11	S17	S19	S13	S18	S20	S14	S15	S12
Evaluation										
1. Recognizes insufficiency of single-ball ev. (problem 1a)	△			△			△		△	0
2. Recognizes insufficiency of single-var. ev. (problem 1b)	△		0	△			△	0	△	0
3. Evidence-based evals. of insufficient ev. (problems 1a and 1b)						△	△	0	△	0
4. Avoids theory-bias in eval. of insufficient ev. (problems 1a and 1b)			△			0	△	-	△	-
5. Recognizes indeterminacy w/ mult. covariates (problems 2a-2d)							-			
6. Recognizes inverse covariation (problem 2b)				△	△	0	0	△	0	0
7. Recognizes less than perfect covariation (problems 2c and 2d)				△	0	△	0	0		
8. Evidence-based evals. of covariation ev. (problems 2a-2d)					△	-	△	0		
9. Avoids theory-bias in eval. of covariation ev. (problems 2a-2d)			△							△
10. Exclusion inf. based on noncovariation ev. (problems 2e, 3a, and 3b)	△			0	△	△	△	0	0	△
11. Evidence-based evals. of noncovariation ev. (problems 2e, 3a, and 3b)	△		△	△		△	△		0	0
12. Avoids theory-bias in eval. of noncov. ev. (problems 2e, 3a, and 3b)			△			△				0
13. Evidence-based evals. of unequal ev. (problems 3a-3d)			△	△		△	△	0	0	0
14. Avoids theory-bias in eval. of unequal ev. (problems 3a-3d)			△			0				0
15. Recognizes relative degrees of covariation (problems 3c and 3d)									-	
Generation										
16. *Imperfect covariation ev.	0	△	(0)	0	0	0	(0)	(0)	(0)	(0)
17. Perfect covariation ev.	△		0	△	△	△	0	0	0	0
18. Controlled covariation ev.			0			△	-	0	0	0
19. Evidence-based expls. of covariation ev.		-	0	0	-	-	0	△	△	0
20. Avoids theory bias in gener. of cov. ev.		(0)		△	-	-	△	(0)	0	0
21. *Single-variable-level noncov. ev.	(0)	(0)		(0)	(0)	(0)	(0)	(0)	(0)	(0)
22. *Imperfect dual-variable-level noncov. ev.	-			0	0	0	0	-	0	0
23. Perfect dual-variable-level noncov. ev.		0	△	△	△	△	△	△	△	△
24. Evidence-based expls. of noncov. ev.		0	△	0	0		△	△	△	0
25. Avoids theory bias in gener. of noncov. ev.	-		0	0	0	-	-		-	0

Note. See text for explanation of symbols.

though only experimental subjects showed progress overall in control of variables in demonstrations of covariation. Finally, with respect to evidence-based responding and avoidance of theory bias, the pattern was the same across both evidence generation and evidence evaluation skills: Control subjects showed some progress overall in focus on the evidence, though less progress than experimental subjects, but only experimental subjects showed progress overall in avoiding theory bias.

DISCUSSION

The microgenetic investigation described in this chapter was not carried out on a large enough scale to permit any broad generalizations and is intended only to be illustrative. While the results show that subjects do make progress, the case study of Randy illustrates that this progress is anything but smooth and straightforward. More and less advanced strategies clearly coexisted in Randy's cognitive repertoire, and it was impossible to predict with certainty which would surface at any particular point.

Yet, gradually the more advanced strategies became more prevalent. Nor was the effect of the interviewer's questioning straightforward. The attempts on the part of the interviewer to get Randy to consider new possibilities sometimes seemed unsuccessful at the time they were made, and yet their influence became apparent several sessions later.

Though in this chapter we only examined subjects' progress in the balls problems, it should be kept in mind that all subjects had the opportunity to apply their skills in evidence generation and evidence evaluation each week to the less structured race cars problem described at the beginning of the chapter. This opportunity undoubtedly contributed to the progress shown by control subjects in the balls problems, but the specific exercise in generating and evaluating evidence regarding the balls that experimental subjects experienced each week enhanced their progress beyond that of control subjects.

At the level of specific skills, the results presented in this chapter suggest that with exercise, subjects typically make progress in skills of generating covariation and noncovariation evidence, in focusing their attention on the evidence, in recognizing insufficient evidence, in understanding inverse covariation, and in inferring exclusion from noncovariation. More difficult, however, was avoiding false inclusion, which is the chief impediment to understanding exclusion and recognizing the indeterminacy when multiple covariates are present. With respect to skill in coordinating evidence and theories, only the experimental subjects made overall progress in avoiding the biasing effects of their own theoretical beliefs on their evaluation and generation of evidence. This difference between experimental and control subjects is significant in that only in the balls problems, which the experimental subjects encountered each week, were subjects asked to coordinate the same body of evidence with contrasting theories. In the race cars microworld that control subjects investigated each week, the subject was not asked to evaluate evidence relative to particular theories, and the biasing effects of the subject's own beliefs on his or her generation and interpretation of experiments were not challenged by an interviewer's probes. These results support the conclusion drawn earlier based on Study 4 results: Exercise in relating the same body of evidence to contrasting theories plays a facilitative role in the development of skills in coordinating theory and evidence.

It should be emphasized that presentation of the Study 5 data in the form of sets of individual skills was intended only as an organizational vehicle and not meant to imply the view that these skills develop as discrete, independent entities, independent of one another. As Randy's case study showed, the various areas of skill development affected one another, sometimes in facilitative and other times in detrimental ways. They clearly did not, on the other hand, progress as an interrelated whole. Nor, it was equally clear, were we observing skills that emerged once and for all at a single point in time and remained firmly in place thereafter. As our current examination of Study 5 subjects' performance in the race cars problem is suggesting, when appearance of a skill eventually becomes consolidated within a specific context, the mastery of that skill in another context that might seem comparable is unlikely to appear automatically and more likely to entail a similar period of uneven performance and gradual development.

This discussion of our microgenetic examination of the skills investigated in this volume should conclude with the caution that the microgenetic study involved subjects of only a very small age range, an age range during which the skills being investigated are just beginning to develop naturally. It cannot be assumed that the results obtained with subjects of this age range will generalize to younger or older subjects. Based on the work with third graders in Studies 3 and 4, and in particular the difficulty they displayed in focusing attention on the evidence, we can assume that the method would have met with at best limited success with subjects of any younger age. With respect to older subjects, the earlier studies establish that many adults exhibit an initial level of performance no more advanced than that displayed by most of the Study 5 subjects. Whether their progress with exercise would be greater or less than that displayed by the fifth and sixth grade subjects in Study 5 is an empirical question. Predictions of greater and lesser amenability to change both seem plausible, and the answer may be particular to age, sex, educational, and socioeconomic groups. Though we cannot answer the question here, its significance is clear, and we return to the issues of mechanisms of change and the role of education in Chapter 13.

IV

THE CONNECTION OF THEORY AND EVIDENCE

Deanna Kuhn and Bonnie Leadbeater

12

THE INTERPRETATION
OF DIVERGENT EVIDENCE

The picture we have portrayed thus far is one of development progressing toward complete differentiation of theory and evidence— an end point of perfect objectivity in which theory and evidence are treated as totally independent entities, each preserving its own identity and boundaries while being evaluated against the other. In fact, however, virtually all modern philosophy of science rejects such a model, acknowledging if not emphasizing the complex interdependence of theory and evidence (Feyerabend, 1975; Hanson, 1958; T. Kuhn, 1962; Lakatos, 1970; Popper, 1965; Toulmin, 1953, 1961). That which is chosen for observation, the methods and tools of examination, and the interpretation of what is observed are all framed and influenced by theory of both the broad world-view and more local types.

In the research reported in this chapter, we asked whether subjects' thinking about theories and evidence develops toward a recognition of this interdependence. Our initial hypothesis was that such recognition, if it occurred at all, would be a late-developing phenomenon—that first a person would need to develop beyond the fusion of theory and evidence observed among our younger subjects to the differentiation and coordination of the two, before being able to connect them, in the sense of appreciating the subtle respects in which they are interdependent.

Our method for this investigation is in some sense the complement of the method used in Study 4, in which we presented subjects with two conflicting theories and asked them to relate these theories to a single body of evidence. In the present study, we presented the subject with two discrepant pieces of evidence regarding an event and asked the subject questions that probed his or her understanding of the nature of the discrepancy and how it might be reconciled. Rather than a simple physical event, for which the influence of theoretical perspective on interpretation of the phenomenon would be more subtle and difficult to appreciate, we chose to focus on a historical event, a war between two fictitious countries. This event was one in which the discrepancies could quite reasonably be attributed to the divergent theoretical perspectives of the authors of the two pieces of evidence—each a narrative account of the war. We asked subjects to give their own account of the war as well as asked them several questions that probed how they interpreted the two discrepant accounts of the war. Did they see the discrepancy as one that needed resolution, that is, did they believe that both accounts could not be right? Or did they see the two accounts as reflecting the differing theoretical perspectives of their authors and not necessarily requiring or capable of resolution? In other words, did they recognize an extent to which facts are relative to contexts of interpretation and the realms of fact and theory therefore interconnected?

STUDY 6 METHOD

Subjects

Subjects were 97 children, adolescents, and adults, equally representing both sexes and divided into five groups. There were 20 sixth graders with a median age of 11 years, 9 months (range 11, 4 to 12, 6); 18 were ninth graders with a median age of 14 years, 8 months (range 14, 6 to 15, 4); 20 were twelfth graders with a median age of 18 years, 2 months (range 17, 7 to 19, 0). These subjects came from a large suburban public school system in a middle- to upper-middle-class vicinity. Another 19 subjects were graduate students in education at a large urban university. Their median age was 30 (range 21 to 46). A final group of 20 nonstudent adults was recruited through personal contacts of the interviewer and was chosen to represent the general adult population. Their median age was 34 (range 29 to 42). Their educational backgrounds were more diverse and overall greater than those of the adults in the preceding studies: 2 had high school diplomas, 8 had some college, 4 a college degree, and 6 had done graduate work.

Procedure

The subject was invited to follow along on a written script as the following two accounts of the Fifth Livian War were read by the interviewer:

A BRIEF ACCOUNT OF THE FIFTH LIVIAN WAR
BY J. ABDUL
NATIONAL HISTORIAN OF NORTH LIVIA

On July 19th, 1878, during a period set aside by North Livia to honor one of their national leaders, the ceremonies were interrupted by a sneak attack from the South Livians, beginning the Fifth Livian War. Because the North Livians were caught by surprise, they were unprepared at first and the South Livians won a few early battles. But then the tide turned heavily in favor of the North Livians. Before the North Livians could reach a final victory, however, a neighboring large country intervened to prevent further bloodshed.

Despite their early setbacks, the later sweeping victories of the North Livians showed that they would have won, had the fighting continued. As a result of this war, the South Livians finally recognized that anything they gained from the North Livians would have to be worked out through peaceful negotiations. Thus ended the Livian Wars.

A BRIEF ACCOUNT OF THE FIFTH LIVIAN WAR
BY M. IVAN
NATIONAL HISTORIAN OF SOUTH LIVIA

In the last war, North Livia had beaten South Livia, taken some of its land, and refused to leave. South Livia could no longer tolerate this situation and spent large sums of public funds to strengthen its military defenses. On July 20th, 1878, the Fifth Livian War began. The war took place with rapid, dramatic victories for South Livia, resulting in great national celebration. After these dramatic victories, the South Livians suffered some minor losses. But then a neighboring large country intervened to prevent further bloodshed.

Despite their later setbacks, the final victory of South Livia seemed assured because of its overall position of strength. As a result of this war, the South Livians felt a new self-respect. They had always felt embarrassed by their previous defeats but now they had proven that they were the equals of the North Livians on the battlefield. Because the South Livians had achieved military respect, they were willing to work out future differences through peaceful negotiations, thus ending the Livian Wars.

Order of presentation of the two accounts was counterbalanced across subjects. The two printed sheets, each containing one of the accounts, were left in front of the subject to refer to. When the subject indicated he or she was ready, the subject was first asked to "describe in your own words what the Fifth Livian War was about and what happened." After the subject's account, these questions were asked:

1. Are the two historians' accounts of the war different in any important ways? (If yes) How are they different?

2. Could both of the historians' accounts of the Fifth Livian War be right? (If no) Why not? (If yes) How can that be?

STUDY 6 RESULTS

Subjects' own accounts of the war were first of all evaluated globally with respect to whether or not the subject constructed a single account of what happened. In addition, each statement in the subject's account was classified as either a simple statement or a metastatement. A *simple statement* is a statement about the event described in the two accounts. A *metastatement* is a statement about one or both of the accounts. Thus, "The South Livians suffered some minor reverses" is a simple statement, while "According to the first account, the South Livians suffered some minor reverses" is a metastatement (in which a simple statement is embedded).

Based on the two probe questions, subjects' responses were classified into one of the levels described below. This sequence of levels is an elaboration of an earlier version developed on the basis of administration of the same task to an adult sample (Kuhn, Pennington, & Leadbeater, 1983).

Level 0

This level is characterized by the complete absence of differentiation between theory and evidence. The two accounts of the event are not differentiated from the event itself. Hence there is no awareness of the process of theoretical interpretation as yielding accounts of the event that differ from the event itself or from each other. For example:

> (Could both accounts be right?) I don't understand. You mean what they're saying here, could this be true? Yeah, I guess so. Sure.

Level 1

At this level, the subject refers to the two accounts and the event itself as distinct entities. However, no acknowledgment is made of the possibility that either or both accounts could deviate from what actually took place (and hence, again, theoretical interpretation is accorded no role). To the extent any differences in the accounts are noted, they are not regarded as discrepancies. Rather, one or both accounts is seem as simply incomplete, not including material mentioned in the other. For example:

> (Are the two accounts different?) I don't think they are, to tell you the truth. (Could both accounts be right?) True, they could be right. (How is that?) By their telling about the war itself, both sides and how it was fought and the outcome.

Level 2

At this and remaining levels, the accounts are regarded as at least partially discrepant. At Level 2, however, the only realm of discourse is that of objective, material facts and events. The accounts are thus regarded as discrepant in the sense that they give different renderings of the facts. The subject shows no ability to reconcile the discrepant accounts, or else claims to be able to do so only if additional factual information were supplied by a third party. No recourse is made to the process of theoretical interpretation as an explanation of the differences or an avenue for reconciling the accounts. For example:

(Are the two accounts different?) Oh, totally different, yeah. (In what ways?) Well the North historian attributes their early victory to a sneak attack and the South historian doesn't mention anything at all about a sneak attack. The South claimed major victories and the North claimed that they recovered from the early days to turn the die totally in their favor and the South said it was only some minor reverses. Each is claiming victory. (Could both accounts be right?) No, I don't believe so. (Why not?) Because they're so opposed. The two viewpoints are totally different and they can't *both* be right!

Level 3

At this and remaining levels, subjects show awareness of theoretical interpretation as having played a role in construction of the accounts and as a vehicle for reconciling them. Very different weights are assigned to this role at each level, however. At Level 3, the subject sees the accounts as largely the product of theoretical interpretation, but in a way that trivializes the product of such interpretive activity, reducing it to merely "that historian's personal opinion," which is "as right as anyone else's." No vehicle is recognized for evaluating such theories against any external evidence or any other standards for evaluation. Despite the importance accorded to theoretical perspective, then, there exists no vehicle for reconciliation of the accounts. For example:

> (Are the two accounts different?) The first one seems to want to provoke more sympathy and the other one wants to show the military strength of their country. (Could both accounts be right?) It depends on to whom it's right. To the South Livians it's right, and to the North Livians it's right. They could both be wrong to a third party.

Level 4

At this level, theoretical interpretation is again recognized as having played a role in construction of the accounts. Two distinct realms of discourse are addressed, however, one of subjective perspective and one of objective fact (in contrast to Level 3 in which recognition of the subjective realm leads in effect to renunciation of the objective, and Levels 2 and below in which only the objective realm is recognized). At Level 4, the subjective realm is clearly subordinated to the objective. The discrepancies between the two accounts are regarded as due to superficial differences in perspective, superimposed on an underlying factual reality of what actually happened. The two accounts therefore are reconcilable (in contrast to Level 3), with respect to this realm of underlying objective fact. For example:

> I think that the primary difference is in emphasis that would seem to relate to the same sort of facts but each side telling it its own way. (Could both accounts be right?) To a degree. I think the interpretations at the end are different but with that exception, yes. (How could it be that both accounts could be right?) Well, each one is telling and emphasizing different facts and ignoring the facts that the other stated.

Level 5

At this level, a coordination and balancing of the objective and subjective realms is achieved. The recognition of subjectivity does not lead the subject to renounce objectivity, as at Level 3, nor is subjectivity reduced to a superficial superimposition of perspective on a factual reality, as at Level 4. Rather, facts are regarded as existing within a frame of reference that includes the cultural and historical contexts and belief systems in which events are observed and interpreted. It is only relative to such frames of reference that facts can be understood. In contrast to Level 4, the accounts are not easily reconciled in the sense of erasing the differences between them. Each is recognized as a valid interpretive effort, and multiple interpretations of events are to be expected. For example:

> (Could both accounts be right?) Yes. How they saw it could have been right. How they saw it in their eyes, in their thinking. If these men are from two different cultures, how they were brought up I think is important—how they live, how their government is set up is different, you know how they look at things. (How would you know if they were right?) I guess you really wouldn't know. I guess you have to depend on them to tell the right story. It's interpretation.

Differences among the five levels are summarized in Table 30.

Level Usage by Age Group

Presented in Table 31 are the frequencies of subjects classified at each level by subject group. Percentage agreement between two independent coders in assignment of subjects to levels was 89%. Subjects at Levels 0, 1, and 4 always produced a single account, with the noting at most of what were asserted to be minor differences, while subjects at Levels 2, 3, and 5 did not attempt to

Table 30
Summary of Differences among Levels of Response to the Livia Problem

Level	Is discrepancy recognized?	Nature of discrepancy	Is discrepancy reconcilible?	Relationship between theoretical interpretation (I) and fact (F)
0	No	–	–	F predominates
1	No	–	–	F predominates
2	Yes	Facts	No	F predominates
3	Yes	Opinions	No	I recognized and predominates
4	Yes	Emphases	Yes	I recognized but F predominates
5	Yes	Perspectives	No	F regarded within framework provided by I

Table 31

Classification of Subjects by Levels of Response
to the Livia Problem

Group	Level					
	0	1	2	3	4	5
Sixth graders	7	8	5	0	0	0
Ninth graders	2	5	7	4	0	0
Twelfth graders	0	1	4	8	6	1
Adults	0	0	2	6	10	2
Graduate students	0	1	3	3	9	3

reconcile the two accounts into a single version. Percentage of the subject's statements classified as metastatements rose from 0% at Level 0 to a high of 45% at Level 5. No sex differences appeared.

DISCUSSION

The data presented in this chapter are not sufficient to establish as definitive the sequence of levels presented above. The association between age group and level reflected in Table 31, however, are consistent with the order reflected above. The "radical relativism" reflected in Level 3 begins to appear by ninth grade, becomes most prevalent among twelfth graders, and then declines in prevalence among the adult groups. Still, these age trend data leave unresolved a number of important questions. Does such a response reflect a necessary stage in a sequence of development of epistemological concepts? Might at least some people bypass Level 3 radical relativism and first recognize subjectivity in the more moderate form we identified as Level 4? Or could the two reactions to the recognition of subjectivity occur in an order the reverse of the one reflected above?

A number of other investigators concerned with the development of epistemological concepts (Broughton, 1978, 1983; Kitchener & King, 1981; Perry, 1970; Sinnott, 1981) have identified a stage of such radical or unbounded relativism as an initial response to the recognition of multiplicity of viewpoints and the realization that knowledge is not static and absolute. As discussed in greater detail in a recent article (Leadbeater, 1986), the theories of adult cognitive development proposed by such investigators differ significantly with respect to the precise nature of this relativism and the nature of its eventual resolution. To what are facts regarded as relative? The radical or completely unbounded relativism reflected in the platitudes "Everyone to their own opinion" and "What's true for him may not be true for her" regards the frame of reference to which facts are relative as the beliefs and attitudes of the particular individual, reducing the concept of truth to an empty one. Very different is "conceptual relativism" (Mandelbaum, 1982), in which this frame of reference is regarded as the historical, cultural, and ideological context in which a judgment is made. Because such frames of reference are interpretable outside the subjective beliefs of a single individual, they afford criteria for evaluation of judgments and beliefs.

What the investigator regards as a resolution to the development of relativism in individuals' epistemologies depends very much on the epistemological framework the investigator him or herself adopts. Our Level 5 end point most closely reflects a hermeneutic epistemological perspective (Packer, 1985) in its endorsement of the view that facts do not stand independently of the frames of reference created by the ideological, cultural, and historical contexts in which they arose. The results presented in this chapter suggest that at least a few individuals develop such a perspective by late adolescence or adulthood.

More broadly, the present results add another dimension to our understanding of the development of scientific thinking, the topic of all of the preceding chapters. The development of scientific thinking skills becomes meaningful and significant only if accompanied by an adequate conceptualization of science and the nature of scientific investigation. A stance resembling the one we have described in which theory and evidence are melded into a single representation of "the way things are" is reflected in the failure of subjects classified at the lower levels in the present study to recognize the possibility of more than a single reality. How does such a person react to the discovery that conflicting assertions about reality are made by reasonable people each of whom offers "scientific" evidence in support of their assertions? Must such a realization lead to unbounded, unreasoned relativism, in which criteria for meaningful scientific inquiry and interpretation vanish, or to the limited conception of science in which the inquiring activity of the scientist him or herself is dismissed as mere subjectivity intruding undesirably into the world of hard, objective fact? Alternatively, can an understanding of science develop in which the interconnection of theory and evidence, of fact and interpretation, is appreciated, with neither being sacrificed to the other? The results presented in this chapter suggest that such an understanding is not attained by most people. Without some such understanding, their interest in and respect for the process of scientific inquiry must be, at best, vulnerable. In the next, concluding chapter, we consider the results presented in this and the preceding chapters with respect to the broader issues they raise regarding scientific thinking, cognitive development, and education.

V

CONCLUSION

Deanna Kuhn

13

SUMMARY AND CONCLUSIONS

In the preceding chapters we have presented results that support a view of the development of scientific thinking as centering around the development of skills in the coordination of theories and evidence. Ideal coordination of theories and evidence can be compared to the ideal role-taking that Kohlberg and his associates, following Rawls (1971), have described as characterizing mature moral judgment (Kohlberg, 1981, 1984). The moral judgment applies whatever the particular role in the conflict that one occupies, such that the same judgment would always be made under the "veil of ignorance" of not knowing one's own identity in the conflict. In the same way, the evaluation of a piece of evidence in relation to different theories is not altered by which theory one favors. Conversely, multiple pieces of evidence relevant to a theory are given comparable consideration irrespective of their compatibility with the theory, that is, those inconsistent with the theory are not slighted in favor of those consistent with the theory. In the absence of such ideal coordination, distorting effects of one's own theoretical preferences on the interpretation of evidence occur.

COORDINATING THEORY AND EVIDENCE

What are the skills required to achieve this ideal coordination? The research described in the preceding chapters points to three key abilities:

1. First, and most fundamental, is the ability to think *about* a theory, rather than only think *with* it. In the latter case, a person uses theories as a means of organizing and interpreting experience but is not aware of their existence. If the person has no awareness of the theory, that is, is unable to represent it as an

object of cognition, he or she cannot evaluate the bearing of evidence on it. Furthermore, if a theory is only used rather than contemplated, the possibility of the theory's being false and of the existence of alternative theories is not conceived. In such a case, the person can be said to "have" or to "hold" the theory only from the third-party perspective of an observer. Such a person does not "have" a theory in the sense of knowing that he or she has it or of having any awareness or control of the manner in which that theory guides his or her thinking.

2. Second, the person must be able to encode and represent the evidence to be evaluated as an entity distinct from representation of the theory. If new evidence is merely assimilated to a theory, as an instance of it, the possibility of constructing relations between the two, as separate entities, is lost. In other words, theory and evidence must be differentiated, such that there is a concept of evidence standing apart from the theory and bearing on it. In the absence of such a concept, evidence, like theory, exists only from the perspective of an observer. From the subjective perspective of the person, the evidence is part of the theory. It consists of instances of the theory, instances that both can be explained by the theory and serve to illustrate it. Theory and evidence remain undifferentiated.

3. Third, the person must be able to temporarily bracket, or set aside, his or her own acceptance (or rejection) of a theory in order to assess what the evidence by itself would mean for the theory, were it the only basis for making a judgment.

Those who possess and apply these skills will have attained a considerable measure of (though probably never total) control of the processes of interaction between theory and evidence as they occur in their own thinking. They might choose to regulate these processes in such a way as to reflect Bayesian principles of inference in which interpretations of evidence are adjusted as a function of prior theories, but if so they know that such adjustments are being made and are in control of their application. If they chose to disregard the probabilities attached to prior theoretical beliefs and interpret the evidence independent of them, they would be able to do so.

In the preceding chapters, we have presented results from a series of studies indicating that these skills are weak among children below adolescence, that they show some development from middle childhood to adulthhood, but that they remain at far less than an optimal level of development even among adults. In the studies reported in Part III, evidence with respect to two different theories was embodied in the same physical objects, and subjects were asked to compare the implications of the evidence for one theory versus the other, in other words, to coordinate the same set of evidence with multiple theories. Both of these conditions, we thought, would make it difficult for the subject to apply different standards in relating the same evidence to the two different theories. While these conditions succeeded in focusing the attention of all but the very youngest subjects on the evidence, subjects very often interpreted identical evidence to mean one thing in relation to a theory that was favored and something else, often quite different, in relation to a theory not favored. This fluidity in the criteria utilized in the interpretation of evidence suggests that in the cases of both the favored and nonfavored theories, the evidence is not adequately differentiated from the theory itself. It does not retain its own identity, its constancy of meaning, across a range of theories to which it might be related.

The lack of differentiation between theory and evidence manifested itself both when the subject's own theoretical beliefs and the evidence to be evaluated were compatible and when they were not. When theory and evidence were compatible, in responding to the interviewer's request to evaluate the evidence, subjects often vacillated between reference to the evidence itself and reference to their theories. For such subjects, evidence is equivalent to *instances* of the theory that serve to illustrate it, while the theory in turn serves to explain the evidence. Referring to the theory is thus as good as referring to the evidence itself in interpreting what this evidence indicates. The two meld into a single representation of "the way things are."

When theory and evidence were not in accordance, a majority of subjects seemed unable to acknowledge the discrepancy, to say in effect, "This is what the theory says; this is what the evidence you have shown me indicates, and either the theory must be wrong or the evidence you have presented must be wrong, but it is not necessary that I decide which." Instead, subjects displayed a number of strategies that functioned to maintain theory and evidence in alignment with one another. Most often, they maintained this alignment by "adjusting" the evidence, either by ignoring discrepant evidence entirely or by attending to it in a selective, distorting manner. If discrepancies were acknowledged, an auxilliary theory was sometimes invoked (e.g., the influence of another variable) to explain them away.

Alternatively, especially when the theory was held with only moderate strength, subjects maintained alignment of theory and evidence by adjusting the theory, usually *before* they were willing to acknowledge the implications of the evidence. In other words, a theory that articulated a plausible link between antecedent and outcome needed to be in place before the subject would acknowledge evidence of the covariation between antecedent and outcome. Similarly, a theory explaining why the antecedent "has nothing to do with" the outcome needed to be in place before the subject would acknowledge evidence of noncovariation. Thus, we witnessed the adjustment of theories to fit evidence, as well as the "adjustment" of evidence to fit theories, but in neither case is either the discrepancy itself or the adjustment made in response to it acknowledged by the subject, and the subject appears to lack conscious control of the operation of these adjustment mechanisms in his or her thinking.

We observed the operation of similar sorts of mechanisms in other tasks we posed to subjects. In generating their own evidence to show that a theory is correct or incorrect, subjects more readily generated evidence that demonstrated the correctness of a theory they believed true and more readily generated evidence that demonstrated the incorrectness of a theory they believed not to be true. When asked to generate evidence that did not accord with their theoretical beliefs, subjects sometimes altered their own theories to match the evidence they had generated. In probing subjects' representations of both the evidence and their own original theories by asking them to recall each, we observed subjects who recalled their own theories inaccurately, representing them as consistent with the evidence that had been presented when they in fact had not been. Likewise, we observed subjects who in reconstructing the evidence represented it as more consistent with their theories than it in fact had been. Both of these tendencies reflect additional mechanisms for maintaining theory and evidence in alignment with one another.

Most of the characteristics just described were present to a greater extent in younger than older subjects, indicating the presence of some development in the skills we have investigated during the years from middle childhood to adulthood. We have suggested that exercise in relating evidence to multiple theories is a primary factor in the development of skills in coordinating theory and evidence. There is another aspect to such development, however, and that is the development of skills in the interpretation of evidence, given that it is sufficiently differentiated from theory. In the next section, we summarize the set of such skills identified in the present research. Let us clarify, first, however, that we see the two kinds of skills both as co-developing and as mutually reinforcing one another as they develop. To the extent a person has acquired explicit and well-developed criteria or rules for interpreting evidence, these criteria are less likely to be compromised by the biasing effects of theoretical preference. Conversely, to the extent a person is able to dissociate evidence from the context of his or her own theoretical beliefs, and regard that evidence as an independent entity in its own right, a concern for consistent and explicit criteria for interpreting evidence will be enhanced.

THE INTERPRETATION OF EVIDENCE

Covariation Evidence

Subjects in the studies we have presented were asked to examine a number of different forms of evidence, ranging from very simple covariation of antecedent and outcome to complex asymmetric arrays requiring comparison of ratios for correct interpretation, and to indicate the implications of that evidence for one or more theories. Conversely, they were asked to generate evidence that would have particular implications for a theory. If there were one ability we might assume that we could count on as already well developed among subjects of the ages assessed in this study, it would be the ability to infer a causal relation from simple covariation evidence. Human infants as well as animals are capable of detecting covariation and responding differentially to covariation and noncovariation, and indeed organisms unable to do so would be severely hampered in adapting to their environments. Almost all of our sixth graders (though not third graders) were able at least some of the time to make explicit reference to covariation as the basis for an inference of causality. Yet, the present work has shown a number of respects in which older children, adolescents, and adults are limited in their understanding of covariation and its connection to causality.

Overcoming False Inclusion

Most strikingly evident in our results is what can be referred to as the overinterpretation of covariation information, or, to use the term we have employed throughout the preceding chapters, *false inclusion*. Subjects of all ages showed a tendency to implicate any covariate as causal, with theoretical belief clearly playing a major motivating role. Because it was present when the outcome occurred, a particular covariate must have played a role in that outcome, even though one or more additional covariates were present. For some subjects, a single co-occurrence of antecedent and outcome is sufficient to warrant an inference of causality, as evidenced strikingly by the willingness many of our subjects showed to make an inference of causality based on the single instance of evidence that we presented initially.

Though its prevalence showed a decline with age, false inclusion in its more subtle forms is an inferential error that even very sophisticated thinkers fall prey to. When other covariates are not salient and one's theoretically preferred causal candidate is particularly compelling, the error becomes hard to resist. Our results suggest, nonetheless, that another factor contributing to the prevalence of false inclusion for many subjects may be an inadequate understanding of covariation. Covariation of two variables signifies that they vary together, that is, variation in one is accompanied by variation in the other. If no variation occurs in one of the variables, the concept of covariation becomes meaningless. Yet, many of our subjects were quite willing to make a causal inference based on just such a lack of variation—for example, one or more light-colored balls with good outcomes in the absence of any evidence regarding dark-colored balls. Furthermore, when evidence regarding both variable levels was available, many subjects believed that a causal interpretation could be made separately for each variable level. Light-colored balls, the subject would claim, for example, "make a difference" to outcome (as they always have positive outcomes), while dark-colored balls (which are evenly distributed between outcomes) do not. If asked about the relation of color "overall" to outcome, such a subject was likely to conclude that it "some-times" makes a difference (i.e., depending on which color is being considered).

In a similar way, a subject evaluating a set of three light-colored balls with good outcomes and three light-colored balls with bad outcomes might conclude that color "sometimes makes a difference" (in the case of the three good outcomes) and sometimes does not (in the case of the three bad outcomes). Taken to its extreme, the "sometimes" concept of relations between variables means that each individual co-occurrence or non-co-occurrence of variable level and outcome can be interpreted in isolation. This of course amounts to false inclusion in its most blatant form. Such errors, we should emphasize, are particularly likely to be theoretically motivated. "Here is some evidence," the person says, "that I can point to as supporting my preferred theory, and therefore the theory must be right." Necessary (though probably not sufficient) for overcoming the "sometimes" conception of relationships that can foster such bias is an understanding of covariation as reflecting exactly what its name implies: "co-variation" of two variables, such that changes in one are accompanied by changes in the other. In the absence of at least some variation in each variable, covariation cannot exist (nor can causality be demonstrated).

A firm understanding in this respect could also diminish the kinds of errors subjects made most commonly in the asymmetric evidence evaluation problems, which require comparison of two ratios (and therefore processing of all four cells in the 2×2 matrix produced by all combinations of the dichotomous antecedent and outcome variables). Very few subjects demonstrated a command of the comparison of ratios strategy, but what is more important is the willingness subjects displayed to make inferences based on inadequate strategies in which the frequencies in only two of the four cells are considered. Use of the very common two-cell strategies in effect reflects the same misunderstanding described above. Information with respect to only one variable level is interpreted, while information with respect to the other variable level, which is available in this case and is of course critical to correct interpretation, is ignored. The subject does not recognize that variation in both variables is necessary for covariation to be inferred. Subjects employing two-cell strategies in the asymmetric evidence problems displayed a lack of metacognitive knowledge regarding the strategies necessary for correct solution to the problem, whether they were or were not capable of executing those strategies. We have more to say shortly regarding the role of metacognitive skills in the kinds of reasoning we have examined.

Generating Evidence for Inclusion

Given the readiness all of our subjects displayed to interpret covariation evidence as indicative of causality, we might anticipate that they would have no difficulty in generating covariation evidence to demonstrate the correctness of a causal theory. In fact, the results of the problems in which we asked subjects to generate their own evidence to show that a variable makes a difference are consistent with the many studies in the literature on formal operations: Subjects fail to construct conclusive proofs of the effect of a variable because in demonstrating the covariation of one variable with outcome, other potentially causal variables are left uncontrolled. This well-documented tendency of subjects, particularly before adolescence, to fail to control variables has been regarded as reflecting the subject's failure to attend to these variables and therefore to recognize the possibility that, left uncontrolled, these variables may exert their own effects on outcome.

The explanations subjects in our work offered of the evidence they generated, however, suggest another interpretation. Rather than ignoring these "uncontrolled" variables, our subjects appeared to be attempting to construct a body of evidence that would reflect the operation of these variables as well. In other words, they wanted to display how the evidence should appear if all the variables they believed operative had their alleged effects, not just the single variable on which the demonstration was to focus. In order to generate a set of evidence that provides a conclusive demonstration of the operation of this single variable, it is necessary that the subject set aside his or her beliefs regarding the remaining variables and focus only on the single variable whose effect is to be demonstrated. This ability to set aside, or bracket, one's own theoretical beliefs is of course the same bracketing ability that is essential to unbiased evidence evaluation and that was listed earlier in the chapter as a third ability underlying the full coordination of theory and evidence.

Prediction

The ability to consider the effects of a single variable at a time is essential also to the generation of correct predictions based on multivariable evidence. As we saw in Study 2, subjects often matched the global combination of variable levels represented in the evidence to the global combination of variable levels in the instance whose outcome was to be predicted, rather than analyzing the existing evidence in terms of the effects of individual variables. This "matching" strategy was also observed in the research by Downing, Sternberg, and Ross (1985), referred to in Chapter 2. In real-world contexts, people who think only in terms of similarities between the patterns represented in constellations of variables may be correct in their predictions some of the time (and hence receive partial reinforcement for use of this strategy). But they are clearly severely hampered in making sense of the world around them, both in detecting regularities that may be present in their environments and in predicting future events based on the past.

Noncovariation Evidence

Mastering Exclusion

In sharp contrast to the ease with which they recognized covariation and used it to infer causality, subjects found noncovariation evidence difficult both to interpret and to generate. Exclusion inferences, justified by reference to the noncovariation of antecedent and outcome, were made occasionally by a minority of third graders and became much more common between third and ninth grade, but some adults failed to display a command of exclusion. A basic problem in interpreting noncovariation and seeing it as the basis for exclusion is understanding the distinction between a variable making *no* difference and a variable making a difference in the opposite direction of the direction initially conceived. Subjects asked to generate evidence that a variable makes no difference often produced evidence reflecting covariation between antecedent and outcome in the direction opposite of that predicted by their own causal theory. In the case of a variable for which their theory was noncausal, they sometimes indicated a direction in which the hypothetical other person might expect the relationship to lie and then, to generate evidence demonstrating that this variable makes no difference to outcome, simply reversed this direction. The concept of no relationship, or independence, between variable and outcome remained elusive. Similarly, in evaluating noncovariation evidence presented to them, third and sixth graders frequently articulated their inability to draw a conclusion from such evidence: "I can't tell if it makes a difference, because both the ones with it and the ones without it came out good [or bad]."

Interpreting Mixed Evidence

Once the ability to see noncovariation as a basis for exclusion emerges, a phenomenon appeared commonly among sixth and ninth graders that can be regarded as the overinterpretation of noncovariation (parallel in some sense to what we identified earlier as the overinterpretation of covariation). Any time that covariation between antecedent and outcome was less than perfect, even if a large majority of outcomes conformed to a covariation pattern, the subject rejected the possibility of a relationship between variable and outcome. Such subjects thus fail to note any pattern in the evidence they evaluate, even when a quite strong covariation pattern is present, and hence fail to make any distinctions among the different sets of evidence they are asked to interpret, some of which show independence of variable and outcome and others of which show substantial covariation. The instances of nonconformity to a covariation pattern that the subject notes may violate his or her theory of the causal mechanism connecting variable and outcome. Yet, the subject declines to consider such exceptions as due possibly to random or other unexplained sources of variability and, as a result, fails to see any pattern at all in the evidence. Though this pattern of response declined among older subjects and was absent among the college group, its prevalence among sixth and ninth graders is noteworthy, especially since, as we discuss shortly, this age range is likely to be a critical one for science education. If all but perfect associations among variables were ignored, a good many of the basic phenomena in science probably would never have been discovered.

Conquering False Inclusion

More common than the failure to see a relationship where one exists, however, is the inclination to see a relationship where none exists, and herein lies the heart of the difficulty with respect to the skill of exclusion. Though subjects may have the kinds of problems indicated at the beginning of this section in understanding the concepts of noncovariation and independence, the most serious impediment to the mastery of exclusion is probably the seductive pull of false inclusion. As we emphasized in the discussion of the evaluation of covariation evidence, the tendency is very prevalent to see any even single instance of co-occurrence of antecedent and outcome as potential evidence for an inference of causality: "Here is *some* evidence that supports the theory." When a single instance is treated as sufficient to warrant an inference of causality, there is, of course, no possibility of exclusion, for the inference of exclusion depends on the detection of a pattern of nonassociation, or independence, in the occurrence or nonoccurrence of variable level and outcome over a number of instances. To develop the critical skill of exclusion, then, the person must relinquish the versatile but false power (to serve as evidence for just about any theory one chooses) that is afforded by false inclusion. This power is well reflected in Randy's interpretation of noncovariation evidence in Study 5: "Mr. C is half right because if he wanted light, three light came out good and if he wanted dark, three dark came out good." Or as another Study 5 sixth grader put it: "No matter what size Ms. S likes, she's right!"

In this section we have summarized a variety of skills identified in the preceding chapters, skills necessary for the accurate evaluation, as well as the generation, of covariation and noncovariation evidence. As we suggested earlier, two kinds of development co-occur and reinforce one another. One is skill in evaluating the implications of evidence, described in this section. The other is skill in coordination of theories and evidence, described earlier in the chapter. Evidence must be sufficiently differentiated from theory for the skills described in this section to develop. In turn, to the extent these skills are firmly in place, the biasing effects of theoretical preference are less likely to intrude into a person's thinking in ways over which the person lacks awareness or control. However, elimination of the distorting effects of theory on the evaluation of evidence may not be an endpoint in the development of scientific thinking. As we suggested in Chapter 12, at least some people may go on to develop a more sophisticated concept of the interplay between theory and evidence, one in which evidence is again subordinated to the theoretical framework within which it is regarded, but this time in a controlled way the subject is aware of and appreciates.

THE DEVELOPMENT OF SCIENTIFIC THINKING SKILLS

Thinking *about* theories, and about how evidence bears on them, in contrast merely to thinking *with* them, we have suggested, is a tremendously important distinction. In both cases, theories guide the interpretation of new evidence and are revised in the face of it, though the responsiveness of theories to new evidence may not be as great as it ought to be. The person who only thinks with theories lacks any awareness or control of the interaction of theories and evidence in his or her thinking. The person who has achieved the ability to think about theories and about how evidence bears on them has achieved a considerable degree of awareness of and control over this interaction. We have suggested that this ability is "metacognitive" in a very important, core sense of the term.

In scientific thinking, this awareness and control are simply assumed as givens. In examinations of the nature of scientific thinking and discovery, the very elementary skills in relating evidence to theories that we have investigated in this volume tend to be taken for granted, even when the scientists being considered are children. Our findings show such an assumption to be anything but warranted and suggest that mastery of these skills reflects an extended process of development. The metaphor of child as scientist that we considered in Chapter 2 may therefore be fundamentally misleading, if it is taken in the sense of the child as an intuitive scientist with the same conceptual skills as the accomplished scientist. Though the child may resemble the scientist in the sense that Carey (1986) and others have described the substituting of new theories for old ones, the process in which existing theories and new evidence interact—the process of theory revision—may well not be the same in the child and the scientist. Our results suggest that the young child's skills as a scientist—skills in ways of coming to know the world, or, in the terms we use, skills in the coordination of theories and evidence— are significantly different from those of the adolescent, the lay adult, or the scientist. Such skills are ones, therefore, that are usefully conceived in a developmental framework.

The skills we have summarized in the preceding sections are related to those identified in earlier work on inductive inference and formal operational reasoning, as discussed in Chapter 2. In addition to some of the particular skills, such as control of variables, that are involved in both the present work and the literature on formal operations, the idea of reflection on one's own thinking figures prominently in Inhelder and Piaget's theory of formal operations as well as in the present work. Unlike Inhelder and Piaget, however, we do not see the development of these thinking skills as deriving from an underlying logical competence. They are clearly general skills, in the sense of being definable across a wide range of content. Yet, as discussed in Chapter 2, we see them as emerging in pragmatic, goal-related contexts (Cheng & Holyoak, 1985), in terms of which they are initially defined. The resulting pragmatic, goal-related schemes both provide an inductive apparatus through which new information is interpreted and themselves undergo development, of a sort that our results help to describe.

In Chapter 2, we suggested that Inhelder and Piaget regarded these skills in too "formal" a way, as completely generalized, abstract operations that function in a uniform way independent of the particular content about which a subject is reasoning. They thus did not regard their subjects' theories about the phenomena they were exploring as directing or even affecting the experimentation process. Rather than presume the existence of broad, general strategies that the child acquires and then presumably is able to apply to any content domains that are relevant, we have taken the child's own specific theories within such content domains as starting points and then examined the processes by means of which they are coordinated with new information. These theories themselves, as we have seen, may account for a good deal of variance in whether a given strategy is or is not exhibited in a particular instance. Furthermore, where it appears that we are more likely to encounter generality (rather than in the strategies themselves) is in the processes in terms of which theories and new evidence interact and in the manner in which these processes develop.

TEACHING THINKING SKILLS

When we turn to the matter of teaching thinking skills, the generality/specificity question remains at the core of the debate. Interest in teaching thinking skills has grown enormously in the last decade (see Baron & Sternberg, 1987, Chipman, Segal, & Glaser, 1985, or Nickerson, Perkins, & Smith, 1985, for reviews). A focal issue of work in this area has been whether thinking skills can be taught in general form or only within the context of particular subject matter. From our perspective, a prior concern must be identification of the skills themselves, which too often has been undertaken by conceptual/rational analysis alone, without empirical grounding. How do we know that the set of skills a particular author identifies as defining good or critical thinking are the ones it would be most valuable to try to teach or the ones most fundamental to the thinking that students engage in in their lives within or outside of school? Empirical study of the kinds of thinking that take place in both academic and informal contexts and, especially, of the *directions in which such thinking typically develops,* we believe, provides a fundamental knowledge base that can inform efforts to teach thinking, and we hope the research described in this volume will make a contribution in this regard.

In addition to the generality/specificity issue, another, related issue that has received less attention but is just as significant is the distinction between teaching students *about* thinking versus engaging them *in* it. There exists a long and distinguished theoretical literature in the field of education, dating back to the beginning of the century, reflecting the view that the only effective way to teach students to think is to engage them in thinking. Dewey's classic *How We Think* (1910) certainly reflects this view, as does the writing of other respected educational theorists of his time. Symonds, for example, in *Education and the Psychology of Thinking* (1936), wrote:

> In order to learn to think one must practice thinking in the situation in which it is to be used and on material on which it is to be exercised. . . . In short, practice in thinking itself is necessary for the improvement of thinking. (pp. 235–236)

This view remained prominent several decades later. In the early 1960s, a report by the Educational Policies Commission of the National Education Association titled *The Central Purpose of American Education* claimed, "The purpose which runs through and strengthens all other educational purposes—the common thread of education—is the development of the ability to think." The report went on to claim how this ability should be fostered:

> The rational powers of any person are developed gradually and continuously as and when he uses them successfully. There is no evidence that they can be developed in any other way. They do not emerge quickly or without effort. . . . Thus, the learner must be encouraged in his early efforts to grapple with problems that engage his rational abilities at their current level of development, and he must experience success in these efforts. (1961, p. 17)

Given this notable consistency in viewpoint on the part of educators over seven or eight decades, it is striking to discover that there exists scarcely any empirical research that pertains to it. Instead, from some of the earliest experiments in teaching thinking skills by E. Glaser (1941) and Osborn (1939), to current programs, emphasis has been on teaching students *about* thinking. In other words, the teacher attempts to provide students with principles or rules of sound thinking that they can then apply in their own thinking and, perhaps as well, attempts to illustrate common thinking errors that the students will then be likely to recognize and avoid in their own thinking. Experimental psychologists engaged in the study of thinking skills (Baron, 1985; Nisbett & Ross, 1980) likewise have tended to endorse this approach.

The major problem with such programs is that they risk suffering the same fate as so many intervention efforts in education and psychology: The competencies that are the object of instruction may be displayed in the narrow contexts in which they are taught but largely fail to generalize to a wider range of contexts in which they are equally appropriate. These all-too-characteristic failures of generalization limit the practical utility of such efforts and also their scientific interpret-ability. One remains unsure what students have grasped in the original teaching situation and to what extent the process that transpired resembles the process by which such acquisitions occur under natural conditions. What is at issue, in other words, is the thorny problem of transfer that has been a central preoccupation of psychology from very early (James, 1890) to modern times (Brown & Campione, 1984).

Anyone who undertakes to teach thinking skills, by any method, would like those skills to transfer as widely as possible. The question is how best to achieve that goal. Accounts of transfer within traditional learning paradigms have focused on stimulus similarity as the critical feature governing the transfer of learned behaviors: To the extent that a new stimulus situation is similar to the one in which the behavior was originally learned, the behavior is likely to be elicited by the new situation. A different way to conceptualize transfer is to focus on the behavior, rather than the setting or stimulus thought to elicit that behavior. Such a conceptualization suggests why exercise of a strategy may be the most effective way to promote its transfer. As we suggested in Chapter 11, exercise of a cognitive strategy is likely to serve not only to perfect its execution but also to promote metacognitive awareness of the strategy itself. Heightened awareness of the strategy itself as a tool in turn may increase the likelihood of the user's recognizing the applicability of the strategy in other contexts. Similarly, increased metacognitive awareness of strategies that operate within limited contexts may promote recognition of the commonalities among these individual context-embedded strategies, thereby increasing their generality and hence their power. In both cases, increased metacognitive control of a strategy acquired through exercise promotes transfer and increases generality. Paradoxically, then, exercise of strategies within very specific, content-delimited contexts may promote their generalization, while didactic teaching of the same strategies in more abstract, general form may fail to achieve this same end.

If these ideas are at all on the right track, they suggest that the educator's role is one of facilitator rather than teacher of thinking skills. Quite the opposite of trivializing the educator's role, this conceptualization enhances it. The goal of getting students to exercise thinking strategies may be clear, but the means may be far from obvious and the goal difficult to achieve. Research has suggested that once problems become familiar, people tend to apply well-ingrained, more or less automatic routines to them, with little intervening thought. Such activity provides no oppportunity for metacognitive deployment of strategic skills. The educator's continuing challenge is thus to pose problems that are novel enough to require conscious, selective deployment of strategies but familiar enough to permit application of strategies within the student's competence. Despite the centrality of the development of thinking skills to the aims of education, until recently we have had only the most intuitive understanding of what a good teacher does in the course of meeting this challenge. Research by Collins and Stevens (1982) and some others is beginning to give us more specific knowledge of the behaviors exhibited by a skilled teacher in this respect. Such research efforts should become more specific as knowledge of the thinking skills in question and the processes by means of which they develop increases.

The focus of the present work has been on the identification of thinking skills involved in evaluation of evidence and the coordination of theory and evidence, and we do not claim to have provided empirical evidence to demonstrate the superiority of an exercise approach to developing thinking skills. The present work does, however, suggest the manner in which cognitive exercise, in particular the exercise involved in relating evidence to a variety of theories, might operate to develop such skills. At the beginning of this chapter we summarized such processes in general terms, and in Chapter 11, through the case study of Randy, we illustrated in more particular terms some of the ways in which they might take place.

THINKING SKILLS AND SCIENCE EDUCATION

Science educators, as we noted in Chapter 1, have long been concerned with the teaching of scientific thinking skills as a central aspect of science education but have been impeded by existence of only a limited body of empirical research identifying the specific skills on which their efforts might focus. Science educators concerned with thinking skills have tended to look to the field of developmental psychology as the major source of theory and empirical data to guide their efforts. The dominant theoretical model utilized as a basis for defining scientific thinking skills has been Piaget's (Karplus, 1974), in particular Inhelder and Piaget's theory of formal operations (Lawson, 1983). The lack of generality of formal operational strategies across a range of content, however, has left science educators wondering whether it is reasonable to suppose that they reflect global developmental stages in scientific thinking, appropriate as the focus of attention of educators wishing to design curricula to develop scientific thinking skills. Moreover, as discussed in Chapter 2, recent research in both science education and cognitive psychology has suggested that children (and adults) bring with them to formal science instruction a variety of naïve, intuitive concepts of phenomena and that these concepts significantly influence their interpretation of new information (Carey, 1986; West & Pines, 1985). The most promising approach, we believe, then, is one that takes what the child already knows or believes as a starting point and then examines the strategies used to integrate new information with these initial understandings. Though involving only very simple kinds of content, it is of course these strategies, and their development, that have been the focus of the present work.

The research presented in this volume has focused on the development of skills essential to even the simplest forms of scientific thinking, and surely these skills should be a central concern of science education. The late elementary and early high school age range examined in the present work is probably the most critical one in terms of science education, and particularly in the development of scientific thinking skills. There may be a potential during this age range for facilitating development of ways of thinking about evidence and theories that is absent before this time and diminished afterward. The evidence that subjects in the present work were asked to evaluate consisted mostly of very simple relations of covariation or noncovariation between dichotomous variables. Most scientific phenomena in fact involve complex relations among many variables that combine and interact to produce chains of causal effects. The kind of approach we have employed in the present work might be adopted in engaging students in the evaluation of more complex forms of evidence involving additive and interactive effects among multiple variables and complex (rather than dichotomous) outcomes. Mastery of the very simple skills in evaluating evidence and coordinating evidence and theories that have been the focus of the present work, however, is a prerequisite to such efforts. As the microgenetic research presented in Chapter 11 illustrated, subjects can be remarkably resistant to giving up the less adequate thinking strategies that they are familiar with. Making contact with these inferior strategies, and getting subjects to see their limitations, must be given as much, if not more, attention than developing the new strategies that will replace them. The challenge posed by instructional efforts should thus not be underestimated.

SCIENTIFIC THINKING AND EVERYDAY THINKING

Though we have cast the present work primarily in the framework of scientific thinking skills, any firm dividing line between scientific thinking and everyday thinking is clearly an arbitrary one. Intuitive thinking has its place in science, but equally important, it is expected that the skills of scientific thinking will manifest themselves to some extent as well in other kinds of thought. And certainly if the teaching of scientific thinking skills is undertaken, the undertakers hope that the skills acquired will generalize beyond the science laboratory. Thinking in scientific contexts represents only a minute portion of all of the thinking that human beings engage in. It is thus more likely to be in the realm of everyday thinking rather than science that deficiencies in the skills we have examined in this volume have their most far-reaching implications.

To the extent the present work is about thinking more broadly defined, it bears on the existing literature in psychology on reasoning and inductive inference, in particular causal inference. We only very briefly summarize these implications here. One is the sizable gap between implicit and explicit mastery of inferential skills that the present work has demonstrated. Another is the demonstration of significant changes in causal inference skills in the age range from middle childhood to adulthood, an important finding particularly in view of the conclusion drawn by a number of developmental researchers that attainment of competence in causal reasoning is complete by the end of early childhood. To experimental psychologists interested in everyday inference, such as Nisbett and Ross (1980) and Baron (1985), the present results may point to the possibility that patterns of developmental change leading to adult modes of thinking have the potential for providing insight into the nature of adult functioning as well as providing a framework for conceptualizing individual variation among adults.

The present results also indicate important individual differences in interpretation of covariation and noncovariation evidence, and hence in causal and noncausal inference. Subjects are quite likely to draw on covariation evidence to confirm a causal theory (or, less often, to disconfirm a noncausal theory). They are less likely to draw on noncovariation evidence to confirm a noncausal theory (or to disconfirm a causal theory). As a result, causal theories are less susceptible to modification based on new evidence than are noncausal theories. Finally, our findings regarding the influence of belief on the evaluation of evidence and processes involved in the coordination of theory and evidence are of relevance to psychologists studying belief formation and modification as well as those studying reasoning and inference. Particularly important in this respect again is the suggestion that developmental analysis may yield insight into adult functioning and, related to this idea, the concept of coordination of theory and evidence as a skill that may show progressive degrees of mastery. Belief bias phenomena, which we have conceptualized as failures in the differentiation and coordination of theory and evidence, are well documented in the cognitive social psychology literature, as we noted in Chapter 2. Developmental study, we believe, suggests a framework in which to conceptualize belief bias and the developmental progression that effects its decline.

The differences in performance we observed across subject groups also have implications with respect to the issue considered at the beginning of this section—the relation between scientific and everyday thinking. Ninth graders exhibited performance significantly different from that of third graders. Equally different, however, and more surprising, were the disparate levels of performance exhibited by young adults in academic versus nonacademic environments. The latter finding suggests that an academic environment facilitates and supports the kinds of thinking skills we have examined. That fact, however, does not diminish their significance in nonscientific contexts. We observed striking variability in the performance of nonacademic adults. Some performed quite like college subjects, while the performance of others was equivalent to that of third or sixth graders. What are the implications of such variability with respect to thinking in everyday life?

In current work, we are attempting to address this question by examining the reasoning of adolescents and young, middle-aged, and older adults about real-world, content-rich topics: What causes prisoners to return to a life of crime after they are released? What causes children to fail in school? After eliciting their causal theories, we ask subjects questions such as: How do you know that this is so, that this is the cause of prisoners returning to a life of crime? If you were trying to convince someone that your view is right, what evidence would you give to try to show this? Suppose that someone disagreed with your view; what might they say to show you were wrong? What could you say to show they were wrong? In other words, we ask subjects to generate multiple, contrasting theories and coordinate evidence with them.

The same kinds of weaknesses in coordinating theory and evidence appear that we have described in the preceding chapters. Subjects often relate a story, or a script, of (in the case of the one topic) a prisoner being released from prison, returning to his community, and being tempted back into crime. Our request for supporting evidence often produces merely an elaboration of the script. Our attempt to elicit alternative theories or counterevidence is often unsuccessful. One of our adolescent subjects put it best. When we asked her for evidence that would support her theory, she replied, "Do you mean can I give you an example?"

We would claim that the key elements in a subject like the one just quoted developing skills in differentiating and coordinating theory and evidence are (a) recognition of the possibility of alternative theories and (b) recognition of the possibility of evidence that does not fit a theory. The first achievement is likely to facilitate the second, as the presence of multiple, contrasting theories makes it difficult to assimilate the same evidence to both of them. In the case of each of these achievements, awareness that things could be otherwise is the key element. A script becomes a theory when its possible falsehood and the existence of alternative theories is recognized. Instances become evidence when the possibility of their lack of concordance with a theory is recognized. And, finally, exercise, we would claim, in generating and evaluating evidence and relating it to different theories is most likely to be the key to developing the skill to fully coordinate the two.

REFERENCES

Alloy, L., & Tabachnik, N. (1984). Assessment of covariation by humans and animals: The joint influence of prior expectations and current situational information. *Psychological Review, 91,* 112–149.

Arkes, H., & Harkness, A. (1983). Estimates of contingency between two dichotomous variables. *Journal of Experimental Psychology: General, 112,* 117–135.

Baron, J. (1985). *Rationality and intelligence.* New York: Cambridge University Press.

Baron, J., & Sternberg, R. (Eds.). (1987). *Teaching thinking skills: Theory and practice.* New York: Freeman.

Becker, J., & Kuhn, D. (1984). Uncertain judgments [Review of D. Kahneman, P. Slovic, & A. Tversky (Eds.), *Judgment under uncertainty: Heuristics and biases*]. *New Ideas in Psychology, 2,* 201–210.

Beilin, H. (1984). Dispensable and core elements in Piaget's research program. *Genetic Epistemologist, 13,* 1–15.

Bindra, D., Clarke, K., & Shultz, T. (1980). Understanding predictive relations of necessity and sufficiency in formally equivalent "causal" and "logical" problems. *Journal of Experimental Psychology: General, 109,* 422–443.

Bower, G., & Trabasso, T. (1964). Concept identification. In R. Atkinson (Ed.), *Studies in mathematical psychology* (pp. 32–94). Stanford, CA: Stanford University Press.

Braine, M., & Rumain, B. (1983). Logical reasoning. In J. Flavell & E. Markman (Eds.), P. Mussen (Series Ed.), *Handbook of child psychology* (Vol. 3, pp. 263–340). New York: Wiley.

Brainerd, C. (1979). [Commentary on L. Hood & L. Bloom, What, when, and how about why: A longitudinal study of early expressions of causality]. *Monographs of the Society for Research in Child Development, 44,* (6, Serial No. 181).

Bredderman, T. (1985). Effects of activity-based elementary science on student outcomes: A quantitative synthesis. *Review of Educational Research, 53,* 499–518.

Broughton, J. (1978). The development of concepts of self, mind, reality and knowledge. In W. Damon (Ed.), *Social cognition* (pp. 75–100) (*New Directions in Child Psychology,* Vol. 1). San Francisco: Jossey-Bass.

Broughton, J. (1983). Not beyond formal operations but beyond Piaget. In M. Commons, F. Richards, & C. Armon (Eds.), *Beyond formal operations: Late adolescent and adult cognitive development* (pp. 395–411). New York: Praeger.

Brown, A., & Campione, J. (1984). Three faces of transfer: Implications for early competence, individual differences, and instruction. In M. Lamb, A. Brown, & B. Rogoff (Eds.), *Advances in developmental psychology* (Vol. 3, pp. 143–192). Hillsdale, NJ: Erlbaum.

Bruner, J., Goodnow, J., & Austin, G. (1956). *A study of thinking.* New York: Wiley.

Bullock, M. (1985). Causal reasoning and developmental change over the preschool years. *Human Development, 28,* 169–191.

Bullock, M., Gelman, R., & Baillargeon, R. (1982). The development of causal reasoning. In W. Friedman (Ed.), *The developmental psychology of time* (pp. 209–254). New York: Academic Press.

Carey, S. (1985a). Are children fundamentally different kinds of thinkers and learners than adults? In S. Chipman, J. Segal, & R. Glaser (Eds.), *Thinking and learning skills* (Vol. 2, pp. 485–517). Hillsdale, NJ: Erlbaum.

Carey, S. (1985b). *Conceptual change in childhood.* Cambridge, MA: MIT Press.

Carey, S. (1986). Cognitive science and science education. *American Psychologist, 41,* 1123–1130.

Case, R. (1974). Structures and strictures: Some functional limitations on the course of cognitive growth. *Cognitive Psychology, 6,* 544–573.

Case, R. (1978a). Intellectual development from birth to adulthood: A neo-Piagetian interpretation. In R. Siegler (Ed.), *Children's thinking: What develops?* (pp. 37–71). Hillsdale, NJ: Erlbaum.

Case, R. (1978b). Piaget and beyond: Toward a developmentally based theory and technology of instruction. In R. Glaser (Ed.), *Advances in instructional psychology* (Vol. 1, pp. 167–228). Hillsdale, NJ: Erlbaum.

Champagne, A., & Klopfer, L. (1984). Research in science education: The cognitive psychology perspective. In D. Holdzkom & P. Ludz (Eds.), *Research within reach: Science education* (pp. 171–189). Washington, DC: National Science Teachers Association.

Chapman, L., & Chapman, J. (1967). Genesis of popular but erroneous diagnostic observations. *Journal of Abnormal Psychology, 72,* 193–204.

Chapman, L., & Chapman, J. (1969). Illusory correlation as an obstacle to the use of valid psychodiagnostic signs. *Journal of Abnormal Psychology, 74,* 271–280.

Cheng, P., & Holyoak, K. (1985). Pragmatic reasoning schemas. *Cognitive Psychology, 17,* 391–416.

Cheng, P., Holyoak, K., Nisbett, R., & Oliver, L. (1986). Pragmatic versus syntactic approaches to training deductive reasoning. *Cognitive Psychology, 18,* 293–328.

Chipman, S., Segal, J., & Glaser, R. (Eds.). (1985). *Thinking and learning skills* (Vol. 2). Hillsdale, NJ: Erlbaum.

Cohen, L. (1981). Can human irrationality be experimentally demonstrated? *Behavioral and Brain Sciences, 4,* 317–331.

Collins, A., & Stevens, A. (1982). Goals and strategies of inquiry teachers. In R. Glaser (Ed.), *Advances in instructional psychology* (Vol. 2, pp. 65–119). Hillsdale, NJ: Erlbaum.

Crocker, J. (1981). Judgment of covariation by social perceivers. *Psychological Bulletin, 90,* 272–292.

Dewey, J. (1910). *How we think.* New York: Heath.

DiSessa, A. (1983). Phenomenology and the evolution of intuition. In D. Gentner & A. Stevens (Eds.), *Mental models* (pp. 15–33). Hillsdale, NJ: Erlbaum.

Downing, C., Sternberg, R., & Ross, B. (1985). Multicausal inference: Evaluation of evidence in causally complex situations. *Journal of Experimental Psychology: General, 114,* 239–263.

Eddy, D. (1982). Probabilistic reasoning in clinical medicine: Problems and opportunities. In D. Kahneman, P. Slovic, & A. Tversky (Eds.), *Judgment under uncertainty: Heuristics and biases* (pp. 249–267). New York: Cambridge University Press.

Einhorn, H., & Hogarth, R. (1986). Judging probable cause. *Psychological Bulletin, 99,* 3–19.

Elstein, A., Shulman, L., & Sprafka, S. (1978). *Medical problem solving: An analysis of clinical reasoning*. Cambridge, MA: Harvard University Press.

Ennis, R. (1975). Children's ability to handle Piaget's propositional logic. *Review of Educational Research, 45*, 1–41.

Ennis, R. (1976). An alternative to Piaget's conceptualization of logical competence. *Child Development, 47*, 903–919.

Fabricius, W., Sophian, C., & Wellman, H. (1987). Young children's sensitivity to logical necessity in their inferential search behavior. *Child Development, 58*, 409–423.

Faust, D. (1984). *The limits of scientific reasoning*. Minneapolis: University of Minnesota Press.

Feyerabend, P. (1975). *Against method*. London: NLB.

Forrest-Pressley, D., MacKinnon, G., & Waller, T. (1985). *Metacognition, cognition, and human performance* (Vols. 1–2). Orlando, FL: Academic Press.

Gelman, R., & Baillargeon, R. (1983). A review of some Piagetian concepts. In J. Flavell & E. Markman (Eds.), P. Mussen (Series Ed.), *Handbook of child psychology* (Vol. 3, pp. 167–230). New York: Wiley.

Gentner, D., & Gentner, D. (1983). Flowing waters or teeming crowds: Mental models of electricity. In D. Gentner & A. Stevens (Eds.), *Mental models* (pp. 101–129). Hillsdale, NJ: Erlbaum.

Gentner, D., & Stevens, A. (Eds.). (1983). *Mental models*. Hillsdale, NJ: Erlbaum.

Gholson, B. (1980). *The cognitive-developmental basis of human learning: Studies in hypothesis testing*. New York: Academic Press.

Glaser, E. (1941). *An experiment in the development of critical thinking*. New York: Teachers College Press, Bureau of Publications, Columbia University.

Glaser, R. (1984). Education and thinking: The role of knowledge. *American Psychologist, 39*, 93–104.

Goodman, N. (1965). *Fact, fiction and forecast* (2nd ed.). Indianapolis, IN: Bobbs-Merrill.

Greenwald, A. (1981). On the conceptual disconfirmation of theories. *Personality and Social Psychology Bulletin, 7*, 131–137.

Greenwald, A., Pratkanis, A., Lieppe, M., & Baumgardner, M. (1986). Under what conditions does theory obstruct research progress? *Psychological Review, 93*, 216–229.

Gruber, H. (1973). Courage and cognitive growth in children and scientists. In M. Schwebel & J. Raph (Eds.), *Piaget in the classroom* (pp. 73–105). New York: Basic Books.

Hamilton, D., Dugan, P., & Trolier, T. (1985). The formation of stereotypic beliefs: Further evidence for distinctiveness-based illusory correlations. *Journal of Personality and Social Psychology, 48*, 5–17.

Hanson, N. (1958). *Patterns of discovery*. Cambridge: Cambridge University Press.

Holland, J., Holyoak, K., Nisbett, R., & Thagard, P. (1986). *Induction: Processes of inference, learning, and discovery*. Cambridge, MA: MIT Press.

Hunt, E. (1962). *Concept learning: An information processing problem*. New York: Wiley.

Inhelder, B., & Piaget, J. (1958). *The growth of logical thinking from childhood to adolescence*. New York: Basic Books.

James, W. (1890). *Principles of psychology* (Vol. 1). New York: Holt.

Jenkins, H., & Ward, W. (1965). Judgment of contingency between responses and outcome. *Psychological Monographs, 79*, (Vol. 1, Whole No. 594).

Jennings, D., Amabile, T., & Ross, L. (1982). Informal covariation assessment: Data-based vs. theory-based judgments. In D. Kahneman, P. Slovic, & A. Tversky (Eds.), *Judgment under uncertainty: Heuristics and biases* (pp. 211–230). New York: Cambridge University Press.

Johnson-Laird, P., Legrenzi, P., & Legrenzi, M. (1972). Reasoning and a sense of reality. *British Journal of Psychology, 63*, 395–400.

Kahneman, D., Slovic, P., & Tversky, A. (Eds.). (1982). *Judgment under uncertainty: Heuristics and biases*. New York: Cambridge University Press.

Kaiser, M., McCloskey, M., & Proffitt, D. (1986). Development of intuitive theories of motion. *Developmental Psychology, 22,* 67–71.

Karmiloff-Smith, A., & Inhelder, B. (1974). If you want to get ahead, get a theory. *Cognition, 3,* 195–212.

Karplus, R. (1974). *Science curriculum improvement study: Teachers' handbook.* Berkeley, CA: Lawrence Hall of Science.

Kassin, S., & Wrightsman, L. (Eds.). (1985). *The psychology of evidence and trial procedure.* Beverly Hills, CA: Sage.

Keating, D. (1980). Thinking processes in adolescence. In J. Adelson (Ed.), *Handbook of adolescence* (pp. 211–246). New York: Wiley.

Keil, F. (1984). Mechanisms in cognitive development and the structure of knowledge. In R. Sternberg (Ed.), *Mechanisms of cognitive development* (pp. 81–99). New York: Freeman.

Kelley, H. (1973). The process of causal attribution. *American Psychologist, 28,* 107–128.

Kitchener, K., & King, P. (1981). Reflective judgment: Concepts of justification and their relationship to age and education. *Journal of Applied Developmental Psychology, 2,* 89–116.

Klahr, D., & Dunbar, K. (in press). Dual search space during scientific reasoning. *Cognitive Science.*

Klayman, J., & Ha, Y. (1987). Confirmation, disconfirmation, and information in hypothesis testing. *Psychological Review, 94,* 211–228.

Kohlberg, L. (1981). *Essays on moral development: Vol. 1. The philosophy of moral development.* New York: Harper & Row.

Kohlberg, L. (1984). *Essays on moral development: Vol. 2. The psychology of moral development.* New York: Harper & Row.

Koslowski, B., & Okagaki, L. (1986). Non-humean indices of causation in problem-solving situations: Causal mechanism, analogous effects, and the status of rival alternative accounts. *Child Development, 57,* 1100–1108.

Krupa, M., Selman, R., & Jaquette, D. (1985). The development of science explanations in children and adolescents: A structural approach. In S. Chipman, J. Segal, & R. Glaser (Eds.), *Thinking and learning skills* (Vol. 2, pp. 427–455). Hillsdale, NJ: Erlbaum.

Kuhn, D. (1983). On the dual executive and its significance in the development of developmental psychology. In D. Kuhn & J. Meacham (Eds.), *On the development of developmental psychology* (pp. 81–110). Basel: Karger.

Kuhn, D. (in press). Cognitive development. In M. Bornstein & M. Lamb (Eds.), *Developmental psychology: An advanced textbook* (2nd ed). Hillsdale, NJ: Erlbaum.

Kuhn, D., & Brannock, J. (1977). Development of the isolation of variables scheme in experimental and "natural experiment" contexts. *Developmental Psychology, 13,* 9–14.

Kuhn, D., & Ho, V. (1980). Self-directed activity and cognitive development. *Journal of Applied Developmental Psychology, 1,* 119–133.

Kuhn, D., Ho, V., & Adams, C. (1979). Formal reasoning among pre- and late adolescents. *Child Development, 50,* 1128–1135.

Kuhn, D., Pennington, N., & Leadbeater, B. (1983). Adult reasoning in developmental perspective: The sample case of juror reasoning. In P. Baltes & O. Brim (Eds.), *Life span development and behavior* (Vol. 5, pp. 157–195). New York: Academic Press.

Kuhn, D., & Phelps, E. (1982). The development of problem-solving strategies. In H. Reese (Ed.), *Advances in child development and behavior* (Vol. 17, pp. 1–44). New York: Academic Press.

Kuhn, T. (1962). *The structure of scientific revolutions.* Chicago: University of Chicago Press.

Lakatos, I. (1970). Falsificationism and the methodology of scientific research programmes. In I. Lakatos & A. Musgrave (Eds.), *Criticism and the growth of knowledge* (pp. 91–196). Cambridge: Cambridge University Press.

Larkin, J. (1983). The role of problem representation in physics. In D. Gentner & A. Stevens (Eds.), *Mental models* (pp. 53–73). Hillsdale, NJ: Erlbaum.

Lawson, A. (1983). Investigating and applying developmental psychology in the science classroom. In S. Paris, G. Olson, & H. Stevenson (Eds.), *Learning and motivation in the classroom* (pp. 113–135). Hillsdale, NJ: Erlbaum.

Leadbeater, B. (1986). The resolution of relativism in adult thinking: Subjective, objective, or conceptual? *Human Development, 29,* 291–300.

Levin, I. (Ed.). (1986). *Stage and structure: Reopening the debate.* Norwood, NJ: Ablex.

Lord, C., Ross, L., & Lepper, M. (1979). Biased assimilation and attitude polarization: The effects of prior theories on subsequently considered evidence. *Journal of Personality and Social Psychology, 37,* 2098–2109.

Mackie, J. (1974). *The cement of the universe: A study of causation.* Oxford: Clarendon.

Mahoney, M., & Kimper, T. (1976). From ethics to logic: A survey of scientists. In M. Mahoney (Ed.), *Scientist as subject: The psychological imperative* (pp. 187–194). Cambridge, MA: Ballinger.

Mandelbaum, M. (1982). Subjective, objective, and conceptual relativism. In J. Meiland & M. Krausz (Eds.), *Relativism, cognitive and moral* (pp. 34–65). Notre Dame, IN: University of Notre Dame Press.

McCloskey, M. (1983). Naive theories of motion. In D. Gentner & A. Stevens (Eds.), *Mental models* (pp. 299–324). Hillsdale, NJ: Erlbaum.

McGuire, W. (1969). The nature of attitudes and attitude change. In G. Lindzey and E. Aronson (Eds.), *Handbook of social psychology* (2nd ed.) (Vol, 3, pp. 136–314). Reading, MA: Addison Wesley.

Meehl, P. (1978). Theoretical risks and tabular asterisks: Sir Karl, Sir Ronald, and the slow progress of soft psychology. *Journal of Consulting and Clinical Psychology, 46,* 806–834.

Mendelson, R., & Shultz, T. (1976). Covariation and temporal contiguity as principles of causal inference in young children. *Journal of Experimental Psychology, 22,* 408–412.

Metz, K. (1985).The development of children's problem solving in a gears task: A problem space perspective. *Cognitive Science, 9,* 431–472.

Moshman, D. (1979). To really get ahead, get a metatheory. In D. Kuhn (Ed.), *Intellectual development beyond childhood* (pp. 59–68) (*New Directions for Child Development,* Vol. 5). San Francisco: Jossey-Bass.

Murphy, G., & Medin, D. (1985). The role of theories in conceptual coherence. *Psychological Review, 92,* 289–316.

Mynatt, C., Doherty, M., & Tweney, R. (1977). Confirmation bias in a simulated research environment: An experimental study of scientific inference. *Quarterly Journal of Experimental Psychology, 29,* 85–95.

National Education Association, Educational Policies Commission. (1961). *The central purpose of American education.* Washington, DC: National Education Association.

Nelson, K. (1985). *Making sense: The acquisition of shared meaning.* Orlando, FL: Academic Press.

Nelson, K., & Gruendel, J. (1981). Generalized event representations: Basic building blocks of cognitive development. In M. Lamb & A. Brown (Eds.), *Advances in developmental psychology* (Vol. 1, pp. 131–158). Hillsdale, NJ: Erlbaum.

Newell, A. (1973). Production systems: Models of control structures. In W. Chase (Ed.), *Visual information processing* (pp. 463–526). New York: Academic Press.

Newell, A., & Simon, H. (1972). *Human problem solving.* Englewood Cliffs, NJ: Prentice-Hall.

Nickerson, R., Perkins, D., & Smith, E. (1985). *The teaching of thinking.* Hillsdale, NJ: Erlbaum.

Nisbett, R., & Ross, L. (1980). *Human inference: Strategies and shortcomings of social judgment.* Englewood Cliffs, NJ: Prentice-Hall.

O'Brien, D. (1987). The development of conditional reasoning: An iffy proposition. In H. Reese (Ed.), *Advances in child development and behavior* (Vol. 20, pp. 61–90). Orlando, FL: Academic Press.

Osborn, W. (1939). An experiment in teaching resistance to propaganda. *Journal of Experimental Education, 8,* 1–17.

Overton, W. (1985). Scientific methodologies and the competence-moderator-performance issue. In E. Neimark, R. DiLisi, & J. Newman (Eds.), *Moderators of competence* (pp. 15–41). Hillsdale, NJ: Erlbaum.

Overton, W., & Newman, J. (1983). Cognitive development: A competence-activation/utilization approach. In T. Field, A. Houston, H. Quay, L. Troll, & G. Finley (Eds.), *Review of human development* (pp. 217–241). New York: Wiley.

Packer, M. (1985). Hermeneutic inquiry in the study of human conduct. *American Psychologist, 40,* 1081–1093.

Parsons, C. (1960). Inhelder and Piaget's "The growth of logical thinking": A logician's viewpoint. *British Journal of Psychology, 51,* 75–84.

Perry, W. (1970). *Forms of intellectual and ethical development in the college years.* New York: Holt.

Piaget, J., & Garcia, R. (1974). *Understanding causality.* New York: Norton.

Pitt, R. (1983). Development of general problem-solving schema in adolescence and early adulthood. *Journal of Experimental Psychology: General, 112,* 547–584.

Popper, K. (1965). *The logic of scientific discovery* (2nd ed.). New York: Harper & Row.

Rawls, J. (1971). *A theory of justice.* Cambridge, MA: Harvard University Press.

Ross, L. (1977). The intuitive psychologist and his shortcomings. In L. Berkowitz (Ed.), *Advances in experimental social psychology* (Vol. 10, pp. 173–220). New York: Academic Press.

Schustack, M., & Sternberg, R. (1981). Evaluation of evidence in causal inference. *Journal of Experimental Psyhcology: General, 110,* 101–120.

Schwartz, S., & Griffin, T. (1986). *Medical thinking: The psychology of medical judgment and decision making.* New York: Springer-Verlag.

Scribner, S. (1977). Modes of thinking and ways of speaking. In P. Johnson-Laird & P. Wason (Eds.), *Thinking* (pp. 483–500). Cambridge: Cambridge University Press.

Sedlak, A., & Kurtz, S. (1981). A review of children's use of causal inference principles. *Child Development, 52,* 759–784.

Shaklee, H., & Fischhoff, B. (1982). Strategies of information search in causal analysis. *Memory and Cognition, 10,* 520–530.

Shaklee, H., & Mims, M. (1981). Development of rule use in judgment of covariation between events. *Child Development, 52,* 317– 325.

Shaklee, H., & Paszek, D. (1985). Covariation judgment: Systematic rule use in middle childhood. *Child Development, 56,* 1229–1240.

Shultz, T. (1982). Rules of causal attribution. *Monographs of the Society for Research in Child Development, 47,* (1, Serial No. 194).

Shultz, T., & Kestenbaum, M. (1985). Causal reasoning in children. In G. Whitehurst (Ed.), *Annals of child development* (Vol. 2, pp. 195–249). Greenwich, CT: JAI Press.

Shultz, T., & Mendelson, R. (1975). The use of covariation as a principle of causal analysis. *Child Development, 46,* 394–399.

Shymansky, J., Kyle, W., & Alport, J. (1983). The effects of new science curricula on student performance. *Journal of Research in Science Teaching, 20,* 387–400.

Siegler, R. (1975). Defining the locus of developmental differences in children's causal reasoning. *Journal of Experimental Child Psychology, 20,* 512–525.

Siegler, R. (1976). The effects of simple necessity and sufficiency relationships on children's causal inferences. *Child Development, 47,* 1058–1063.

Siegler, R. (1983). How knowledge influences learning. *American Scientist, 71,* 631–638.

Siegler R., & Klahr, D. (1982). When do children learn? The relationship between existing knowledge and the ability to acquire new knowledge. In R. Glaser (Ed.), *Advances in instructional psychology* (Vol. 2, pp. 121–211). Hillsdale NJ: Erlbaum.

Simon, H. (1977). *Models of discovery*. Dordrecht: Reidel.

Simon, H., & Lea, G. (1974). Problem solving and rule induction: A unified view. In L. Gregg (Ed.), *Knowledge and cognition* (pp. 105–127). Hillsdale, NJ: Erlbaum.

Sinnott, J. (1981). The theory of relativity: A metatheory for development? *Human Development, 24,* 293–311.

Smedslund, J. (1963). The concept of correlation in adults. *Scandinavian Journal of Psychology, 4,* 165–173.

Snyder, M., & Swann, W. (1978). Behavioral confirmation in social interaction: From social perception to social reality. *Journal of Experimental Social Psychology, 14,* 148–162.

Spears, R., Van der Plight, J., & Eiser, J. (1985). Illusory correlation in the perception of group attitudes. *Journal of Personality and Social Psychology, 48,* 863–875.

Sternberg, R. (Ed.). (1984). *Mechanisms of cognitive development*. New York: Freeman.

Sternberg, R. (1985). *Beyond IQ: A triarchic theory of human intelligence*. Cambridge: Cambridge University Press.

Stich, S., & Nisbett, R. (1980). Justification and the psychology of human reasoning. *Philosophy of Science, 47,* 188–202.

Strauss, S., & Stavy, R. (1982). U-shaped behavioral growth: Implications for theories of development. In W. Hartup (Ed.), *Review of child development research* (Vol 6, pp. 547–599). Chicago: University of Chicago Press.

Symonds, P. (1936). *Education and the psychology of thinking*. New York: McGraw-Hill.

Toulmin, S. (1953). *Philosophy of science*. New York: Harper & Row.

Toulmin, S. (1961). *Foresight and understanding*. New York: Harper & Row.

Trolier, T., & Hamilton, D. (1986). Variables influencing judgments of correlational relations. *Journal of Personality and Social Psychology, 50,* 879–888.

Tschirgi, J. (1980). Sensible reasoning: A hypothesis about hypotheses. *Child Development, 51,* 1–10.

Vygotsky, L. (1962). *Thought and language*. Cambridge, MA: MIT Press.

Wason, P. (1960). On the failure to eliminate hypotheses in a conceptual task. *Quarterly Journal of Experimental Psychology, 12,* 129–140.

Wason, P. (1966). Reasoning. In B. Foss (Ed.), *New horizons in psychology* (Vol. 1, pp. 135–154). Harmondsworth: Penguin.

Wason, P., & Johnson-Laird, P. (Eds.). (1968). *Thinking and reasoning*. Harmondsworth: Penguin.

Wason, P., & Johnson-Laird, P. (1972). *Psychology of reasoning: Structure and content*. Cambridge, MA: Harvard University Press.

West, L., & Pines, A. (Eds.). (1985). *Cognitive structure and conceptual change*. Orlando, FL: Academic Press.

Williams, M., Hollan, J., & Stevens, A. (1983). Human reasoning about a simple physical system. In D. Gentner & A. Stevens (Eds.), *Mental models* (pp. 131–154). Hillsdale, NJ: Erlbaum.

Wright, J., & Murphy, G. (1984). The utility of theories in intuitive statistics: The robustness of theory-based judgments. *Journal of Experimental Psychology: General, 113,* 301–322.

INDEX

DATE DUE
